P9-DFW-795

920.72 Holl

Holland, Barbara.

They went whistling :

APR 1 9 2001	MAR 2 4 2008	
MAY 1 0 2001		
JUL 1 0 2001		
JUL 2 0 2001		
SEP 1 7 2001		
10/08/01		
NOV 1 2001		
NOV 3 0 2001		
SEP 2 6 2002		
MAR 0 8 2006		

MAR 2 7 2001

VESTAL PUBLIC LIBRARY

0 00 10 0233050 2

1-607-754-4243

Vestal Public Library
Vestal, New York 13850

They
Went
Whistling

Also by **Barbara Holland**

Bingo Night at the Fire Hall: The Case for Cows,
Orchards, Bake Sales, and Fairs

Endangered Pleasures: In Defense of Naps,
Bacon, Martinis, Profanity, and Other Indulgences

One's Company

Wasn't the Grass Greener:
A Curmudgeon's Fond Memories

Hail to the Chiefs

Secrets of the Cat

Mother's Day

A whistling woman and a crowing hen,
Both will come to no good end.

—Old Proverb

They Went Whistling

Women Wayfarers, Warriors, Runaways, and Renegades

Barbara Holland

Pantheon Books, New York

Copyright © 2001 by Barbara Holland

All rights reserved under International and Pan-American Copyright Conventions. Published in the United States by Pantheon Books, a division of Random House, Inc., New York, and simultaneously in Canada by Random House of Canada Limited, Toronto.

Pantheon Books and colophon are registered trademarks of Random House, Inc.

Library of Congress Cataloging-in-Publication Data

Holland, Barbara
    They went whistling: women wayfarers, warriors, runaways, and renegades / Barbara Holland.
        p.   cm.
    Includes index.
    ISBN 0-375-42055-X
    1. Women adventurers—Biography.   2. Adventure and adventurers—Biography.   I. Title.

CT9970 .H65 2001
920.72—dc21   [B]   00-056495

Random House Web Address: www.randomhouse.com

Book design by Johanna S. Roebas

Printed in the United States of America
First Edition
9   8   7   6   5   4   3   2   1

To all women who take their own lives in their hands and step over the edge.

I defined a woman's duty, "To look the world in the face with a go-to-hell look in the eyes; to have an idea; to speak and act in defiance of convention."

—Margaret Sanger, 1914

"One is a much less lighthearted traveler with a foal at foot."

—Dervla Murphy, 1974

Contents

Introduction

Grace O'Malley, as handy with a blunderbuss as she was at the helm, commanded her own successful fleet of pirate ships.

Daisy Bates lived for fifty years in the Australian desert with the Aborigines simply because they were more interesting than the husband and son she'd left behind.

Gudrid Thorbjarnardottir led the third Viking voyage to America and camped out on its wild shores long enough to produce the first known European-American baby.

Dr. James Barry, a surgeon in the British army, after a dashing and distinguished career on several continents, retired to London with full honors, died, and was discovered to have been a woman all along.

Dian Fossey went to live alone among gorillas and took such fierce draconian measures against poachers that she was found with her skull split by a poacher's knife.

Joan of Arc led the French to victory against the English and broke the back of the Hundred Years War. Margaretha Geertruida Zelle took up exotic dancing, called herself Mata Hari, and was executed as a spy by a French firing squad. Queen Jinga of Angola conquered the surrounding countries and snatched the slave business away from Portugal. Beautiful Charlotte Corday stabbed Marat to death in his bath because she thought he was bad for France. Alexandra David-Neel spent years journeying and studying Tibetan religion and language before she tackled the high mountain passes to get to Lhasa, the holy city shut tight against foreign women.

It can be done. It just doesn't happen often. Women aren't supposed to take their lives in their hands, light out on their own, and have independent adventures. People fought long and hard for our right to hold jobs, even good jobs, the right to divorce our husbands, and the right to vote and even run for elective office, but we will never win the right to be Marco Polo or Don Quixote or Che Guevara or Lawrence of Arabia.

Of course, most men never kick over the traces and strike out on their own, either, unless you count starting a software company or investing in dubious stocks, but they feel that one of these days they just might. Most women know they wouldn't. Women stay where they belong and behave themselves, or misbehave in traditional feminine ways; adultery may be wicked but adventures are perverse. Unnatural. Women are Penelope, not Ulysses. The words say it: an "adventurer" is a man who goes forth on daring escapades; an "adventuress" is a woman who preys on rich men and other people's husbands.

This is nobody's fault. It's the nature of our task in life. A woman with children—and for most of history, normal life resulted in children—is more or less forced to be a mother; being a father has always been optional. A man can do his duty by the future of the race in ten minutes, and then go forth to bound from oasis to oasis on a zebra, or explore Antarctica or the moon, or conquer the known world, or, having planted his youthful seed, retreat to the desert and sit praying on a sharp rock for forty years. The seed, as every farmer knows, is step one, and essential, but the following steps take more time and attention. If things are to keep going into the future, a woman must not only carry and bear the children, but see them fed and doctored and clothed and civilized, preferably in the cradle of a stable society where she's dug out a respectable place for them.

Women swept off on adventures by their menfolk, like the settlers of the American West, went anxiously and, as soon as they got down from the wagons, made the men build a church and a school for socializing the young. Women worked together to make a settled world where their children could find responsible mates, and produce their own children and raise them, and the genetic material survive and civilization as we know it totter on.

The motherhood business drags on into a second generation: What use to have raised this one if no one wants to breed with it? Only rich and powerful mothers can be peculiar. Cleopatra was far from respectable and probably murdered one or both of her little brother-husbands, but who would object to marrying one of her four illegitimate children by Julius Caesar and Mark Antony? She was the queen. I'm told I had a spinster great-aunt, long ago in Cuba, who lived alone on an immense walled plantation and raised what were called at the time "great apes." Naturally there were salacious rumors about her relationship with her charges, but she was so rich it didn't matter. If she'd had children, whatever their paternity, she could have bought them mates.

Ordinary women must strive for acceptability, have a place to live, see that the lawn is mowed, and keep in touch with a circle of friends. Women's lives simply bend that way. Women invented the house. Without women, men would still be sleeping under a rocky outcrop and wandering away in the morning. Women needed a permanent roof under which to raise children and marry them off to the neighbors' children. Today even women without the slightest interest in reproducing live as if, any minute now, they might find themselves with a houseful of infant dependents. They buy furniture and maintain social bonds and cooperate, weaving a nest-shaped world. As men identify with their cars, instruments of speed and change and distance, women identify with their houses, motionless and sheltering, and preen them like birds preening their feathers, and decorate them with bits of colored glass.

Browsing through literature, the reader can plainly see that each man is different from all other men, singular by reason of what he does, while women differ only in hair color, beauty, and chastity, and the less they do, the better. The youngest reader learns this basic lesson: the protagonist is male. Babar is a boy elephant, Stuart Little is a boy mouse, Peter is a boy rabbit, the Black Stallion is a stallion, and even The Little Engine That Could is a boy engine. Sometimes a female hovers wringing her hands in the background, like Kanga among Christopher Robin's friends, but she doesn't get to do anything. Girls, even girl kittens or ponies, don't do things. In modern books they're allowed to play team sports at school, but the stories lack the classic punch, and besides, unlike Peter Rabbit, these heroines follow directions. They may squabble with each other but they don't question authority. Even young heroines meant to be odd, wild, and creative, like Harriet the Spy and Anne of Green Gables, do what they're told without losing their tempers or running away from home: good potential motherhood material.

Acceptable hero women should be driven not by dreams of glory but by a nurturing concern for others: the Virgin Mary, Florence Nightingale, Clara Barton, Harriet Tubman, Mother Teresa—mothering their way into history. In the index to Kenneth Clark's definitive *Civilisation,* based on the awe-inspiring television series on what we've done since the dawn of time, we find the names of 395 men and eleven women, including the Virgin Mary, several lesser saints, and Dorothy Wordsworth, the poet's sister.

Men, while not directly responsible for this state of affairs, have never had any interest in changing it; comradeship is all very well but it doesn't compare with clean shirts and hot meals waiting when you come home from the wars. Men are the side-beneficiaries of the system, and have always encouraged it. They can bring considerable pressure to bear on a woman who acts up—the ultimate pressure, in fact, by refusing to marry her, as mothers have warned their daughters for millennia. Both men and women approve the passive female virtues and crack down hard at the first signs of restlessness; when Joan of Arc was a child, her father threatened to drown her in the Meuse if she tried to join the army, and today when the president's wife takes an active stand on policy, the electorate howls for her blood.

The Old World of Europe was set in its ways, but the blank spaces of America might have given its women more leeway. It didn't. In 1881 the noted historian Benson J. Lossing, LL.D., undertook to sum up the dramatis personae of our first 250 years in his comprehensive *Eminent Americans*. He includes 384 notables, of whom eleven are women.

One was Martha Washington, because she married George, and one was Mary Philipse, because when George was twenty-four he met her at a party and "his young heart was touched by her charms." (Then she married someone else and died in England at ninety-six.) Of the remaining nine, two were missionaries' wives who briefly accompanied their husbands to "carry the Gospel to the pagans of the world." Pocahontas makes the list because she saved Smith's life (it would be idle to wonder whether she'd be there for saving some endangered housewife).

xvii

Lossing's favorite eminent female was Lucretia Maria Davidson, a little girl who wrote poetry; her earliest known work, written at age nine, is an epitaph for a pet robin. She longed for an education, but studying wrecked her frail health, as studying so often did to girls, and killed her at seventeen, in 1825. Her last work is as follows:

> *That thought comes o'er me in the hour*
> *Of grief, of sickness, or of sadness;*
> *'Tis not the dread of Death—'tis more;*
> *It is the dread of Madness.*

Five to go.

Catherine Ferguson was born a slave, and when she was freed she taught religion to small children until a kindly pastor helped her open a Sunday school, where male preachers came to conduct services.

Isabella Graham was a young widowed mother who, with the help of some influential men, also opened a school, and handed out tracts about being kind to the destitute, and "walked daily among the poor."

Lucretia Mott was an abolitionist, but Dr. Lossing quickly excuses this unseemliness by assuring us that "During all her public ministrations she never neglected her home duties. She was an exemplary old-fashioned housekeeper" and could still thread her own needles at eighty-six. (Prudently, he doesn't mention that after the Civil War she took up the cause of women's suffrage, which was far from a nice thing to do.)

Rebecca Motte was a hero of the American Revolution, because when her house was occupied by the British, she lent the American general her son's bow and arrows so he could burn it down and smoke out the Brits; apparently abetting the destruction of her house was the female equivalent of a glorious death on the field of battle.

Then there was Ann Lee, a dreadful embarrassment. Since all four of her children died in infancy, she was a relatively free agent, and converted to the doctrine of John Wardley, a Quaker who believed in the holiness of celibacy and the wickedness of marriage. His followers, "because of the great agitations of their bodies when religiously exercised," were called Shakers. Lee was clapped in jail as a lunatic, and had visions, got released, got jailed again for high treason, and later set up quite a thriving colony of what Dr. Lossing calls her "deluded followers," who believed she was the Second Coming, and immortal. He's sure that she fleeced them of their worldly goods, but chalks that up to insanity rather than cleverness. (Later historians say she was a pioneer for justice and equality, women's rights and true democracy, which would have made her even more disreputable in Lossing's eyes. He includes her only with reluctance, not to say loathing.)

Actually, plenty of women were doing more exciting things than Lossing lets on, but he would have considered it indelicate to mention the wild and reckless Confederate spy Belle Boyd; or Annie Oakley, the grandstanding sharpshooter; or the outlaw Belle Starr, horse thief and host to the western criminal classes; or "Mad Ann" Bailey, daredevil scout and messenger in the Indian wars. Not even Anne Hutchinson, pious wife and prolific mother though she was, is nice enough for him. When Governor John Winthrop threw her, middle-aged and pregnant, out of the Massachusetts Bay Colony for doing her own praying and preaching in defiance of the local theocracy, calling her "a woman of haughty and fierce carriage, a nimble wit and active spirit, a very voluble tongue, more bold than a man," she lost her chance with Lossing. (She marched off through the woods to start up Rhode Island, where she could pray all she wanted to, and, after her husband died, tried Long Island, where Indians killed her and five of her children, to the great joy of the Massachusetts authorities, who felt God had served her right. No doubt Lossing would have agreed.)

With Lossing, if a lady couldn't be eminent politely, she couldn't be eminent at all.

At the close of the twentieth century, *National Geographic* published its definitive timeline of the human race from 30,000 B.C. to A.D. 2000. No woman appears on it. Elvis Presley made the cut, as did Joseph-Nicéphore Niepce, who took the first photograph, and Ottaviano dei Petrucci, who printed the first book of music. *National Geographic* was looking for innovators, and apparently women didn't innovate. Or perhaps they did, but their breakthroughs were considered too humble to matter. Probably a woman first put food in a container to cook it, instead of just throwing it into the fire and hooking it back out when it was sufficiently charred. Probably cooking food at all was a woman's idea, and keeping a domestic fire going, and crushing the grain between a couple of rocks instead of between our teeth. No doubt a woman figured out how to fasten our clothes on with thongs instead of just clutching them around our shoulders. And what of needles and thread, the uses of flax and wool, and carding and spinning and weaving? Must we assume men thought of all this first, and then instructed their wives accordingly? And anyway, which would you rather have, food and clothes, or a printed book of music? But no woman signed her name to these lowly inventions and domestic life has always slipped by under the radar. Laden with toddlers and nursing infants, women trudged along behind, shielding the young from adventures.

Now, rather abruptly over the course of the twentieth century, women are allowed to have careers and professions and consider it a great step forward. We call it freedom. Perhaps it is. Unless it's just a change of cubicles and roles, and children weeping by cell phone instead of around the neck.

The wonder is that some women out of the millions have always managed to thumb their noses at nature and society and slash their way out on their own trails.

Their motives were often inscrutable, but except perhaps for top-level courtesans like the Empress Theodora and Pamela Harriman, they weren't looking for money. Looking for money has always been a major spur to the maverick male; for gold he has sailed the seven seas and scaled the mountains and trampled whole civilizations under foot, but the wild women seem satisfied with bus fare to the next continent. Claustrophobia is a main propellant, especially among the women of the foggy little British Isles. Quite a few of the breakaways had been pent to the bursting point with domestic responsibility—and who, after finally burying her ailing old parents, would opt to be pent again? Others lit out sanctioned by odd jobs in odd places, like Anna Leonowens at the court of Siam or Margaret Mead in Samoa; or they found religious or romantic excuses to live beyond the rules, or they simply had an idea and chased it over the horizon. Some were brilliant or inspired or beautiful. Some were plain as bread.

What follows is a brief look at a small handful of the willful wildlings, with no attempt at psychosocial explanations or larger meanings. They were who they were, a thorny and various little band not easily arranged in a communal flowerbed and covered by conclusions, and they did what they wanted to do.

They
Went
Whistling

Warriors

Women were always infiltrating armies, sometimes as women, sometimes as men. Currently, the American armed forces welcome them under their own names and gender but don't quite know what to do with them. A long-standing wrangle continues in undertones: Should they be allowed into actual combat, or stay at headquarters to answer the phones?

A recent Speaker of the House of Representatives declared that women are by nature unsuited to combat, since if they stayed too long in the trenches they'd develop diseases peculiar to the female organs, and if it came to hand-to-hand combat, they wouldn't have the upper-body strength to wrestle the foe to the ground.

He was rather a pudgy sort of Speaker who had managed not to go to war personally, but you could see his shining vision of it, war as a man's world, test of muscular strength, endurance, and courage, authenticator of manly skills, path to glory. No place for womenfolk. Suppose they heard bad language or, worse, learned to use it? Suppose they got killed or, worse, killed someone? Women have been known to kill in personal matters or, like mother bears, in defense of the den and cubs, but to have

3

them leave home and go out to kill strangers, for impersonal reasons of state, is strangely repulsive. How would you feel if your mother did something like that? Women on the battlefield are there to nurse the wounds, not to cause them.

The whole subject is distasteful and people tiptoe around it, talking nonsense. The few women who insist on training for combat jobs report harassment at all levels, and their gentlemen comrades never invite them to come along for a drink after work and never forget their smallest error.

Women are supposed to be less aggressive than men, and for the most part they do start out that way. Mothers watching a hatch of siblings can see that the girls are more likely to wheedle, negotiate, or weep, while the boys snatch and kick shins. What men experience as a fine, invigorating adrenaline rush, women feel as fear, and react prudently; what men see as a challenge, women see as a chance to get hurt. The difference may be only skin deep, though, and reversible. A few victories early in life, or a basically combative nature, a noble cause or a homeland to protect, and women march into battle. After Waterloo, one soldier wrote, "Many females were found amongst the slain." In the sixteenth century a Danish women's unit led by the widow Kenau Hasselaer fought the Spanish army "with great endurance and bravery at the siege of Haarlem." As a commissioned officer in the Irish Citizens' Army, one Constance Markievwicz led the rebels into battle in the 1916 Easter Rising, and in 1973 the Cumann na mbann, an all-girl terrorist combat unit, was formed under the IRA. In World War II the Russian sniper Tania Chernova killed two dozen Germans with great relish, blew up the German headquarters, and killed an SS agent in a hand-to-hand scuffle.

Mostly, though, they slipped through unnoticed. Nobody can count the women warriors, because unless they were rich and well-connected they went in disguise, chopping their hair short and slipping off to the Crusades without saying goodbye. Sometimes they were discovered. More often, probably, they weren't.

Here and there we catch a glimpse of women important enough to go to war under their own names, though it's rarely more than a glimpse, as if the historians averted their eyes politely from a spectacle so unseemly. Some of them are dismissed as mythical.

The Amazon River was named by the sixteenth-century explorer Francisco de Orellana, who said the fierce Tapuyan women there fought side by side with their men. The myth of the warrior Amazons, if it is a myth, has been wonderfully durable. Skeptical historians claim that originally it was part of a funny story about a topsy-turvy world where everything was backwards, like whistling women and crowing hens, but the tale took root and grew.

In Greek mythology, the Amazons cut off their daughters' right breasts so they wouldn't interfere with the bowstring. In the *Iliad,* they live in Phrygia and Lycia, where Priam meets them. One story goes that their queen, Penthesileia, brought a regiment of her warriors from Thrace to help Priam, and got killed by Achilles. In the story of Hercules, one of his labors was to get his hands on their queen's girdle, after which he easily conquered them.

The Scythians called them Oeorpata, "man-killers." It was said that they mated with men of other peoples, kept the daughters, and sent the sons back to their fathers, having no use for them. It was said that Alexander the Great was plagued by an Amazon who wanted to have a child by him.

Amazons invaded Greece itself. According to the highly unreliable historian Herodotus, the Greeks defeated them at the

5

river Thermodon and took as many prisoners on board their ship as they could possibly squeeze in. Once at sea, the prisoners killed off their captors but, not knowing the first thing about ships, blew ashore at Cremni on Lake Maeotis. They landed, and seized themselves a herd of horses, and rode off in search of plunder.

The local Scythians were so impressed they decided they wanted children mothered by these fierce females. Craftily, they picked a detachment of handsome young men and sent them off to camp near the Amazons, with instructions not to fight but to run away when attacked. And every day they moved their camp a little closer. Presently the inevitable happened, friendships were struck up, and the two camps merged in amity. Herodotus says the men were quite unable to learn the Amazon language, but the women quickly picked up theirs.

The Scythian suitors begged their ladies to come home with them, where they had property, and settle down to a respectable married life. "The Amazons replied, 'We and the women of your nation could never live together; our ways are too much at variance. We are riders; our business is with the bow and the spear, and we know nothing of women's work; but in your country no woman has anything to do with such things—your women stay at home in their wagons occupied with feminine tasks, and never go out to hunt or for any other purpose. We could not possibly agree.'"

After further debate, it was decided that the Scythian men would go home and pack up as much of their possessions as they could carry, and come back, abandoning their home commitments and casting their lot with their ferocious brides. The women said that since they'd done so much damage to the populace where they were, they'd have to settle elsewhere. So they traveled east for three days and then north for three more, and claimed the land they found. Here, the women kept to their old ways, hunting and fighting, either with or without their menfolk, wearing men's clothes, and making their own laws. (We aren't told who changed diapers and washed dishes, but we can guess.) One of their stricter laws "forbids a girl to marry until she has killed an enemy in battle; some of their women, unable to fulfil this condition, grow old and die unmarried."

Naturally the whole story has to be fiction, though as of this writing, archaeologists are still trying to figure out why the Scythian women were buried with quite such heavy-duty armor and weaponry; they think perhaps it had some abstract ceremonial significance. Still, for mythical creatures, Amazons certainly hoodwinked a number of influential people and picked up a lot of convincing details on their travels through history.

The Romans were fanatically methodical and organized and wrote everything down, which would be a blessing for the historian if they hadn't written such outrageous lies about their own nobleness and their enemies' sliminess, and shredded all records to the contrary. The smear job they did on Cleopatra is a fine example and still convinces most people, with a little help from art and Hollywood.

The Cleopatra we inherited from Roman propagandists is the ultimate siren, eyes made up like a raccoon, as in the 1917 Theda Bara movie, dressed in diaphanous scarves or, in romantic nineteenth-century paintings, nothing but an asp. She is pure sexual temptation, forever famous as poor, infatuated Antony's downfall. Contemporary Romans claimed Antony was only one of thousands of lovers; they said she was "the wickedest woman in the world," utterly degenerate, sexually insatiable, and a physical wreck from making love to her slaves all day and drinking herself sick all night. (Being Romans, they assumed this is what any unsupervised woman would do.)

Among the upper classes in Rome, women were used like markers in a card game. Whenever an alliance went sour and a new friendship replaced it, which was once a month or so, all parties concerned were expected to divorce their current wives, who were relatives of their former allies, and marry the sisters and daughters of their new friends. Sometimes there were tears and lamentations, sometimes rejoicing, or the odd case of suspected poisoning, but mostly people did as they were told. Out in the hinterlands beyond Rome, though, Romans occasionally stubbed their toe on a woman outside the system who did whatever she pleased, and it made them nervous.

Cleopatra was born in 69 B.C., third child of Ptolemy XII, and her early years were instructive. Her father, called the Flute Player, was quite useless; his subjects paid no attention to him, and he kept having to go to Rome to borrow money to put down rebellions. Probably he took Cleopatra along, when she was twelve. In any event, she early absorbed the fact that Rome's friendship was the top priority of the day, and that paying cash for Roman protection was emptying the treasury, and perhaps there was a less expensive way to their hearts. She also learned not to trust her immediate family an inch.

While the Flute Player was off begging in Rome, his oldest daughter grabbed the throne, and then somehow got assassinated, and the second daughter grabbed it, so her father had to bring some Roman help and execute her. This left Cleopatra as the eldest, and not much got past her. Somehow she found herself an education, something her family had never been interested in; the Arab historian Al-Masudi, unaffected by Roman propaganda, called her "a princess well versed in the sciences, disposed to the study of philosophy." Plutarch says she spoke nine or ten languages, including the language of her Egyptian subjects, which no other Ptolemy had ever condescended to learn. (They were Macedonian Greeks and proud of it.)

When she was eighteen the Flute Player died and left Egypt to her and her ten-year-old brother and fiancé, Ptolemy XIII. Little Ptolemy was under the thumb of an ambitious court eunuch named Potinus, who started ordering everyone around, took control of the army, and drove young Cleo clear out of town.

Rome was the traditional place to look for help, and happily Rome showed up on the doorstep, in the person of Julius Caesar, who'd sailed to Alexandria hoping to collect some of the Flute Player's debts. Cleopatra needed a word with him. She had herself wrapped up in some bedding and delivered to Caesar as merchandise, under the nose of Potinus's guards.

Caesar was charmed by her wit and resourcefulness, and presently quite undone by the pleasure of her company. (George Bernard Shaw's *Caesar and Cleopatra* gives us a version that would have pleased the most slanderous Roman historian, with a wise and fatherly Caesar and a very young and silly little queen, but this is absurd. She was merry company, it's said, but never silly. You could get killed being silly.) Using her best blandishments, she persuaded Rome's most powerful leader to kill Potinus, bring the rebellious army into line, and patch things up with her brother to cement her position.

All of which he did, at considerable effort and expense. Shortly thereafter, Ptolemy XIII, smartly dressed in heavy golden armor, was found drowned in the Nile. (Perhaps his foot slipped on the bank or something.) So Caesar married her to her surviving brother, Ptolemy XIV, who was only twelve and easily ignored, and there was our heroine in the driver's seat and pregnant with Caesar's only child, a wise career move. (Caesar, with a stern and warlike image to maintain, never publicly confessed to fatherhood, but he didn't deny it either.)

She called the baby Caesarion and took him to Rome, where they were Caesar's guests, and fabulous parties were thrown, and the besotted leader indiscreetly put up a golden statue of her in the temple, causing a scandal that fueled the plots against him.

Alas, he wasn't so besotted as to name Caesarion his heir. Instead he picked his great-nephew Octavius, of whom we shall hear more later. Cleo took the baby back to Alexandria where, shortly thereafter, yet another family tragedy struck and her husband-brother met an untimely end. No one seems quite sure what ailed him.

She named the baby co-ruler and settled down to run the country.

Poets and playwrights ignore the following years, since there was no famous lover involved, nor, apparently, even a casual bedmate. Certainly the records we inherited from Rome wouldn't tell us she was just and wise and shrewd and the first of her line to be loved and admired by her subjects. Here and there the voice of a non-Roman historian creeps in, though, and we learn that she'd inherited a bankrupt and rebellious kingdom and turned it into the richest state in the Mediterranean, and even traditionally quarrelsome Alexandria lived in peace and harmony. Her aqueducts and other engineering projects were praised; grain was distributed free to the poor in times of hunger; her foreign alliances held firm; the budget was balanced. It was said, in countries far from Rome, that she was a messiah sent to free the world from Roman rule and establish a golden age of peace and plenty.

This is not Hollywood's Cleopatra, or history's either: a ruler ahead of her time, negotiating profitable trade deals, meeting with ambassadors, and adjusting taxes to relieve the poor. After the trouble with Potinus, it's reasonable to suppose she trusted no prime ministers and burned the midnight oil alone. If we had the uncensored records, she might stand shoulder to shoulder with Elizabeth I in the history books, instead of lolling in asses' milk and dying for love.

So prosperous had she made her country that presently another Roman leader came to call, looking for money so he could invade Parthia.

Shakespeare gives Mark Antony a famous and poetic speech in *Julius Caesar,* but in real life he wasn't the poet type. He was a good soldier, popular with his troops, and never said no to an all-night party, after which he sometimes threw up, at least once in front of a large audience gathered to hear him speak. Cranky old Cicero said he was "odious."

He was a Triumvir. The Romans were still tinkering with the notion of the Triumvirate, or three equal rulers, which, considering the testosterone content of your basic Roman male, was an ill-starred concept. Antony ruled with Octavius and someone named Lepidus, who prudently crept offstage early.

He was still married to his third wife, Fulvia, but when he saw Cleopatra on that royal barge, dressed as Venus and lounging under a golden canopy, Fulvia fled from his thoughts.

Cleopatra knew exactly what he'd come for, and at breakfast the next morning she agreed to finance his Parthian campaign in return for his military protection and, for good measure, the death of Arsinoe. Arsinoe was her last surviving sibling, and she'd been lurking in Ephesus, saying she was the real queen of Egypt, and Cleopatra knew her family well. (The Ptolemies had been marrying only their sisters and brothers for hundreds of years, and we're told that even a couple of generations of this

11

results in a weedy and feeble human product, but the Flute Player's four daughters were as tough, resourceful, and ambitious as they come, and not bad-looking either.)

Antony hung around. His hostess, whose own tastes were more fastidious, graciously dropped everything to drink and gamble with him, and hunt and fish and play practical jokes, and feast at banquets prepared around the clock. Occasionally she tried to coax him to more cultural pursuits, but they weren't his style.

For some reason, back in Rome, his wife Fulvia raised an army against Octavius. He beat her easily, but it made him cross, so Antony had to go back to Rome and divorce Fulvia and marry wife number four, Octavius's sister Octavia. Meanwhile, Cleopatra had twins, a boy and a girl.

Antony then remembered his Parthian invasion, but somehow he now needed even more help. He and Cleopatra met in Antioch and fell into each other's arms, and she said she'd build him a fleet and feed his troops if he gave her most of Lebanon, Syria, Jordan, and southern Turkey. For a star-crossed lover, she cut a shrewd deal.

Off he set for Parthia, where he was pulverized and lost almost half his army and the survivors were in a fair way to freeze and starve. Cleopatra had another boy, Ptolemy Philadelphus, and then rushed to Antony's aid with food and blankets. Unfortunately, the same mission had occurred to Octavia.

Antony told his wife to go back to Rome and mind her own business. Octavius was furious.

Then Antony set up a grand ceremony in Alexandria to present the four children, announcing that Cleopatra was the Queen of Kings and Caesarion King of Kings and the real heir to Rome. He made his own children royalty, too, and bestowed some countries on them. Then he divorced Octavia.

This was a declaration of war. We don't know whether it was his idea or hers, but somehow it seems more like her. He wasn't a planner. It was a long shot, but the winner would rule the Western world. Everyone prepared to fight.

Octavius ran into trouble at the start, trying to raise taxes to pay for a war against the popular Antony. A good politician, he blamed everything on Cleopatra, the evil, dissipated, foreign, and sexually rapacious villain who had quite addled our dear Antony's wits. Antony was bewitched, poor thing, and needed Octavius's army to bring him to his senses and stamp out the lecherous serpent.

This slow start was probably the window the lovers missed; they might well have invaded Italy at once, before Octavius convinced the people and raised the money; they might have rallied support on the road to Rome, and ended up sharing the world. Instead, they retreated to Greece to prepare their forces and Cleopatra's fleet. This was probably her fault; she seems to have been inordinately fond of her ships, while Antony was more the foot soldier. They had cost her a fortune and she wanted to use them, and sail with them, whistling, against the Rome that had humiliated her father; what could she have done on foot?

It was a mistake. Octavius picked off their scattered troops in western Greece and trapped them at Actium.

Just what happened at the Battle of Actium is up for grabs, and the winner, as always, got to tell it his way. In the midst of the action, Cleopatra, commanding from her flagship, took her fleet and left the scene; Antony followed her, and the fight turned into a rout. His army surrendered. The *Encyclopaedia Britannica,* which takes rather a dim view of women in general, states flatly that it was treachery and she'd sold Antony out to Octavius. (It doesn't say who told them, but we can guess.) An earlier *Britannica* adds that she'd agreed to assassinate her lover in exchange for Octavius's clemency, though it doesn't say why; she could hardly have believed he'd trade Egypt for a simple hit-job he could do himself.

One or two other sources suggest that her flight wasn't treachery but simple womanly cowardice. Nobody says that it might have been misguided prudence; she had Egypt's entire treasury in those ships, enough money down in the hold to build another fleet or two and fight again another day.

In any case, it was a disaster. Back in Alexandria, she had a two-storey mausoleum thrown up and stuffed it with treasure, in case bribery was in the cards, and enough firewood to burn the place down if it wasn't. She and her two serving maids barricaded themselves on the second floor.

Authoritative sources tell us Antony killed himself because she'd sent to tell him she was dead, but maybe he just felt rotten about the whole debacle. He disemboweled himself, not very skillfully, and lived long enough to get carried to the mausoleum and hoisted to the second floor somehow, where he died in Cleopatra's arms. (The *Britannica* states firmly that he killed himself because she'd told him, as a favor to Octavius, that she was dead, but doesn't explain why, in that case, he'd take the trouble to get his dying self hauled up into her hideout. I suppose, when the *Britannica* asked Octavius, he didn't have a good answer ready.)

Octavius marched into town and sent soldiers to trick their way into the mausoleum and take Cleopatra prisoner, complete with her treasure. He called on her there, and she tried all her evil tricks and blandishments on him; the Greek historian Plutarch says that at thirty-nine "her old charm, and the boldness of her youthful beauty had not wholly left her and, in spite of her present condition, still sparkled from within." Octavius, being so much purer and nobler than Antony, thrust her from him and spurned her loathsome advances. He told us so himself, and everyone believes it, so it must be true.

Having played her last card in vain, Cleopatra, along with her serving women, dressed up in her very best finery and died.

That asp, one of our most cherished beliefs, sounds like pure Octavius. For starters, there's the problem of finding an asp on short notice and getting someone to smuggle it in in a basket of figs. Next, there wasn't a shred of evidence, no sign of snakebite, and no asp. Plutarch examined the medical records and says, "What really took place is known to no one, since it was also said that she carried poison in a hollow bodkin . . . yet there was not so much as a spot found, or any symptom of poison upon her body, nor was the asp seen within the monument." In fact, the women looked simply splendid, and the signs of asp-bite are quite unsightly, even supposing one asp could do in all three of them. Some people suggest a cobra instead, but a cobra big enough for the job would need to be six feet long and hard to carry, thrashing around in a basket of figs. Heavy, too; did the dying women haul it to the window and pitch it out, and if so, why?

Poison seems the obvious answer. Cleopatra knew a thing or two about pharmaceuticals; nobody did find out what happened to that second husband, and she'd written a book on cosmetics full of ingredients unknown to Estee Lauder. In provisioning her hideout, she'd had plenty of time to prepare for the final contingency.

The snake, however, suited Octavius. In Egypt it was a symbol of royalty, but in Rome it was creepy. After he'd killed Caesarion and annexed Egypt as his own personal colony, he marched triumphant through Rome with an effigy of Cleopatra and pictures of her simply crawling with snakes, as befitted such a slimy and treacherous villain. The asp passed into history.

After all, Octavius went on to become the Emperor Augustus, and surely an emperor wouldn't tell us a fib.

Cleopatra was the last great Hellenistic ruler and the last major threat to Rome for a long time. She gambled and lost. She might have won and, with her children, changed the whole world. Many things might have been different under a rule less military, more scholarly and tolerant; for instance, how would Christianity have developed without Roman soldiers to crucify Jesus?

And of course, if she'd won, she could have written her own records, instead of leaving her reputation to Octavius and Hollywood.

She wasn't the last woman to annoy the empire.

Queen Boudicca—Latinized as Boadicea—of Britain was real, which distinguishes her from her predecessors in the Isles, who weren't. Everything we know about Britain before Caesar's arrival we learned from a massive, comprehensive history written considerably after the fact by Geoffrey of Monmouth. Geoffrey lists and details the exciting careers of no fewer than seventy-six monarchs of pre-Roman Britain. Unfortunately all seventy-six of them are entirely imaginary, including the original of King Lear; the luckless monarch devoured by a sea monster; King Bran, whose head was cut off but took no notice whatever and reigned independently of the rest of him for eighty-seven prosperous years; and the resourceful King Lludd, who saved his people from two horrific plagues, one of wizards and one of shrieks. The wizards he got rid of with a literal bug-spray, pelting them with a brew of insects mashed up in water; the shrieks, which sounded off on the first of May and drove everyone insane, he persuaded to turn into pigs and drown in a tub of mead. Then, after he overcame a giant in hand-to-hand combat, peace fell upon the kingdom.

Boudicca's reality limited her exploits, and since as far as we know she had no tragic romantic attachments, no American has ever seen a movie about her. British schoolchildren still know her from the romantic statue that Victoria's Prince Albert caused to be erected on the Thames, near the Houses of Parliament; she's driving two wild horses and wearing the long flowing garments always considered proper combat wear for ladies. Most memorable in the schoolchild's eyes are the long knives that stick out from the wheels of her chariot. One of the few things we know for sure about Boudicca is that she didn't have any knives on her chariot wheels, but symbols go far in the immortality business.

In such school texts as still teach history that far back, the Romans simply marched into Britain, which was full of ignorant and dirty Pagan tribes almost indistinguishable from their livestock, and set about peacefully civilizing them with roads and baths and decent clothing, rather the way American schoolchildren learned about America shouldering the white man's burden in the Philippines.

Reality is rarely so tidy. Britain was divided into a multitude of small kingdoms, and some of the local kings and queens signed treaties with the conquerors and some didn't. The elite Druids, their long-haired women brandishing torches and the men chanting horribly, had a good shot at overthrowing the newcomers, but in the end they were massacred and their sacred oak groves destroyed; whatever they may have said about themselves, the Romans weren't any nobler than your average conqueror. Furthermore, all those roads and buildings they considered civilization called for a good deal of hard work and heavy lifting on the part of the conquered, who resented it.

17

Prasutagus, king of the Iceni, in the Norfolk area, had honored his treaty with Rome, but when he died without a male heir, the Roman officials considered the treaty canceled and closed in to take over his territory and anything else he'd left lying about, including his widow, Boudicca, and their two daughters. The Romans flogged the queen and raped the daughters. History doesn't tell us why; it seems like excessive force, and out of character. Very likely she and her daughters, all unarmed as they were, put up a fight and had to be subdued. They were imprisoned, but apparently not very securely, because when next heard from Boudicca was appealing to the discontented Iceni and the neighboring Trinovantes to follow her in an open rebellion.

We can almost feel the adrenaline rush of rage that propelled her. She must have been traveling from village to village, stopping at isolated farmsteads, standing in ox-carts, shouting herself hoarse into the drizzle and fog of southeast England, pounding her fist, the veins standing out in her neck, her long red hair damp and straggly. She was no Cleopatra; she hadn't the clout, or an army, and no longer even the following of the provincial queen she'd once been. She was deposed and powerless, but nobody told her to go home and tend to her knitting, as they would have in more civilized centuries, and somehow she fired up a motley, discontented, disorganized rabble. She fired up quite a lot of them. All East Anglia followed her, armed with God knows what; it was forbidden under Roman law for the Britons to own weapons, but they must have carried something, if only clubs and pitchforks. She led them into battle.

The Romans were caught off guard. After lulling them with friendship at Colchester, Boudicca's horde suddenly poured down from the north and destroyed the settlement. They ambushed and massacred much of the disciplined and well-armed Ninth Legion.

The Roman governor hurried to defend London, sending orders to the Second Legion to march against the rebels. The Second Legion prudently disobeyed. The governor's force was too small to hold London; he retreated, and Boudicca captured both it and Verulamium and burned them to the ground. With Colchester, this left seventy thousand dead, conquerors and collaborators alike.

Some quite disagreeable atrocities may or may not have ensued, such as respectable women stripped and hung up and their breasts cut off and sewed to their mouths before they were skewered through and through, and the whole celebration marked by pagan rites and feasting. Or so it was alleged by Rome.

The Romans paid the rebels back with interest, though. The following year, perhaps A.D. 61, the governor gathered ten thousand men and forced a showdown. The queen's men outnumbered his, but her ragtag rebels were no match for professionals in body armor. Rome, as usual, won. The Britons had brought along their families, in wagons, to watch, and the wagons blocked their retreat and trapped them. Some eighty thousand of them were killed, and perhaps four hundred Romans.

As a lesson, the citizens were wiped out right down to their smallest chicken. Boudicca, a widow with a handful of farmers behind her and no strong ally at her side, had defied the almighty Roman Empire, won a few rounds, and then lost everything. Cleopatra might actually have won; Boudicca never had a chance. Her war cry had been "Death over slavery!" She took poison.

The physical strength necessary for traditional warfare with broadsword and longbow was an obstacle for most fighting women, so they made do with fire, poison, sex, and sabotage. Occasionally, though, we hear of a woman holding her own in single combat.

Marco Polo, who was either widely traveled or wildly imaginative, tells of a certain princess in the land he calls Great Turkey. Her father is Kaidu, the great Khan's own brother. "He has many cities and castles, and is a great prince. He and his people are Tartars alike; and they are good soldiers, for they are constantly engaged in war."

"Now you must know," he says, "that king Kaidu had a daughter whose name was Ai-Yaruk, which in the Tartar is as much as to say, 'The Bright Moon.' This damsel was very beautiful, but also so strong and brave that in all her father's realm there was no man who could outdo her in feats of strength. In all trials she showed greater strength than any man of them.

"Her father often desired to give her in marriage, but she would none of it. She vowed she would never marry till she found a man who could vanquish her in every trial; him she would wed and none else. And when her father saw how resolute she was, he gave a formal consent in their fashion, that she should marry whom she list and when she list. The lady was so tall and muscular, so stout and shapely withal, that she was almost like a giantess. She had distributed her challenges over all the kingdoms, declaring that whosoever should come to try a fall with her, it should be on these conditions, *viz.,* that if she vanquished him she should win from him an hundred horses, and if he vanquished her he should win her to wife. Hence many a noble youth had come to try his strength against her, but she beat them all; and in this way she had won more than ten thousand horses.

"Now it came to pass in the year of Christ 1280 that there presented himself a noble young gallant, the son of a rich and puissant king, a man of prowess and valiance and great strength of body, who had heard word of the damsel's challenge, and came to match himself against her in the hope of vanquishing her and winning her to wife. That he greatly desired, for the young lady was passing fair. He, too, was young and handsome, fearless and strong in every way, insomuch that not a man in all his father's realm could vie with him. So he came full confidently, and brought with him one thousand horses to be forfeited if she should vanquish him. Thus she might gain a thousand horses at a single stroke! But the young gallant had such confidence in his own strength that he counted securely to win her.

"Now you must know that king Kaidu and the queen his wife, the mother of the stout damsel, did privately beseech their daughter to let herself be vanquished. For they greatly desired this prince for their daughter, seeing what a noble youth he was, and the son of a great king. But the damsel answered that never would she let herself be vanquished if she could help it; if, indeed, he should get the better of her then she would gladly be his wife, according to the wager, but not otherwise.

"So a day was named for a great gathering at the palace of king Kaidu, and the king and queen were there. And when all the company were assembled, for great numbers flocked to see the match, the damsel first came forth in a strait jerkin of samite; and then came forth the young bachelor in a jerkin of taffeta; and a winsome sight they were to see. When both had taken post in the middle of the hall they grappled each other by the arms and wrestled this way and that, but for a long time neither could get the better of the other. At last, however, it so befell that the damsel threw him right valiantly on the palace pavement. And when he found himself thus thrown, and her standing over him, great indeed was his shame and discomfiture. He got him up straightway, and without more ado departed with all his company, and returned to his father, full of shame and vexation, that he who had never yet found a man that could stand before him should have been thus worsted by a girl! And his thousand horses he left behind him.

"As to king Kaidu and his wife they were greatly annoyed, as I can tell you; for if they had had their will this youth should have won their daughter.

"And you must know that after this her father never went on a campaign but she went with him. And gladly he took her, for not a knight in all his train played such feats of arms as she did. Sometimes she would quit her father's side, and make a dash at the host of the enemy, and seize some man thereout, as deftly as a hawk pounces on a bird, and carry him to her father; and this she did many a time."

We assume she never did find a man worth marrying, though owning eleven thousand horses and going forth on all those excellent and bloodthirsty adventures with her father probably reconciled her to spinsterhood, if she needed reconciling.

Not every woman is strong enough to pluck a man off his horse and ride away with him. Most resorted to what historians indignantly consider treachery. As in the Old Testament, they waited until the enemy was asleep and then cut off his hair, or his head, or burned down the house. They sent hit men, like Mary Queen of Scots disposing of the luckless Darnley.

Jeanne la Flamme of Brittany, fourteenth-century heroine of that stubborn, unassimilated land of Celts, Druids, and dolmens, personally cooked the entire French camp, asleep in its tents during the siege of Hennebont. The nineteenth-century poet La Villemarqué—who has been suspected of taking liberties with what he swore were authentic ancient ballads—says contemporary Bretons sang:

> *Jeanne la Flamme is the most intrepid on the face of the earth,*
> *truly!*
> *Jeanne la Flamme set fire to the four corners of the camp;*
> *And the wind spread the conflagration and lit up the black*
> *night;*
> *And the tents were burned and the French roasted,*
> *And three thousand of them turned to cinders, and only a*
> *hundred escaped.*
> *Now, Jeanne la Flamme smiled the next day at her window,*
> *Looking over the countryside and seeing the camp destroyed,*
> *And smoke rising from the tents all reduced to little heaps of*
> *ashes.*
> *Jeanne la Flamme smiled;*
> *'Oh what a fine weed-burning! My God!*
> *My God! What a fine weed-burning! For every grain we will*
> *have ten!*
> *The ancients were right when they said there's nothing like*
> *Gauls' bones,*
> *Like Gauls' bones, ground up, to make the harvest grow.'*

Whether this chant was actually contemporary or not, the events did happen, and Jeanne was certainly fleet-footed and cat's-eyed in the dark, to ignite all four corners of a three-thousand-man camp, striking the sparks with a flint and steel and nourishing them with tinder, and then vanishing into the night before anyone woke up. Thus was female warfare at the grassroots level, canny and secret.

Royalty could fight by daylight. In Siam, in the sixteenth century, Queen Suriothai rode into battle with her husband in their war with Burma. Mounted on her favorite war elephant, she saw an enemy aiming a deadly blow at her husband and maneuvered her mount to slip between them, taking the blow herself. It killed her, but she'd saved the king, and a splendid picture it makes in the mind. Surely she was beautiful—how else be a queen?—and sumptuously dressed in bright silks, and carried a jeweled sword. She was also a world-class elephant-rider, and must have spent years training in the martial arts of the day. Her husband must have loved her dearly, to allow her to ride beside him to war; no doubt he built her a glorious tomb; no doubt the whole nation mourned.

Modern warfare rarely offers such graceful glimpses. Raising the flag at Iwo Jima was a grand moment, surely, but it lacks poetry.

Another scenic historical moment was the 1896 victory in Ethiopia. The French and the British had African colonial empires, so Italy wanted one too. Ethiopia looked good, being convenient to their colony in Eritrea. The Italian prime minister announced that the Ethiopians were "barbarians whose material progress and spiritual salvation cried out for the high ministry of Roman civilization."

This was a familiar tune in the nineteenth century, but the prime minister was misinformed. The country had been firmly established since biblical times and had a rich culture of its own and the continent's only native written language. Converted to Christianity in the fourth century, they retreated from the spread of Islam and went into seclusion in their highlands, where they stayed for twelve hundred years, quietly producing illuminated manuscripts.

The Italian governor of Eritrea, General Baratieri, said he would swoop down and conquer the savages and bring their king, Menelik, "back in a cage." Instead he and his men got lost, and trapped, and horribly surprised by the quantity and ferocity of the Ethiopian forces. Menelik himself commanded his crack imperial guard of twenty-five thousand, and his wife, the Empress Taitu, led three thousand infantry and six hundred cavalry. The Ethiopian forces came on in wave after wave of red, orange, and green flags, glittering helmets, and shields decorated with lions' manes. They fought, one Italian survivor remembered, "like madmen," some with European guns and some with swords and spears, all howling *"Ebalgume! Ebalgume!"* (Reap! Reap!) At one point, discouraged by the loss of men, Menelik wanted to order a retreat, but his wife talked him out of it and persuading him to send in his imperial guard for a final, decisive assault. It carried the day. The surviving Italians were routed and utterly disgraced, conquered not just by savages but by savages taking their orders from a woman.

Not since Hannibal had an African army defeated a European one. As the nineteenth century closed down, Ethiopia was the only African country still free of European civilizers; and that glorious day, March 1, is still celebrated as a major holiday.

Forty years later, Mussolini made a particular point of overrunning the place to expunge the humiliation.

The queens and empresses fight no more. It's possible, if you stretch it, to imagine Elizabeth II leading a cavalry charge on horseback and slashing around with her sword, but not popping up from the hatch of a tank and spraying the fleeing enemy with an assault rifle. It's not the same. The once-creative game of warfare has gone technological on us, and its scope for independent adventure has withered.

Across the continent from Ethiopia, in Dahomey, now Benin, three crack regiments of a thousand women each were the flower and pride of the army, committed to fight to the death. It was a fine army, too, conquering the neighbors and buttressing a powerful kingdom. In 1862, Sir Richard Burton, the tireless traveler, reported that they fought with blunderbusses, flint muskets, bows and arrows, or their bare hands. They were experts in the sneak attack and their endurance under battle conditions was simply splendid; European visitors invited to their training maneuvers watched them sprint and scramble barefoot through piles of thornbushes representing defenses, to emerge bloody but cheerful. Their ranks continued to swell, welcoming only the country's finest, until the kingdom collapsed into a French protectorate and later a mere colony.

Being a shoeless foot soldier isn't everyone's idea of adventure, but at least a girl got to travel and probably commanded a lot more respect than those who stayed home pounding grain.

It helped that everyone knew they were women. In Russia, the women of the "battalion of death" fought in the 1917 Revolution, but they fought as women. Women who went to war disguised as men faced, on top of swords and bullets, never-ending problems of privacy and basic hygiene.

In the early 1600s, Catalina de Eranso escaped from a nunnery and joined the Spanish army, calling herself Alonso Diaz Ramirez de Guzman. She acquitted herself gallantly in combat in Chile and Peru, and not only did her superior officers not notice her sex, her own brother, in the same wars, didn't recognize her, just as in a Shakespearean comedy. She was wounded, and exposed, and sent back to Spain, but far from being disgraced, she became a national pet and the Pope granted her a special dispensation to go on wearing men's clothing as a token of her courage.

In the 1700s, a good handful of spunky Englishwomen found their way to war. Phoebe Hessel was wounded at Fontenoy but survived and lived to be a hundred and eight; Mother Ross of the Second Dragoons was buried with full military honors; Hannah Snell got out of line and took five hundred lashes from the sergeant without revealing her identity, and was later wounded at Pondicherry; Mary Anne Talbot, called "the British Amazon," served as both soldier and cabin boy before she took to drink.

In the American Revolution, Deborah Sampson signed up with the 45th Massachusetts as Robert Shurtleff and won everyone's admiration for her fearlessness under fire. She was good-looking, and countless young women fell in love with her; her comrades teased her for her beardlessness, and called her "Molly." She took a bullet in the thigh but managed to fend off the doctor by digging it out herself. Later, she was wounded in the shoulder, and again escaped medical inspection. Then she came down with camp fever and seemed to be dying; this time the doctor got to her. As she wrote, "Thrusting his hand into my bosom to ascertain if there was motion at the heart, he was surprised to find an inner vest tightly compressing my breasts, the instant removal of which not only ascertained the fact of life, but disclosed the fact that I was a woman."

The kind doctor kept her secret, and moved her into his own house. However, such were Deborah/Robert's charms that the doctor's female friends and relations kept proposing marriage to her, and the doctor went privately to her commanding officer, who went to George Washington, who issued her discharge papers.

Back in New England she stayed in uniform and called herself Ephram Sampson for a while, flirting with the local girls, and then put a dress on and married Benjamin Gannett. They had three children, but Benjamin had never served in the army and she always looked down on him as a bit of a slacker.

Presently she put on the uniform again and hit the lecture circuit, performing the manual of arms and describing the horrors of battle. Her death in 1827 was attributed to her old war wounds, but it seems clear she wouldn't have traded them for peace.

Women dressed as men to fight in the American Civil War. Nobody knows how many. Only a hundred and twenty-seven have been officially documented, but plainly there were hundreds more; doctors, nurses, prisons, and burial squads kept turning them up. At least four women fought at Antietam; Clara Barton treated one Mary Galloway there. As always, the important thing was to stay well and unwounded. Mary Scaberry, otherwise Charles Freeman of an Ohio regiment, was hospitalized with fever, discovered, and expelled for "sexual incompatibility," but Sarah Emma Edmonds of the 2nd Michigan Infantry was luckier and lived to write a popular memoir, *Nurse and Spy,* without mentioning that she was Franklin Thompson at the time. Some were estranged from their families, but others wrote letters home, letters sometimes kept in the attic as a shameful family secret—like Rosetta Wakeman's.

Wakeman enlisted in the 153rd New York for the adventure and the change from a hardscrabble farm in upstate New York; as she wrote home, she was "tired of staying in that neighborhood." As Lyons Wakeman, she spent much of the war on guard duty around Washington, D.C., where she met several women similarly under cover, two spies and a major who had ridden into battle giving orders and urging her men forward and was now in prison for violating regulations by being female. Wakeman pined for action, and was finally sent south to Louisiana and the misbegotten Red River Campaign. She wrote, "I was under fire about four hours and lay on the field of battle all night."

In her letters she seemed almost to look forward to a gallant death in battle, but the climate killed more than the bullets did and she died in a New Orleans military hospital of chronic diarrhea. Somebody there kept her secret, though, and she was buried in grave number 711 as Lyons Wakeman.

Longest of all was the illustrious military career of Dr. James Barry. Barry enrolled as a medical student at Edinburgh University in 1808, age fifteen or sixteen. After graduating, he joined the British army as a medical surgeon and served with distinction all over the far-flung empire. He soldiered and doctored in Canada, South Africa, India, the West Indies, and among the leper colonies, a popular fellow, though often in scrapes and fistfights. He was quick-tempered and fought a number of duels in the old-fashioned way, with swords, killing at least one opponent. He was known on several continents as a breaker of feminine hearts, but he didn't seem to be the marrying kind. In the course of his service he rose to the considerable rank of medical superintendent-general, and finally retired to London, where he died in the fullness of years in 1865.

The army doctor, on his routine inspection of the body, was particularly startled, since he'd served under Barry in South Africa without suspecting a thing, but neither had anyone else in the military. How Barry survived the physical exam essential for enlisting in the first place is a mystery; perhaps he sent a friend of the correct gender. Once in, he seemed a man of unusual physical modesty, but this was held in his favor, as a gentlemanly trait. When contacted, his astounded classmates at Edinburgh recalled only that he couldn't be persuaded to take up boxing, but no doubt his swordsmanship made up for this delicacy.

Nobody ever found out who she was, though you might consider that, after so long, she'd won the right to be whoever she said she was. Her tombstone reads simply, "Dr. James Barry."

British feminists cheered. They penned many a tribute, one stating: "In her numerous reports she proved herself a skillful doctor, and an enthusiast at her work. She wrote fearlessly and frankly, always ready to expose incompetence and charlatanism, even though it involved her in controversy and opposition. For high courage nothing could exceed the spirit of this woman who was so far ahead of her time that, to achieve her purpose, she renounced her sex."

Perhaps renouncing her sex wasn't so painful. Whoever she'd been at fourteen, at fifteen she buttoned on her trousers and went forth to see the world as an army surgeon, forge a distinguished career, and have considerably more fun than the average housewife in skirts stirring oatmeal in nineteenth-century Scotland.

Menswear

As soon as men and women stopped draping identical bearskins around their shoulders and developed different modes of dress, one for each sex, as identity markers rather than just weather-proofing, their separation was carved in stone. Whatever a man wore, even if it was a flowing ceremonial robe or a floor-length cassock, it meant that he was a man, and in charge here, and for a woman to wear similar garments was an attempt to seize power under false pretenses. It was taboo. It was much worse than wearing nothing at all. Deuteronomy makes it clear: "The woman shall not wear that which pertaineth to a man, neither shall a man put on a woman's garment; for all that do so are abomination unto the Lord thy God." (Considering that He created us stark naked, it seems odd of Him to take such an interest in our later wardrobes.)

To say, as men and women alike still do, that a man should wear the pants in the family means that his word should be law. Pants mean authority. Authority means manhood. In many times and places, small boys were kept in short pants or knickers or even dresses until the proper time, when they crossed over into full manhood in the initiation ceremony of the first long

31

pants. (Pants had their drawbacks, too. In some societies, a boy baby dangerously ill would be dressed as a girl as a precaution, so death wouldn't bother to stop for him.)

Women wore dresses. Through much of history it was felt that, to discourage lustful thoughts in onlookers, women should be considered a single, indivisibly welded unit from the waist down. If a man could see that they had two legs, or even two ankles, then he might make the inference that the legs joined the body at some point, and speculate lewdly thereon. When I was a child we had a brass dinner-bell of a woman in a long brass skirt; within it she was hollow, except for a brass clapper. The perfect lady.

Through the millennia, women's dresses and sometimes layers of petticoats hung down to their shoes or beyond, sweeping up whatever dust, mud, tobacco spittle, or cow dung they passed. They sloshed through puddles; to have lifted them clear might expose what was called "a well-turned ankle" and corrupt the observer's morals. Before the washing machine and dryer, they were often wet and dirty, and a dismal handicap in farmwork.

The handicap may have been part of the point. The properly dressed woman could barely navigate across the parlor floor, let alone jump on a horse and head for the horizon, leaving her husband with no one to wash his socks. If a man were chasing her, for whatever purpose, she couldn't outrun him, with her skirts snatched back by twigs and brambles or sodden with mud, or leap over a fence or across a bog, or climb a tree.

In *Pride and Prejudice,* Elizabeth Bennet, as evidence of her rebellious spirit, walks cross-country to visit her sick sister, and the women of the household are disgusted by her condition on arrival: "'I hope you saw her petticoat, six inches deep in mud I am absolutely certain; and the gown which had been let down to hide it, not doing its office.'" Nice women stayed home.

Strict Islamic societies today emphasize this point by dressing their women like black fire hydrants; peering through a mesh slit, with no peripheral vision, almost incapable of distinguishing rice from melons in the market, they're in constant danger of being blindsided by a truck, which would serve them right for leaving the house in the first place.

During World War II, women recruited to work in the munitions factories while the men were away were allowed to wear pants to work. Pants showed that they were honorary men for the duration of the war. Pants were a badge of merit, a pat on the head for their patriotic sacrifice. After the war they were expected to turn in their trousers and go back to dresses again, demoted. Those who clung to the practical, comfortable trousers were sneered at. It was generally agreed that they looked hideous in them, because the backsides of women, unlike the trim butts of their brothers, were bulbous and ugly and ought to be hidden by skirts. "Women in slacks," wrote Ogden Nash, "Should not turn their backs."

As the twentieth century rolled on, skirts got shorter and the modesty principle vanished, leaving only the pure taboo. Pants still mean authority, and authority in a woman is simply not very nice. Women can wear slacks or jeans on weekends, or to the supermarket or for a hike in the country, but they wear dresses to the PTA meeting, to church, and to work.

For a giddy while in the 1970s women in hard-won managerial positions wore pants-suits to the office, sometimes of the same fabric as a man's—what Joan of Arc's judges called *difformitate habitus,* "monstrous clothing." The idea quickly slunk away. The men in the office were uncomfortable. They wouldn't have said so, and perhaps didn't even recognize it consciously, but a woman in a tailored suit ending in pants rather than a skirt felt to them, however sweetly she smiled, like a threat. A cold, hard, dangerous person. Uneasy, they applied for transfers. The women went back to skirts. An unthreatening woman of lowly status might wear pants, but British prime minister Margaret Thatcher, known to her friends as "The Iron Lady," wore skirts, and the fierce Israeli prime minister Golda Meir reviewed her troops in granny dresses.

A popular television show at the dawn of the twenty-first century centers on a woman lawyer. The creators obviously thought hard about their dilemma: though it's politically correct to show women in the professions, if she actually looked and dressed like a lawyer, viewers of both sexes would be alienated and wish her ill. The solution was to make her a giddy-schoolgirl lawyer, a ditz with long blond hair falling in waifish skeins to her waist. In one episode she appears in court in a skirt so short it barely covers the necessary, and the judge threatens to hold her in contempt. She counters that the skirt is her means of self-expression as a woman. Presumably the viewers sympathized. If she'd chosen to express herself as a lawyer instead, in a pinstriped three-piece suit, sets would have clicked off across the nation.

Dresses and pants produce two totally different mind-sets in the wearer. A woman strolling down the street on a splendid morning might feel like whistling, but whistling in a dress would be absurd. Whistling implies and requires pants, and the swagger that goes with them. Ideally, it calls for pockets to thrust the hands into, or at least a sturdy waistband for the thumbs. In a dress, we feel kinder and gentler, but less capable and much less cocky.

The magic of menswear is so powerfully transforming that, according to Shakespeare, immediately a woman puts it on she's unrecognizable. In his day, both men and women wore starchy neck-ruffs that must have itched; women wore long fitted gowns; men wore shirts with flowing sleeves, elaborate tight-waisted vests, short skirts or bloomers, and long stockings with garters. It was practical and by far the best-looking, most creative, and generally most becoming menswear ever designed, and must have made the gentlemen very happy when dressing in the morning, and on a pretty young woman it must have been wonderfully fetching. Once she put it on, though, her own mother didn't know her. In *The Merchant of Venice,* Portia appears in court thus disguised, pretending to be a learned young doctor, and speaks of the quality of mercy; her husband, standing by, doesn't know who she is. In *As You Like It,* when Rosalind takes off her long gown and puts on stockings and britches and calls herself Ganymede, even at close quarters and during long conversations, neither the young man madly in love with her nor her father, the Duke, thinks she looks even vaguely familiar. In *Twelfth Night,* Viola changes clothes and her beloved twin brother does think she looks familiar but can't place her, except that she looks exactly like him and might be a relative. In *Cymbeline,* Imogen puts on the menswear and her dear husband not only doesn't know her, he knocks her down for impudence; her father doesn't know her either.

None of these ladies wore false beards or masks or wigs, just "that which pertaineth to a man"; if your wife, daughter, lover, or twin sister were dressed like a man, how could she possibly still be your wife, lover, sister, daughter? She is not just a stranger, she's transfigured, like a witch turning into a cat, by changing her clothes. Clothes make the man. Apparently Shakespeare's audience wasn't outraged by the usurpation, knowing full well that the actors were really young men pretending to be women pretending to be men, and thus entitled.

Joan of Arc, however, who really did wear menswear––in her day a belted short jerkin of mid-thigh length, long stockings, and boots (exactly what the well-dressed young woman of the 1960s wore in Manhattan) and sometimes armor too—isn't wearing them in Shakespeare's *Henry VI, Part I,* or at least not in the stage directions; perhaps the other characters in the play couldn't have recognized her, rendering her presence useless.

Joan's admirers and detractors alike, who had no trouble accepting lesser matters like divine visions or satanic witchcraft, couldn't handle the jerkin and stockings. In a medieval painting of her bound to the stake, she's wearing a floor-length red evening gown, cut low in the bosom. In a Victorian compromise, her portrait shows her in heavy armor from neck to hips, and from hips to heels in an orange print skirt. It's slit to the waist so we get a glimpse of armored leg; apparently she only wore it to hinder walking. Perhaps it would have been impious to show a saintly lady, however warlike, without a skirt somewhere in the picture. In some of the statues, she's positively swaddled in draperies. Ingres did draw her in full armor, plated like a celestial lizard, but Fragonard saw her as a buxom, double-chinned matron in a dress that not only reaches the floor but ripples generously out over it on all sides.

Joan has always been vexing, however you inspect her. George Bernard Shaw calls her "the queerest fish among the eccentric worthies of the Middle Ages." If we can believe in her voices and visions, the rest follows naturally, but this involves believing that God, like the interfering partisan gods and goddesses of Olympus, took a fierce interest in the fine points of the Hundred Years War and was rooting for the French, wanted badly to raise the Siege of Orleans and crown the weasely Dauphin, and chose a bizarrely roundabout way to go about it.

The Church itself has doubts. With masterful delicacy, the *Catholic Encyclopedia* says of her visions that their "supernatural character it would now be rash to question." Not foolish, or impious, or ignorant, but "rash," a risky public-relations move.

For those unable or unwilling to believe, the story is even stranger: What else could have impelled this illiterate village teenager to decide to throw the English out of France and set forth all friendless to defy the civil, military, and religious authorities? Not to mention winning all those battles? Shaw, an unbeliever, wrestles valiantly with the question and concludes that some people have desires so strong and imaginations so vivid that they create and believe in the illusions that sustain them: Joan's visions were a sort of out-of-body embodiment of her own wishes, complete with step-by-step instructions.

Maybe. She refused to give the court a physical description of her saintly visitors but stood firm on their reality, heresy or not. *Was she lying?* The *Catholic Encyclopedia* mutters ambiguously ". . . unless we accuse the Maid of deliberate falsehood, which no one is prepared to do . . ." Might we entertain the notion anyway? Is it possible that she simply concocted the whole story of divine tutorial visitors to give weight to her purely secular mission? Without major, even divine, credentials, no village girl would have been allowed to lead troops, or even to speak to the officers in charge; without a heavenly mandate, she would have been roughed up by soldiers and hangers-on and sent back home. Why not invent a mandate?

But however did she manage to do what she did? Mark Twain has no trouble with this, because in his eyes she is "easily and by far the most extraordinary person the human race has ever produced." He says she "stands alone, and must continue to stand alone, by reason of the unfellowed fact that in the things wherein she was great she was so without a shade or suggestion of help from preparatory teaching, practice, environment, or experience." The unique genius is always a bit hard to come to grips with, though; easier to suppose she had divine help.

Or perhaps satanic help. If you were English, it was pleasanter to believe that Joan was a witch than that God was fighting for the French. Even now the theory is held in some learned circles that she was a member of a well-organized coven of witches. This is the angle Shakespeare chose, and produced a most peculiar play.

He calls her "La Pucelle," which sounds rude but means virgin, and she starts out splendidly. She is, of course, a beauty, since heroines must be beautiful, but she explains that she wasn't always; her job as a shepherdess, out in the sun, had made her "black and swart," but exposed to the rays of her vision of the Virgin Mary she was altered, and "That beauty am I blessed with that you see." Charles the Dauphin says he won't believe she's been sent to save France unless she can best him in single combat, which she promptly does, though this was no great feat if reports of the wormy young Charles are true.

The English consider her supernaturally wicked from the beginning. After she defeats him, Talbot mutters, "A witch, by fear, not force, like Hannibal / Drives back our troops and conquers as she lists. . . ." They call her a "shameless courtezan" and "a hag of all" with "lustful paramours."

It's clear that our author doesn't agree. Her speeches are charming and sensible, unlike the weird imprecations of *Macbeth*'s witches, and she repeatedly beats the English heroes at hand-to-hand combat and leads her victorious troops with gallantry. "Of all base passions, fear is most accursed," she cries.

Without warning, in act V, our heroine turns villain. She summons a gang of foul fiends from hell, and it turns out that they, not the Virgin Mary, had supported her victories. She tries to bargain with them for France: "My body shall / Pay recompense, if you will grant my suit." When sex doesn't work, she goes all the way: "Then take my soul, my body, soul and all, / Before that England give the French the foil." No takers. The fiends depart, carrying her supernatural powers with them, so that when she next grapples one-on-one with the Duke of York, he easily takes her prisoner.

The transformation is so complete she's even lost her looks; York says, "See, how the ugly witch doth bend her brows." She curses him, she curses Charles, and later, on her way to the stake, when her poor old father shows up wringing his hands, she curses him too: "Decrepit miser! Base, ignoble wretch! / I am descended of a gentler blood: / Thou art no father nor no friend of mine." Not only a sorceress, but an unfilial snob as well. Deserves to burn.

This abrupt switch from sweet-spoken saint to railing witch must have mystified audiences. It's been suggested that someone else rewrote the last act, or that Shakespeare, in a fit of diplomatic patriotism, rewrote it himself after protests. Maybe, being young and inexperienced, he didn't realize where he was leading himself, and created a noble-minded, fearless, selfless, and thoroughly likable heroine who was going to be handed over to the English for burning, causing English audiences to weep for England's enemy. More likely, several people wrote the play, least of them, if at all, Shakespeare, and none of them knew what to think of her a hundred and sixty years after she went up in flames.

Henry VI, Part I, is a baffling work, and it's small wonder few of us have ever seen it on stage. A shame, though, because the part, for an actress who can manage the transition, is a plum, though not as plummy as George Bernard Shaw's Saint Joan.

Those who are neither French nor Catholic have now demoted Joan to a delusional mental defective, ignorant and probably schizophrenic, who was duped to death by her own hallucinations. This doesn't fit well with her military and political strategies, which Shaw compared to Napoleon's and called "masterstrokes that saved France," so the common wisdom discounts them and demotes her to a kind of mascot, with no more influence on tactics than the regimental flag. Some common wisdom thinks she's mythical, a nursery tale run amok. According to a *Wall Street Journal* survey, 12 percent of all Americans think she was Noah's wife. Some confuse her with Pope Joan.

Pope Joan was educated at Cologne in the ninth century and, falling in love with a Benedictine monk, fled with him to Athens disguised as a man. After he died, she went to Rome, still in menswear and calling herself Joannes Anglicus, and entered the priesthood, presently being awarded a cardinal's hat. She was elected Pope John VIII, in between Leo IV and Benedict III, but died publicly in childbirth in the very midst of a papal procession. For four hundred years over a hundred authors wrote authoritative works about her.

Unfortunately there's not a word of truth in the tale. There never was a Pope Joan, and nobody knows how the myth got started. Maybe it was an instructive parable about the biological unfitness of women for church office.

However uncomfortable she may make us, there really was a Joan of Arc.

She was born in 1412, burned in 1431, and canonized in 1920.

The notion of her as a poor barefoot shepherdess is romantic, but actually she was quite respectable. Her father was indeed a peasant farmer, but his neighbors looked up to him, asked his advice, and elected him to act for them in village matters. The d'Arcs lived in a two-storey stone house with a tilted slate roof that looks quite adequate for a family with five children, and besides, it's still standing, which is more than most of our houses will be able to say in six hundred years.

Joan's first angelic visitor, when she was twelve, was the

Archangel Michael, who kept telling her to be a good girl and then sent the saints Catherine and Margaret as her counselors. They visited regularly for the next four years, though oddly, given the natural human tendency to brag, she didn't mention them to anyone, even her priest, at the time. Finally Michael reappeared and told her to leave the village and go help her king.

He needed all the help he could get. The French and the English had been fighting over the French crown for nearly a hundred years and the English, with those wicked longbows that carried the day at Agincourt in 1415, kept winning. Half France felt the country belonged to the infant English king, Henry VI, and the other half said it was the French Charles VII's, but Charles had never been crowned; there was some doubt about his legitimacy. He was an unattractive creature with a flabby nose, thick lips, and piggy little eyes with bags under them, but God wanted him officialized anyway and sent Joan to do the job. He told her to go to Baudricourt, captain of the fortress at Vaucouleurs, and he'd see her safely on the road.

Through her sheer intensity, which must have been daunting, she persuaded Baudricourt to give her a horse, a dagger for self-defense, and half a dozen men to take her to Chinon, where the Dauphin lurked dispiritedly, surrounded by councilors who were smarter than he was and had their own agendas. It was 350 miles, a nasty trip in February, but she cut her hair short, put on the tunic and tights that would later make so much trouble, and set merrily forth.

She couldn't, as she said herself, tell A from B, but she could dictate a fine subtle letter, and at Fierbois, near Chinon, she sent one to the Dauphin that convinced him to see her. (There's a persistent story that he disguised himself to test her, and, divinely guided, she recognized him at once.) She told him God had sent her to get him his crown, and apparently he believed her, but his advisors didn't. They sent her off to Poitiers to be investigated by a panel of theologians; she answered them bravely and firmly, and they, too, were convinced. They recommended that she be given troops and sent to Orleans. This is perfectly amazing behavior from a panel of theologians; Joan's powers of persuasion must have amounted to genius.

Impressed, the Dauphin had a suit of armor tailored to her girlish measure, lacking only the helmet's visor; she said she wanted her face to be visible. She had a white banner made up, showing Christ sitting on a rainbow accepting the fleur-de-lis of France. She refused the offered sword, because, she said there was a special sword, hidden behind the altar at the church at Fierbois, with five crosses cut into the blade; that one was hers. At Fierbois, they rummaged around and found it, all rusted, in a forgotten chest. This was clearly a miracle, and her stock went up. (She'd stopped at Fierbois to write to the Dauphin. How she knew about the sword is another matter.)

During the preparations, she made friends with the powerful Duke of Alençon, who showed her how to use a lance. Then, with several thousand soldiers and wagons full of food for the hungry city, she led the way to Orleans, under siege by the English, Lord Talbot commanding, for six months now.

As an officer, she ran a tight ship. When she was disobeyed, as she often was, since seasoned commanders are unhappy taking orders from a sixteen-year-old girl in her first battles, she raged furiously: her instructions came from God. God turned out to have a much bolder approach to warfare than the French officers.

Barefaced, she marched into the city and demanded that the English surrender; they laughed. She attacked the English fortresses that guarded the city. At St. Loup, she rode up and found her troops in retreat, spun them around, and led them into battle; they stormed the fortress and burned it. This was the first

English stronghold the French had taken in nearly a hundred years and it brightened their spirits considerably. They took another fortress, and then moved on to Les Tourelles, considered impregnable. The battle there was bloody, with Joan in the thick of it always. While placing a scaling ladder against the wall, she was pierced through the neck by an arrow. They carried her bleeding to shelter; a soldier cut off the arrow's point, and she pulled out the shaft and went back to the fray. Her troops were exhausted and her captains begged for a retreat, but she drove them on over the wall while others set fire to the drawbridge. She called on the English to surrender but their captain found death better than surrendering to a woman; trying to escape, he fell through the smoldering drawbridge and drowned in the moat.

The surviving English departed. Saved, Orleans cheered and cheered.

Assignment two was crowning the Dauphin at Reims, and it called for political maneuvering rather than raw courage. Diplomacy was never her strong point. The Dauphin's advisors weren't best pleased at Joan's popularity with the people, and less pleased at the thought of a king indebted to her rather than to them—though as it turned out they needn't have worried about his gratitude.

He himself didn't know what to think. He never did.

Reims lay deep in English and Burgundian territory, the Duke of Burgundy being on the English team. English strongholds made the way too dangerous for Charles to travel. Very well, then, Joan would take them. At the first, she went straight for the jugular, crying "At them! At them!" and demanding unconditional surrender. She was hit, but picked herself up and led the troops shouting over the wall, and the garrison fell. Then she took Meung, and Beaugency surrendered. English reinforcements arrived, but Joan's men, drunk with success, cut them to pieces, leaving over two thousand dead and taking a thousand prisoners. (Joan herself was very much against the taking of prisoners, though ransoms for the captured were half the fun of medieval warfare; she felt it distracted the soldiers and slowed down the fighting. She thought heavy armor slowed it down too, and that artillery, not arrows, was the wave of the future. Her angelic instructors knew a thing or two.)

On to Reims. The Dauphin's advisors were still against it, but who could argue with all those miraculous victories? With the prospective king in tow, she fought her way fortress by fortress to the city where the first French Christian king had been crowned. When they arrived, the Burgundian captain offered to hold the city against her, but the citizens refused and cheered the wayfarers in.

The English had carried off the great crown of Charlemagne, but a backup crown was found and the holy oil duly smeared on the Dauphin, making him Charles VII.

Great partying followed. Jacques d'Arc made the trip to congratulate his daughter, and the king rewarded him by absolving his village from taxes. Joan was a hero. Asked, "Do you really fight? Are you not afraid?" she answered prophetically, "I fear nothing but treachery."

She wanted Charles to march on Burgundian Paris, but he dithered. Perhaps he felt that now he was king, it was unbecoming to be pushed around by a village girl. She wrote repeatedly to the Duke of Burgundy, urging him to break with the English. Behind her back, Charles signed an ambiguous truce with Burgundy. She was furious. She distrusted treaties and would always rather fight than sign. She was right; Burgundy used the truce time to send for English reinforcements.

The English were recovering. Bedford wrote a nasty letter to Charles, saying he was calling himself king "without cause" and with the help of "superstitious and damnable persons such as a woman of disorderly and infamous life and dissolute manners dressed in the clothes of a man."

Joan and her old friend Alençon dragged the king off to attack Paris, at the time a rather battered and pitiful city. The battle was ill-starred. Joan broke her sword, which her troops saw as a bad omen. She was hit in the thigh by a crossbow bolt; her page was killed and her banner fell to the ground. Gamely, the next day she had herself lifted onto her horse to press the attack; there was a back way into the city where her troops had built a bridge over the Seine. When she got there, she found that Charles, having decided to fight no more, had had the bridge taken apart and the pieces dropped in the river. He retreated toward the Loire, where his army disintegrated. Perhaps he still hoped for a peaceful settlement with Burgundy, and so snatched defeat from the jaws of victory.

Joan was crushed. She managed a few more victories, taking St. Pierre-le-Moustier almost single-handedly, and Melun, and rescuing the terrorized folk of Lagny, but her siege of La Charité-sûr-Loire had to be called off and her captains were ignoring her orders. While at Lagny, she had joined other women in praying over the body of an infant who had died unbaptized; the child revived just long enough to receive the sacrament. This persuaded her followers that she was a saint and her enemies that she was a sorceress.

The end was close. His latest truce with Charles having expired, Burgundy marched on Compiègne. Joan rode to the rescue. Fighting a losing battle outside the walls, she refused to retreat when her troops fled back to the city, and the French garrison commander panicked and closed the gates, locking her out. She was taken prisoner by a Burgundian, who sold her to the English for a tidy sum.

All hands turned against her. Archbishop Regnault said she deserved to be captured "because she would not take advice but would follow her own will." Charles's chief minister was said to be "overcome with delight." The general public was overcome with grief and begged Charles to buy their heroine back from the English, but "king" is not an elective office and he had no comment.

The ingratitude is staggering. Ransom was the name of the game at the time: Charles, who owed her his crown, could have paid it; the prosperous City of Orleans, which owed her its freedom, could have paid it; the Church that gave her its sanction at Poitiers would hardly have noticed paying it; or she might have been exchanged, gratis, for an English prisoner, perhaps the Duke of Suffolk. For that matter, she could have been rescued shortly after her capture by her old comrade-in-arms La Hire, who had troops nearby. Nobody offered. Full revenge would be taken for all her victories, and her courage, and her wounds, and all the cold nights sleeping on the ground. She hadn't a friend in the world.

With good reason. Charles was embarrassed by her help; his ministers were jealous of her popularity; the English were humiliated by their defeats. To the establishment—all the establishments—she was a threat. She's been called the first Protestant, since she claimed to speak directly with God instead of going through Church channels. She's been called the first patriot, since she encouraged Frenchmen to unite as a nation and follow a single king, threatening the feudal system of loyalties so dear to local dukes. For those who believed she was a witch under satanic guidance, she threatened Christianity itself.

Everyone wanted her out of the way, but the English, wary of creating a martyr, needed her thoroughly discredited first by the Church. For five months they held her prisoner in a series of strongholds; though in theory she was the Church's prey, they refused to send her to an ecclesiastical prison because, in case she was acquitted of heresy, they wanted to keep a grip on her. She was guarded night and day by the roughest of soldiers, who abused and insulted her. She tried to escape. Once she got as far as the gates before they caught her; then she jumped from a seventy-foot tower. The fall knocked her unconscious but didn't kill her, offering further proof of witchcraft. After that she was kept chained hand and foot to a huge log. She was nineteen.

The ecclesiastical court met under Pierre Cauchon, Bishop of Beauvais, enemy of Charles, paid high councillor to the English, who hoped for the reward of an archbishopric if he convicted. His superior was Joan's old enemy, Archbishop Regnault.

Her appearance before the court in hose and jerkin caused gasps of horror, but in the six public sessions she answered the church dignitaries and theologians bravely, intelligently, courteously, and stubbornly. She had no legal council. Nothing could be proved against her, and some of the judges wanted the charges dismissed, but Cauchon's career was riding on conviction and he pressed on, taking the trial private and cross-examining her in her cell. He threatened her with torture but held his hand, afraid torture might cast some shadow on his proceedings.

There were seventy charges, full of demons and evil spirits and the wearing of "immodest dress, contrary to the Holy Scripture." To all charges she calmly referred herself to the judgment of God, which further angered the churchmen: she was going over their heads. She tried to appeal the case to the Pope, but Cauchon said, "The Pope is too far away." And she warned that, whatever happened to her, the English would be out of France within seven years.

The evidence boiled down to her refusal to admit that her visions were "false and diabolical," and this marked her as a heretic. Heretics could be turned over to the English civil authorities for burning. (The church could, of course, have simply excommunicated her, but this wouldn't have satisfied Cauchon's ambitions.)

Her voices, she had said, promised she would be rescued. When she was led to the cemetery for her final sentencing and saw no rescue at hand, perhaps through simple exhaustion at the endless haranguing, she made some sort of recantation, though the brief statement she agreed to was unrelated to the many pages the Church later claimed she'd agreed to. Back in her cell, when she found out that she'd only traded the stake for life in an English dungeon, she defiantly put her menswear back on again, meaning she rejected the recantation.

Some scholars swear it was a trap, and that the guards, under Cauchon's orders, stole the dress she'd finally consented to and left nothing else in the cell to wear. This is one of those baffling historical assertions to which we can only answer: Says who? The guards? Cauchon? Joan? No, she put on the hose and jerkin, which must have been fairly appalling after a year in prison, to thumb her nose at the world.

As a relapsed heretic, she was burned at the stake in the Rouen marketplace, holding a makeshift cross and calling on Jesus. Her ashes were thrown in the Seine. Within seven years, the English grip, if not quite gone, was indeed broken and Charles was in Paris.

Maybe she was a saint of miraculous visions. Maybe she was a delusional hysteric. Or maybe, back home in Domrémy, she'd invented the visions and designed for herself the grandest adventure of all. In any case, it's pleasant to remember her on that first long journey to Chinon, straddling her horse in the new freedom of hose and jerkin, hair chopped short and bristly, her breath puffing white in the February air as she whistled along the roads.

People's adventures are dictated by their times. To what unknown islands would Amelia Earhart have flown if, like Joan, she'd been born in 1412? What would Joan have conquered if, like George Sand, she'd been born in 1804? In our own times, only the very rich can have adventures, and hire guides to haul them up Mount Everest so they can perish in unexpected storms, or buy yachts so they can drown in the annual Sydney-to-Hobart race. The source of the Nile has been discovered and the South Pole charted. Not even the most mannerly and well-connected young man can now apply to join King Arthur's Round Table and rescue maidens and slay dragons, not unless the dragons involve Microsoft. Chronology is destiny.

George Sand was another independent, lion-hearted Frenchwoman in menswear, but she was born in tamer days and we remember her only for wearing pants, sleeping with Chopin, and writing novels nobody reads anymore. In the nineteenth century, writing was the only respectable career open for a woman in need of money, but nobody could call it adventure; it consists of sitting still, indoors, for hours and days and years, making marks on a piece of paper. She might have been happier with stagecoach robbery, but a woman with children can't live on the dark side of the law. Still, she did the best she could to strike some sparks from her life.

As a child she ran free in boys' clothes on the family estate in Berry, with horses to ride and room to roam. Her mother, grandmother, and great-grandmother all believed in the equality of women; radicals ran in the family. When George was in Paris, she complained to her mother of the impossible expense of fashionable dresses and ladies' shoes and their unfitness for bad weather and filthy sidewalks, but without them she couldn't go to the theater, salons, clubs, literary gatherings. Her mother wrote back saying that when she and her husband were themselves young and broke, her husband decided to dress her as a boy so she could go places with him—"Oh, anywhere we wanted. And it halved our bills."

If George was always an unusually sweet-natured rebel, perhaps it was thanks to the women who raised her; the most disagreeable social rebels seem to be kicking against their upbringing, but it was laws, not friends and family, that set George's face sideways to society. Seizing the suggestion, she was thereafter seen in all the smart places in the inexpensive but respectable jacket and trousers of a young man, avoiding the stares a pretty woman would draw, watching and listening and smoking a cigar.

But that came only after she'd been blooded in earlier battles.

She was born Amantine-Aurore-Lucile Dupin, which must have made the switch to "George" a great relief. Her father was thrown from a horse and killed when she was five and her mother was a capricious parent, leaving her with her grandmother on the estate, Nohant, whenever she had other things to do. Aurore, as she was then, spent some time in a convent school, and then came back to take care of the old lady, put her trousers on again, ride and shoot and study the trees and plants and creatures at Nohant; her education was only slightly more extensive than Saint Joan's and she could never do even the simplest arithmetic.

At eighteen, inexplicably, she married a cavalry officer

named Casimir Dudevant. He turned out to be a drunk, and a bully, and hit her, and bedded everything that couldn't outrun him, including her maid. They had two children. Solange, the daughter, was a nasty child who turned even more ungrateful and unmanageable in adolescence, but the son, Maurice, if undistinguished, was nicer.

During her years in the country with—and often without—Dudevant, she wore herself out in good works, riding around on horseback through dark and stormy nights with her homegrown herbal remedies to dose the ailing peasantry. The peasantry was ungrateful and virtue wasn't her natural bent. She wrote, "I believe I have never met anyone as stupidly good as I am. I have a perfect right to say so because my character is naturally violent and self-willed."

Dudevant's drinking and wenching got worse, and it seems she wasn't strictly faithful herself, but she hung on for the children's sake, like mothers before and since. Then, after seven years, she steeled herself to make a break for it, run for Paris—leaving the children at Nohant, which she'd inherited from her grandmother—and earn enough money to take control of her estate away from Dudevant and have the children too. Not an easy task under the laws of the time. Husbands ruled.

Paris was a crackling storm center of artistic, literary, and political energy, and Aurore turned herself into George and sprang into its vortex. She would always write lovingly of country life, but after rusticating so long with Dudevant, the cafés and ideas and arguments of Montparnasse must have been heaven. She wrote wicked political satires for *Figaro;* she had a talent for vivid friendships, and presently knew everyone interesting. She was jolly company, and talented, and, they say, lovely. The poet Heinrich Heine, who adored her, rhapsodized over her "velvet-soft, dark, unfathomable eyes," and strangers turned to stare at her. Aside from expense, the reason she went on wearing her gentleman's clothing was so, like Joan among the soldiers, she could be welcomed as a companion without the distraction of her pretty person. Dressed as a man, she was treated as a man, and allowed to argue and speak her mind. Besides, the women of the mid-nineteenth century were forced into the most hideously unbecoming dresses and hair-styles in all of history, so that we automatically feel they must have been as gloomy, pious, and dull as they look; hard to think of them sparkling in witty salons like the elegantly coiffed and rouged ladies of Versailles. Probably George looked much more interesting, if sexually neutral, in jacket and trousers.

We have to take her beauty on faith. However kindly we peer at her portraits, she looks like a basset hound in a bonnet. We're looking at two George Sands, the fiery one who kindled all Paris in the 1830s and forties, in love with freedom and swaggering through town with a cigar, and the surviving portrait of a contented Victorian country dormouse, half asleep.

Her first novel, *Indiana,* came out in 1832; it dealt with a woman married to a beastly man and loved by a nice one, but trapped by the "ignorant tyranny" of the divorce laws. It sold well enough so that she could send for Solange to come join her in Paris, and it made her the pet of the town. Exuberant, she took the poet de Vigny to bed.

Sand has been criticized for having too many lovers, though exactly how many is too many may be open for debate. Probably they seem like a multitude because of their high profiles, all the poets and musicians and novelists in the news, and if she had slept with twice that many footmen and cab drivers nobody would have noticed. One authoritative current reference work states flatly that she was frigid, and the string of bed-mates was her pursuit of the elusive satisfaction; the authority doesn't say how it knows. Sand herself, in the throes of an affair, wrote in her private journal, "Warm, supple body, never again will you hover over me, as did Elisha over the dead child, to bring it back to life. . . . Henceforth in my ardent nights I shall be driven to embrace the trunks of pine trees or rocks in the forest, crying aloud your name, and when I have dreamed my ecstasy I shall fall fainting on the moist earth." If she really was frigid, she had a busy imagination.

There's also a persistent rumor, circulated by a disappointed lover, that she was a lesbian.

Freudians believe that the more normal we seem, the more peculiar we probably are; others are at liberty to believe that Sand liked men and enjoyed their company in bed.

Otherwise her life was fairly orderly. In the evenings she gave small dinners for two or three friends. At midnight she said goodnight and retired to write until eight or nine in the morning, neatly, swiftly, never crossing out a line, covering twenty pages a night without fail. She wrote too much too fast, regularly turning out two novels a year, for a lifetime total of sixty, plus twenty-five plays, an autobiography, and hundreds of short pieces. She worked for money for her children and she loved them like a tiger, fighting Dudevant for them and, when they were away, writing them every day and dreaming every night that they were lost and she was searching the world for them.

Valentine came out the same year as *Indiana,* foreshadowing her social activism with its peasant hero. Then she wrote *Lelia,* and just before it was published Alfred de Musset, a charming young poet known to some as "Mademoiselle Byron" and a fellow contributor to the *Revue des Deux Mondes,* moved into her apartment and bed.

Lelia is a long prose poem concerning a proud and cynical woman who has been scarred by a beastly marriage; she and a starry-eyed young poet fall in love, but her heart is so wounded by her experience that she rejects him and joins a convent. He commits suicide. It sounds harmless enough now, but then it caused widespread consternation. Her message was that women who have married disastrously should be allowed to divorce and marry again, and the idea was more than radical: it meant the end of civilization, the death of marriage, the ruin of the family. One English critic cried, "A few George Sands will soon reduce France to a level with the orang-outang. . . ." The liberal French literati loved it. The *Revue des Deux Mondes* called it "this century's analysis of itself. It is the agonized cry of a society which has denied God and truth, only to look into its own heart and find that its dreams are illusions." Sainte-Beuve, the top literary critic of the time, said she "sounded every abyss of thought" and bore "the weight of an amount of wisdom that would make a man's hair fall out or turn white . . . lightly, easily, without loss of poise." A genius, he said, with a dazzling future.

If she'd been in a reasonable state of mind, the praise might have shored up her confidence and made her take her work seriously, as something more than a means to support her family. Unfortunately by this time she was so besotted with de Musset she could hardly think. She had written *Lelia* when she was living alone and unloved, and for art's sake she probably should have stayed that way, but that was an unthinkable price to pay for art; George loved being in love.

She should have known better, but who ever does? She was twenty-nine, and famous, and experienced; de Musset was not yet a famous poet (back when that wasn't an oxymoron) and seems to have been feckless, spiteful, and a bit of a twerp. Nevertheless, when she should have been leaping from the success of *Lelia* to new heights, she wallowed and agonized over the affair. She wrote half a dozen books in two years, but they were potboilers and damaged her reputation. She wrote because she needed money and her publishers pursued her, but her attention had gone chasing after de Musset. They went to Venice, where he got sick and, when she wasn't nursing him tenderly, she bedded his doctor, which he resented; they separated, reunited, separated again. She wrote him slavish letters. She cut off her hair and mailed it to him in an effort to melt his heart; she offered to cut off her hand and send that too. She thought of suicide, but the vision of Maurice's subsequent grief restrained her. Finally, exhausted, it was she who made the final break and rolled up her sleeves to recover her literary reputation, and her life.

Dudevant, having already tried blackmail and kidnaping, resurfaced, threatening her with a gun; he wanted money. She sued for a legal separation, and won, but he kept appealing until eventually she settled out of court, paying him half her inheritance as the price of freedom.

Then she took up with Chopin, an affair much glamorized by Hollywood. It lasted for eight years and did them both a world of good. George nursed him like a mother whenever his health broke down and took him for summers to Nohant, where he did some of his best work and broadened his range as a composer. Somehow he got along well with Solange, the witch-daughter, and gave her piano lessons. (Sand's dear friend Delacroix gave Maurice painting lessons. Nice to have a mother with good tutorial connections.)

George regained her literary crown, turning from love stories and the divorce laws to the pastoral novels with a social-equality theme that strengthened her reputation, though she still insisted, "My works provide merely temporary amusement and will die with me."

Not everyone agreed. Her novels were called "the Trojan horse in which liberal ideas traveled for the first time into Tsarist

Russia," and Dostoyevsky called her "one of the most brilliant, the most indomitable, and the most perfect champions" of the liberal cause. She was more admired than Dickens. Balzac, Turgenev, Chateaubriand, Henry James, Matthew Arnold, Dumas *père et fils*, Victor Hugo, and Oscar Wilde praised her. Flaubert, an unsentimental fellow, wept while reading *Marianne*. Whitman and Melville absorbed her influence. Has ever a writer so highly regarded fallen so fast and so far? Today the *Britannica* dismisses her work as fairy tales, "so-called rustic novels," and "sentimental socialism." The words "escapist" and "trash" have been used.

Perhaps she wouldn't mind—it was only what she said herself—but Balzac and Flaubert and Dostoyevsky might flinch at the slur on their judgment.

Solange married, and a quarrel about her husband closed down the long Sand-Chopin romance. Sand threw herself into politics. It was 1848, year of unrest and antimonarchical movements, and Sand was a joyful republican and published her own partisan newspaper. When offered, though, she turned down a candidacy for the National Assembly. She wrote to the Central Committee that women weren't ready to take part in political life: "In order for the condition of women to be so transformed, society must be transformed radically," meaning the end of marriage laws that require "tutelage to and dependence on a man" and take away a woman's civil rights and property, leaving her "still a minor at the age of eighty" and "a slave in principle."

In any case Louis Napoleon's coup put an end to the revolutionary movement, and she charmed her way out of a prison sentence for her part in it and took up writing plays. Here again she triumphed—Sarah Bernhardt starred in her *L'Autre*—and touched a chord with her contemporaries that eludes us today. And still she turned out her two novels a year, along with a four-volume autobiography; and still she had time to sit and talk for hours with friends. More time now, as romance ebbed out of her world while her spirits and health flourished.

Her friendships were as enthusiastic as her loves and, in a society that relished wicked gossip and the barbed wit, she was all gentleness and kind words. She and Franz Liszt would sit at opposite ends of a table working in quiet communion, occasionally looking up to chat. (They had been friends for years, and been on holiday together, and Paris spread rumors of an affair, but she retorted, "Liszt loves no one but God and the Holy Virgin, who does not resemble me in the slightest degree.")

Her late-blooming friendship with Flaubert delighted them both, and they corresponded voluminously. She sent him a picture of herself; he framed and hung it and called it the greatest honor ever bestowed on his house. Lovingly he called her, "Oh you, of the third sex!"

George Sand held the peculiar idea that she could be a man as well as a woman, alternately or simultaneously. As a woman, she was gentle and compassionate, nursing orphaned baby birds at Nohant as well as all her ailing friends and lovers, and de Musset called her *"la femme la plus femme"* he had ever known. But she often referred to herself in journals and letters as a man— "a man of letters" or "an average sort of fellow." Her journal contains long dialogues between the male and the female George Sand. Her menswear flaunted her right to be taken seriously and respected as a man, or at least a genderless person a man might sit down with, talk and listen to, drink and smoke and fall silent with in manly companionship. She didn't see why it was necessary to be of only one sex and lose the benefits of the other; why not have it all?

A character in one of her novels protests, "You can never imagine what it's like to have a man's force of genius in you, and yet to suffer the slavery of being a girl." Sand found a way out by simply choosing both, and somehow convinced a number of notable people.

Balzac praised her by listing all her splendid traits and talents and concluding, "Ergo, she is not a woman." Flaubert said he "cried like a calf" at her funeral, and called her a "great man"; Turgenev said, "What a brave man she was, and what a good woman." In the introduction to his biography of her, André Maurois calls her *"un tres grand homme."*

It's absurd, of course; we're locked into our genders and only surgery can release us, and when it does there's no return; we can't step back and forth at will between pants and petticoats. It's tempting to ask, Why not, exactly? But that way lies anarchy.

Sand's dream of androgyny, like her novels, died with her. Women in menswear still violate taboo and raise hackles, perhaps even more so since they've invaded the male professions. When Hollywood wants to tell us that a character is hard as nails and cold as ice, Wardrobe still puts her in a tailored suit with lapels and trousers, and we know the plot will ruin and humiliate her, and serve her right, too.

My sister, librarian in a prison, wears a necktie to work, the better to control her unruly clientele.

Animals, who wear no clothes, identify one another by scent and can read a résumé, even a whole biography, in a single sniff. Humans can know one another only through the arrangement of yard goods, so we've woven them into the very essence of self and given them magical powers.

Most women in pants have worn them for practical reasons, of course, rather than to make a statement. The hard-drinking, tobacco-chewing Calamity Jane, for instance.

She was born Martha Jane Canary, in Missouri, in 1852, oldest of six children. In her own words, "As a child I always had a fondness for adventure and out-door exercise and especial fondness for horses which I began to ride at an early age and continued to do so until I became an expert rider being able to ride the most vicious and stubborn of horses. . . .

"In 1865 we emigrated from our homes in Missourri [sic] by the overland route to Virginia City, Montana, taking five months to make the journey. While on the way the greater portion of my time was spent in hunting along with the men and hunters of the party, in fact I was at all times with the men when there was excitement and adventures to be had. By the time we reached Virginia City I was considered a remarkable good shot and a fearless rider for a girl of my age."

She was thirteen. Her parents both died shortly after reaching Montana and she was on her own, moving to Utah and then to Wyoming. At eighteen, "Joined General Custer as a scout at Fort Russell, Wyoming, in 1870, and started for Arizona for the Indian Campaign. Up to this time I had always worn the costume of my sex. When I joined Custer I donned the uniform of a soldier. It was a bit awkward at first but I soon got to be perfectly at home in men's clothes.

"Was in Arizona up to the winter of 1871 and during that time I had a great many adventures with the Indians, for as a scout I had a great many dangerous missions to perform and while I was in many close places always succeeded in getting away safely for by this time I was considered the most reckless and daring rider and one of the best shots in the western country. . . .

"When on returning to the Post we were ambushed about a mile and a half from our destination. When fired upon Capt. Egan was shot. I was riding in advance and on hearing the firing turned in my saddle and saw the Captain reeling in his saddle as though about to fall. I turned my horse and galloped back with all haste to his side and got there in time to catch him as he was falling. I lifted him onto the horse in front of me and succeeded in getting him safely to the Fort. Capt. Egan on recovering, laughingly said: 'I name you Calamity Jane, the heroine of the plains.' I have borne that name up to the present time. . . .

"During the month of June I acted as a pony express rider carrying the U.S. mail between Deadwood and Custer, a distance of fifty miles over one of the roughest trails in the Black Hills country. As many of the riders before me had been held up and robbed of their packages, mail and money that they carried, for that was the only means of getting mail and money between these points. It was considered the most dangerous route in the Hills, but as my reputation as a rider and quick shot was well known, I was molested very little, for the toll gatherers looked on me as being a good fellow, and they knew that I never missed my mark."

Her friend Buffalo Bill Cody added, "In 1876, Jane, by a daring feat, saved the lives of six passengers on a stage coach traveling from Deadwood to Wild Birch, in the Black Hills country. The stage was surrounded by Indians, and the driver, Jack McCall, was wounded by an arrow. Although the other six passengers were men, not one of them had nerve enough to take the ribbons. Seeing the situation, Jane mounted the driver's seat without a moment's hesitation and brought the stage safely and in good time to Wild Birch."

There's a picture of her when she served under Custer, in uniform. It's far too big for her and the sleeves are bunched up into folds, but there are certain things you simply can't do in a dress, which is perhaps the main point of dresses.

Outlaws

Lizzie Borden took an axe
And gave her mother forty whacks,
And when the job was nicely done
She gave her father forty-one.

Actually, it was only eighteen for her stepmother and eleven for her father, and perhaps she didn't do it. She was acquitted, but the prosecution was bumbling and the whole trial was a zoo, with the kind of frenzied media coverage and public obsession we associate with our own times, over a hundred years later. Who hacked up the Bordens remains an open question to the kind of Web-site proprietors who can't sleep nights for worrying old bones.

Lizzie was a respectable spinster who lived with her parents and taught Sunday school, and the jury just couldn't buy it: such women don't do such things. Poison, maybe; hatchets, no. Or not usually. Only the other day a woman was executed in Texas for killing two people with a pickax, which seems old-fashioned and unfeminine; most women don't even carry pickaxes. There wasn't any question of her guilt, but the public grieved anyway over what she'd done to the image of womanhood. Violence is for men. By and large, crime is for men.

The not-for-profit domestic murder, aside from being against the law, isn't what we think of as crime. It's not a career. The woman who's poisoned her brute of a husband isn't likely to develop a taste for it and take up poisoning as a way of life. Reading the headlines, we're shocked but not startled to learn that a woman has killed her lover or husband or even her child, but if she were running an international drug cartel or terrorist ring, we'd be startled. An emotional murder is acceptable because women are known to be emotional, but a life of calculated, deliberate crime, crime for gain, is distasteful in a woman. It's no way to bring up a child.

The Mafia is not godmothered; neither do women, as a general rule, shoot the clerk while robbing convenience stores, though a woman in love with the actual perpetrator may be waiting at the wheel of his car; nor do we often excavate a woman's backyard and turn up the bones of dozens of strangers. Gambling rings, investment scams, bank robberies, cattle rustling, snake-oil sales, burglary, art forgery, protection rackets, street-corner shell games, flimflams with a marked poker deck or loaded dice, doped racehorses, televangelical swindles, phony uranium mines, phony money, kidnaping, safe-cracking, highjacking—it's a man's world out there.

And, ah, how glamorous they've been, from Robin Hood to Mack the Knife, Jean Lafite to the OK Corral. If they were successful they could afford to dress like Alfred Noyes's "Highwayman," who came riding, riding, up to the old inn door:

>He'd a French cocked hat on his forehead, a bunch of lace at his chin,
>>A coat of the claret velvet, and breeches of brown doeskin.

62

Outlaws to set a maiden daydreaming over her chores, hoping to be snatched up and carried away. Few men daydream about glamorous lady shoplifters.

Full many a man has turned to crime for the merry hell of it, but women try to stay on the sunny side of the law; they never know when children will turn up and need an unfouled social nest to grow in. Not that women don't need money, but traditionally they've angled for it with their personal charms and those of their relatives, scheming like Jane Austen's matriarchs to wring the top dollar and the top social position out of the marriage market, since they hadn't a prayer of earning their own money in the job market.

Female crime was always pathetically street-level, like Moll Flanders shoplifting lace to sell. The most enterprising tried blackmail. Others fenced a bit of stolen goods, peddled drugs or gin at the back door, rolled a drunk, picked a pocket and spent the proceeds on food for the baby, not because they were noble mothers but just because it's the nature of the creature to have babies and feed them.

Prostitution has traditionally formed the broad, solid base of employment for women not otherwise provided for, and when it's illegal this could be called a life of crime; but except at the highest levels, where it's no longer considered crime but only a stylized form of barter, it's a dismal and dangerous way to live. Many die young; few get rich. It's not a career often chosen by those with better choices.

Crime, for women, has always been more a pathetic desperation measure than a lark. Or almost always.

Grace O'Malley was an Irish pirate in the days of Good Queen Bess, and there was nothing remotely pathetic about her life of crime. She was a lion of a lady, powerful and fearless and so clever that she lived to be over seventy in spite of the gallows, the dungeons, and the blazing battles she fought.

Her father was Owen ("Black Oak") O'Malley, elected chieftain of the Barony of Murrisk and scion of a long line of seafaring merchants. The O'Malley galleys and three-masted caravels had been trading with Scotland and Spain since early in the twelfth century. You could assume that after four hundred years the family blood ran more than half seawater, and when Grace was a little girl she begged her family to let her sail on one of their ships to Spain. Her mother said, as mothers will, that this was no life for a young lady, so Grace, as such girls will, went and cut off her long hair and came back and asked her parents to reconsider, since she was plainly no longer a girl. The family gently nicknamed her "Grainne Mhaol," Grace the Bald, and as far as we know they let her sail to Spain.

In 1546, when she was around sixteen, she was married to Donal O'Flaherty, a good match since he was next in line to be The O'Flaherty, chief of his clan and of all Iar-Connacht. They were probably well-matched in other ways, too; he was known as Donal of the Battles for his tendency to crack heads, and apparently a few years after the wedding he found it necessary to murder a step-nephew who stood in the way of his sister's son's chieftainship.

Grace and Donal had three children, Owen, Murrough, and Margaret, but this didn't slow her down. She seems to have had superhuman energies and before she was out of her teens she was outstripping Donal of the Battles in political maneuverings and tribal intrigue as well as the familial fishing and trading. Donal's family had been forbidden to use the port and trading center of Galway, which was under English control, so they plied their way around Munster, Ulster, Scotland, Spain, and Portugal. As a sideline to regular trade, Grace would lurk with her fast galleys near a port and swoop down on the plodding merchant ships, offering them a safe passage for a price or, if they objected, board and plunder.

England was having trouble with the Irish, who were reluctant to be English, a problem that went on to work its way into the very genes of all concerned. Henry VIII had declared an Irish policy of "surrender and re-grant," under which the clan chiefs would submit to the English crown, promising to behave themselves, and then the crown might give them back their lands and titles, unless they could think of someone worthier to give them to instead. The titles were a problem, because the chieftains were traditionally chosen by the clans' elite citizens, who elected a successor to the current chieftain; the English were passionately dedicated to primogeniture, the succession of the eldest son, a hard-won law closely treasured by all the reigning eldest sons in the land, who told everyone it was the will of God. Since the Gaelic system was obviously ungodly and immoral, the English appointed whom they pleased.

Some Irish clans had submitted and some hadn't and some had been subdued, and naturally the neighbors took sides, and the English were underfoot, and it was an interesting time to be Irish, ripe with opportunity, since who could say who should be plundered and who shouldn't?

In 1564, one of Donal's relatives, Murrough ("Battleaxes") O'Flaherty, fought and trounced the English Earl of Clanricarde. The English considered striking back, but then decided it wasn't worth the expense, so instead they accepted Battleaxes' submission and promise to keep the Queen's Peace in exchange for the chieftainship of Iar-Connacht and the title of The O'Flaherty. So much for the incumbent and for Grace's Donal, the appointed heir.

This did nothing to soothe the disinherited couple's famous tempers, and they captured the island castle of Caislean-an-Circa. The Joyce clan retaliated by storming the place, and Donal was killed defending it. The Joyces rejoiced, but prematurely; freshly widowed, Grace fought on like an angel of vengeance and finally drove them out in full retreat.

Apparently she set up housekeeping in this fortress, as much as she could be said to be in residence anywhere, because presently an English force out of Galway surrounded and held her in it under close siege. Along with the usual siege problems like eating rats, Grace and her band ran out of ammunition, which would have meant immediate defeat and death if she hadn't noticed that the castle roof was made of lead. She ordered the roof stripped off and melted for ammunition and gave the English ships such a merciless pounding that they retreated to the mainland to continue the siege out of firing range. Undaunted, Grace secretly set up a series of beacons among them, then sent a scout through a hidden passage to fire them up. Guided by the flares, her fleet sailed into the shore and bombarded the English until they gave up and scuttled back to Galway.

Grace was Donal's widow and Donal had been a substantial man; in theory a chieftain's widow was entitled to a third of her husband's estate, but in practice this rarely happened, even to women as dauntless as Grace. With two grown sons to place in the world and little to offer them, she went back to the land of the O'Malleys, along with two hundred followers as loyal to the mistress as they'd been to her husband. She established herself on Clare Island in Clew Bay, with a splendid view of the shipping lanes, and proceeded to prosper mightily.

Her business tactics were flexible. Depending on the situation, she could offer legitimate pilot services, charge protection money for safe passage, or simply board and plunder.

She and her band of fighting sailors were none the less religious for their professional activities, and they were on a Saint Brigid's Day pilgrimage to a holy well on the island when a gale blew up and they got word of a ship foundering. They dashed to their fleet and sailed off into the howling winds to assess the possibilities, but when they arrived the ship had smashed up and left nothing of interest except a half-drowned young man named Hugh de Lacy. For lack of more valuable souvenirs, they carried him home and Grace nursed him back to health. According to the stories, they fell in love, but what might have been a gentle interlude in her life was quickly interrupted when the MacMahons of Ballycroy killed Hugh one day while he was out deer-hunting.

Apparently, at the time, if you couldn't think of any particular reason not to kill someone, you figured you might just as well kill him as not, but the MacMahons might have paused to consider that Grace's patronage was a very particular reason indeed not to kill Hugh de Lacy. She tracked them down where they were on a pilgrimage on Cahir, and those she decided were personally responsible for Hugh's death she killed with her own hands. Then, for good measure, she sailed to their castle, Doona, in Blacksod Bay, tossed out or killed everyone in residence there, and moved her own people into the vacated and probably bloodstained rooms. This gave rise to one of her many traditional names, "The Dark Lady of Doona."

She was no blundering, crashing warlord, though, and many of her maneuvers were delicately feminine rather than murderously direct.

When she gazed around the environs of Clew Bay, she saw that all the lands and waters for far and wide were in the hands of her O'Malley clan except for a single alien pocket, the country ruled from Rockfleet Castle by Richard-an-Iarainne, or Iron Dick Burke. So, being then only in her mid-thirties and no doubt a handsome woman, glowing with health and freshness from her life on the sea, she married Iron Dick. It was a stroke of fairness in a way, since Dick was none other than the nephew in whose interests Donal O'Flaherty had killed his step-nephew, clearing the way for Dick's accession; now Donal's widow moved into Donal's nephew's lands.

The English, as noted, had the liveliest contempt for the barbaric laws of their semisubject land, and surely one of the most uncivilized was the "one-year certain" marriage law, under which a marriage, after a year's trial, could be simply dissolved by either party as having been a mistake. In England, then and for hundreds of years to come, a wife was her husband's absolute property, like a cow or a sheep, and the conquerors must have been disgusted and even frightened to think that an Irishwoman could dismiss her husband simply by saying so and just because she wanted to.

Grace moved into Rockfleet Castle and set her O'Malley foot down firmly on its corridors and lands, and settled her trustiest henchmen into its spare rooms. A year later, when Iron Dick was returning from a hard stint smiting enemies here and there, Grace O'Malley stood on the rampart, cupped her hands around her mouth, the wind whipping her skirts and hair, and shouted down at the weary warrior, "I dismiss you!"

It was a valid divorce and a bloodless coup, and now when she surveyed the wide view she could see that the O'Malleys ruled the length and breadth of Clew Bay and all the lands around. It may seem like a small kingdom now, but kingdoms were smaller then.

Iron Dick had left a memento, and presently she had another son, called Tibbot of the Ships.

Fairly or unfairly, the Irish have a reputation for not letting a good story shrink in the telling, and we may hear more about Grace than was reliably documented at the time. The official word on Grace survives from her brushes with the English authorities; she's wondrously absent from the Irish chronicles. Perhaps they found her an embarrassment and an unsuitable role model. We do have stories in full measure, though, and stories have been recently dignified as "oral history," so no shame is attached to repeating them. Tibbot, it's said, was born while Grace was returning from a legitimate trading mission. The next day she was resting up below when their ship was attacked by Turkish pirates. The captain came to tell her to prepare for the worst, as the fight was going against her. She thrust the infant from her breast and leaped up crying, "May you be seven times worse this day twelve months, who cannot do without me for one day!" Seizing her blunderbuss, she stormed up on deck and blazed away bravely at the Turks. Emboldened or maybe embarrassed, her men took heart, redoubled their efforts, and won the day; she disposed summarily of the Turks and took their ship home to add to her flourishing forces.

For the next seven years she made such a flaming nuisance of herself in Irish waters that the English, forgetting their previous failure, sent a force to besiege her in Rockfleet Castle. For three weeks she lay low, no doubt planning and organizing, and then burst forth in a ferocious counterattack that drove the humiliated Captain Martin and his men howling for cover.

Young Tibbot grew but seemingly didn't take after his

mother; he next appears hiding behind her while she stormed the Stauntons' Kinturk Castle. According to oral history, she roared at her youngest, "Is it cowering behind my backside you are—the place where you came from?" (The seafaring life does not encourage genteel language.) He was suitably shamed, the Stauntons suitably routed, and Grace taxed their lands to the tune of an ox, a pig, and a barrel of meal from every family.

Her valor seems to have been helped by extraordinary good luck, but occasionally the luck slipped, and in 1577, while on a raid against the Earl of Desmond, she was finally taken prisoner. The Lord Justice of Munster described her as "a great spoiler, and chief commander and director of thieves and murderers at sea to spoille this province," and held her in prison in Limerick before transferring her to the dungeons of Dublin Castle itself, the mark of a very important prisoner indeed and a spot from which few people ever reappeared. Almost miraculously, Grace rode away home, having promised to behave herself, though it's unclear why anyone would have believed her. She must have had tremendous powers to charm and persuade, besides her more physical talents.

Oddly, no official went on record marveling that this commander of thieves and murderers belonged to the gentler, weaker sex. Perhaps such ladies seemed less peculiar in the sixteenth century than they do now.

The problem with oral history is the same as with ordinary lies: the stories tend to tangle their feet and trip over themselves; the sequence of events is impenetrably murky; and the villain who died in act two turns up alive and well in act three. Iron Dick, so dramatically divorced in 1567, turns up again ten years later, described as her husband, though apparently she does all the talking. She must have found him useful after all, whatever their private lives.

Her own O'Malley clan had submitted to the English, but Iron Dick was next under local law to be The MacWilliam, though the current MacWilliam had also submitted and sworn to abide by primogeniture instead of the barbaric clan elections. Luck had been on Grace's side, but history was running against her and the situation was delicate, calling for détente with the English.

Shortly after her release from Dublin castle, she appeared of her own free will with Iron Dick in tow to offer her services in submission to Sir Henry Sidney, along with three galleys and two hundred fighting men. (Henry's more famous son, Sir Philip Sidney, had come to Ireland with him and was said to be fascinated by Grace, though most of the letters he wrote about her were lost.)

Her submission seems to have worked, because in 1580 the incumbent MacWilliam died and after a certain amount of scuffling Dick was allowed to succeed him and the following year was even knighted, an odd honor to bestow on the husband of such a wife and perhaps a mark of how Grace had beguiled the Sidneys. She was fifty now, and peace threatened to settle over her. According to rumor, she even began to give herself airs, which can't have come easily to her after the life she'd led, but her gentility was short-lived. Within three years Iron Dick was dead, of natural causes, apparently the least natural way to go in those days. Grace, on her own again, immediately "gathered together all her own followers and with a thousand head of cows and mares departed and became a dweller in Carrikahowley," lands that were apparently hers by Irish right if not by English law.

The new English governor of Connaught, Sir Richard Bingham, was quite obsessed by the sanctity of primogeniture, and since Grace was nobody's eldest son, he took steps to wipe her out. She must have been slowing down a bit, because in 1586 he captured her, had her tied up with ropes, and confiscated her thousand horses and cows and everything else except the clothes she was wearing. And then he built a special gallows for her use alone.

Details are vague; somehow she slithered out of that one too, but she had little left to live on and Bingham wasn't finished with the family yet. Owen, Grace's eldest son, had prudently withdrawn with his tenants, followers, and cattle to a fortified island stronghold. Sir Richard sent out a considerable force, which stood on the mainland hallooing that they were hungry and needed help. With misguided hospitality, Owen sent boats to bring the troops over to the island, where he wined and dined them handsomely. After dinner, they captured Owen and eighteen of his top men, took five hundred horses and a thousand sheep, leaving the rest of the tenantry to starve. They hanged his men, including an old gent of ninety. Owen they tied up and stabbed; "cruelly murdered," Grace wrote, "having twelve deadly wounds."

Unsurprisingly, she lent her ships, her wits, and her presence to the tumultuous years that followed; Bingham called her "a notable traitoress and nurse to all rebellions in the Province." When her second son, Murrough, sided with Bingham against her, she personally sailed to his town while he was away and burned it, took all the cattle she could round up, and killed several of his men when they resisted. She was not a mother to be trifled with.

Grace had followers and sailors to support; and now, having taken away her lands and cattle and farming livelihood, Bingham undertook to harry her ships and prevent her earning a living at sea either. Grace wrote to Queen Elizabeth, a letter of great subtlety and cunning in which she explained her own warfares as essential to protect her people against her neighbors, who "constrained your highness's fond subject to take arms and

by force to maintain herself and her people by sea and land."
Her letter then boldly asks for a pardon for her surviving sons
and her jailed brother Donald, and blithely requests that in spite
of her "great age" she be allowed to roam the seas freely and "to
invade with sword and fire all your highness's enemies."

Before the answer could arrive, Bingham jailed Tibbot and
wrote to Elizabeth denouncing Grace as a traitor. Grace threw a
few things in a suitcase and sailed straight off to see the queen in
person.

No other Irish rebel would have considered stepping on English soil, let alone marching into the sumptuous court itself and
accosting Elizabeth the Great, perhaps the shrewdest and most
powerful monarch in the history of the world. How did Grace
work her way through the wall of chancellors and advisors and
court procedures? What did she wear? What does an aging lady
pirate from Connaught wear to stand before the queen of England? Who styled her hair? Did she have suitable jewels, or
were all her investments in cattle and ships? Had she ever curt-
sied before? Did the elegant courtiers snigger when she appeared, and did she silence them with a single look? Above all,
what did they say to each other, these two brave women?

There's no question that Elizabeth was impressed. The de-
tailed letter she fired off to Bingham slaps him down in no
uncertain terms: Tibbot and Donald are to be released; Tibbot
and his brother Murrough are to be shown particular favor, and
Bingham shall "in all their good causes protect them to live in
peace to enjoy their livelihoods." Furthermore, "we require you
to deal with her sons in our name to yield to her some mainte-
nance for her living the rest of her old years." And she is to be
free on the seas to "fight in our quarrel with all the world."

Everything Grace wanted, freely offered and asking none of

the usual guarantees or collateral in return. Grace had charmed the great queen, a woman well vaccinated by the charms of professional charmers. Perhaps she envied Grace. She was a woman of formidable forces herself, and she'd confined them in the cage of diplomatic gamesmanship all her life. She might have preferred piracy and a blunderbuss. She was sixty; Grace was sixty-three. What did they see in each other's faces?

Bingham wasn't pleased. He tried to ignore the royal instructions, but when Grace threatened to go back to the queen he gave in on most points, though he knew her too well to turn her loose entirely; he billeted great numbers of hungry troops with her and sent a captain and a company of soldiers to sail with her wherever she sailed. This cramped her style, but presently Bingham was replaced by Sir Conyers Clifford, who must have been more amiably disposed, because it's recorded that Grace and Tibbot fought nobly on his behalf and were well rewarded for their efforts. Grace, however, continued to freelance on the side, just to keep her hand in.

She probably died around 1603, at Rockfleet, under the ramparts she'd climbed to shout down her divorce of Iron Dick. We're told that the key to longevity is maintaining an active lifestyle in old age; the last recorded mention of Grace O'Malley reports an English patrol seizing one of her galleys on its way to raid and plunder the McSweeneys.

History closed over Grace in silence. If she'd been a patriot confining her activities to the intrusive English, she'd be a national hero like Boadicea, with statues on every flat surface, but she seems to have played a nonpartisan game, purely for personal gain, which is unbecoming to a lady, as her mother would have told her, and puts her firmly beyond the pale.

We hear more about the pirates Anne Bonny and Mary Read. Unlike O'Malley, commanding her own ships and still unrepentant at seventy-three, they're admissible by being both fittingly subordinate—crew, not captains—and unsuccessful. They turn up often, as bit players in a jokey historical sidebar: women aping men, swearing, drinking, gambling, and killing people, always good for a scholarly laugh.

Anne Bonny was the daughter of an Irish lawyer and his housekeeper; her arrival seems to have embarrassed her father into leaving County Cork and seeking his fortune in the Carolinas. He succeeded, and found himself a fine plantation. Anne grew up a mettlesome girl who, they say, once lost her temper with a household servant and killed her with a carving knife. (This colorful touch may have been added later to flesh out a rather thin story.)

Tempted by the father's plantation, a no-good sailor and occasional pirate named James Bonny married Anne, but her father thwarted him by disinheriting her. The two nevertheless ran off together, relocating to the Bahamas, where Bonny made quite a good thing out of denouncing former shipmates as pirates and collecting the rewards from Governor Rogers. Disgusted, Anne took up with handsome Jack Rackham, called Calico Jack for his striped trousers, his trademark in the piracy business.

Calico was an honorable pirate and offered to buy Anne from Bonny for cash, but Bonny appealed instead to Governor Rogers, his friend from the stool-pigeon business, and Rogers said Anne should be flogged for her faithlessness and returned to her husband. That night, Anne and Calico stole a sloop from the harbor and set merrily forth to pillage and plunder, with Anne dressed as a sailor. It's said she was a wicked shot and wielded a mean cutlass, as well as the heavy ax used in boarding captured shipping.

Peculiarly enough, a second woman in sailor's clothes served in the same crew. Mary Read was English, and had fought in the English navy as a man. When Calico's men—and woman—captured the ship she was on, she joined them.

She was tough. It's said that during an attack, the male pirates turned coward and all but one hid from the action while Mary and Anne did the fighting. Mary yelled at the cowards to come out and fight like men. They didn't, so she shot them, which must have left the ship woefully short-handed. Another tale relates that when her lover was being intimidated by a fellow crew member, Mary challenged the man to a duel, an odd formality perhaps on a pirate ship, and took him out neatly with a well-aimed stab from her cutlass.

Without O'Malley's luck, the party lasted only two years. In 1720, the governor of Jamaica sent a heavily armed ship and captured theirs—too easily, Anne sniffed; her comrades had resisted feebly. Both women were conveniently pregnant and given the usual stay of execution on that count, but the men were hanged at once. Calico Jack was allowed to see Anne one last time, and her final words to him were: "I'm sorry to see you here, but if you had fought like a man you wouldn't be going to hang like a dog." (Or so they say she said.)

Mary Read died in jail of a fever. Anne's well-earned execution was delayed over and over, and then she disappears from the records. Some people believe that her father pulled some influential strings, ransomed her, and took her back to the Carolinas, where she changed her name and, we presume, went on to lead a blameless life.

If we admit to these two from a single ship who were captured, stripped, identified, and recorded, how many more slipped through with better luck?

*   *   *

One by one the pirate ships burned to the waterline, or sank and turned into shadowy hatcheries for deepwater fish. Bank robbery never recaptured the glory days, though a few romantics tried it.

Bonnie Parker was a moony little girl, a poetry-reader, a romantic, a type of child unfamiliar now but common enough in the early years of the twentieth century; a child for whom adulthood loomed hideous with boredom and respectability. She could have been my daughter, or yours; she could have been me. She lived in the bleak dusty hopelessness of west Texas, in a world where girlhood could have only one outcome, and she wanted to be a doomed heroine in Sir Walter Scott or a doomed princess in *The Idylls of the King.* She wanted to die for love like Barbry Allen or Heathcliff's Cathy. She wanted to be a poet. What she got instead was life with her widowed mother, brother, sister, and grandparents in a Dallas suburb unenticingly named Cement City, a job as a waitress, and, not all that much later, fame and death as Bonnie of Bonnie and Clyde, the notorious Barrow Gang.

She was a pretty little thing, just five feet tall and ninety pounds, with strawberry-blond curls, dimples, and a lightly freckled nose. She loved her mother dearly and did well in school, singing in the chorus and winning prizes for her essays and poetry recitations. And she had the romantic girl's weakness for bad boys. At sixteen she married sixteen-year-old Roy Thornton, but she couldn't bear to leave her mother, so Roy moved in with the family, more or less. While Bonnie worked as a waitress in a café, Roy came and went in a most unspousal way until finally she threw him out. Her mother wanted her to divorce him, but by then he was in prison for robbery and Bonnie felt it wouldn't be sporting of her, under the circumstances; she always showed a delicacy of feeling rare in the career criminal.

The café where she worked closed after the Crash of '29 and she couldn't find another job, so she offered to stay with a neighbor who'd broken her arm and needed help. The neighbor was a girlfriend of Clyde Barrow's. Clyde came to visit and, over a pot of cocoa in the kitchen, Bonnie and Clyde fell in love.

He was a weedy young man, not much bigger than Bonnie, one of eight children of an illiterate tenant farmer. His passions were music, snappy cars, sharp clothes, and guns—he gave all his guns pet names—and his temperament was volatile; normally mild and mannerly, he could switch in an instant to white-hot killing rages. He might have been the young Elvis Presley, without the glamorous career waiting in the wings. He'd dropped out of high school and, in cahoots with his older brother, Buck, progressed from turkey-rustling to burglary to car theft, avoiding jail by means of his harmless looks and ingratiating smile. By the time he met Bonnie, though, the law was closing in.

They nailed him in Bonnie's mother's living room. Mrs. Parker, apparently the least judgmental of parents, was upset, but Bonnie reassured her. The scenario that would lead unswervingly to her death was already written in her mind: the "laws" had it in for poor Clyde. They were out to get him. They were the villains, the Sheriffs of Nottingham, and Clyde their Robin Hood victim. She, Bonnie, would stand loyally by him till death, if necessary, though as soon as these current trumped-up charges were cleared, he would surely, surely get an honest job and go straight.

Clyde was transferred to a prison in Waco. Bonnie followed him. He'd put her name down as his wife, so she was allowed to write and visit. One of his cellmates had a plan: Bonnie would go to his parents' house while they were at work, retrieve the hidden door-key, follow his directions to the chest where they kept the pistol and the bullets, and smuggle them into the jail.

It was her first crime. She took a cousin with her for moral support, and with admirable coolness followed the directions like a professional. The gun was buttoned neatly into her dress, hard and chilly between her breasts, and delivered to the conspirators. They broke out as planned, eluded their pursuers on foot, hot-wired a car, and left Waco behind, picking up fresh cars and switching license plates as they fled toward Illinois.

Bonnie was the heroine. She had proved herself, and proved her love. She was a person of consequence for the first time in her life, wanted by the law for burglary and aiding a jailbreak. Maybe she also saw herself as the girl in "Curfew Shall Not Ring Tonight," a sentimental ballad she would have known, whose heroine saves her lover from Cromwell's executioner by swinging from the bell in the church steeple, muffling the clapper with her bare hands and muting the fatal curfew.

Prosaically, she went home to Dallas to wait for word from Clyde.

Robbery was thin pickings during the Depression. The cash registers of the small-town stores and the vaults of the banks were hardly worth opening, the Great Drought of the thirties dried up farm incomes, and no paid jobs could be found to flesh them out. For sustenance, a sensible young crook might have opted for his jail term instead of crime. Clyde and his friends had bad luck and worse judgment; they did get sixty dollars from a railroad ticket office, but most of the time they found only pocket change. At a ladies' clothing store they made off with nothing but some silky underwear for their girlfriends.

Presently they got caught and hauled back to Waco. Clyde, now twenty-one, said he was only eighteen and his mother backed him up, but just the same he was sent to a prison farm with a fourteen-year sentence. Bonnie wept and wrote to him daily.

Then she stopped writing. She found another waitress job and started seeing another young man, as if the fates had stayed their hand to give her a chance to save herself, or braked the wheels so she could get off and go somewhere else. She almost did.

For Clyde, the hard work on the prison farm was torture; he persuaded a friend to chop off a couple of his toes with an ax so he could go rest in the prison hospital. In the meantime his mother had been hounding the authorities for his release, and at last the governor came through with a parole. Clyde paused only long enough to bum money from his sister for some sharp new clothes before he turned up on the Parker doorstep. If he'd served his whole sentence, or even a few more years of it, Bonnie might have been freed for a different life, but now she gave him a hero's welcome. Her mother was dismayed, but she loved her daughter and held her tongue.

Clyde hooked up with a couple of other aspiring toughs, Raymond Hamilton and Ralph Fults. Bonnie told her mother she'd found a job in Houston and joined the gang to serve as lookout, scout, and driver; Clyde always chivalrously kept her out of the actual robberies. The first job was to get some guns, so they tackled a small-town hardware store. The watchman set off the alarm and they fled out into the countryside, over roads soggy from the spring rains, with the police in pursuit. When the car bogged down to its hubcaps in mud, the luckless bandits took off on foot across the fields. Finding a group of mules, they climbed onto them and urged them forward with their heels, which seems like an idea of Bonnie's, a vision of them galloping away into the night like Young Lochinvar—but the mules, being mules, laid back their ears and stood still.

The police found the car and tracked them into the field. Crouching in a ditch, bullets zinging over their heads, Clyde told Bonnie to lay low while he made a break for it to pick up another car and come rescue her. He sprinted away between two policemen who were reloading their guns. (If the Barrow Gang had bad luck, the law's luck was worse, and the early escapades have a ring of the Keystone Kops colliding with the Marx Brothers.) Fults and Hamilton also ran, but Bonnie huddled obediently in the cold, muddy culvert all day and the following night, waiting for Clyde. At daybreak she walked to the highway and held out her thumb for a ride. The driver who picked her up was one of the posse.

She called her mother from jail, and her mother was going to try to borrow money to bail her out but the jailer's wife, who must have been a kindly soul, told her not to: the grand jury would certainly dismiss the case for lack of evidence, and in the meantime Bonnie should stay where she was and consider where her life was heading.

The others, without her, managed to get in deep trouble. Fults gallantly took the rap for the hardware store and went to the state prison, while Clyde and Hamilton enlisted Frank Clause. The three took on a gas station and gift shop out on the highway, and while the store owner and his wife were emptying the safe of the money and jewelry, nervous Raymond Hamilton's finger twitched on the trigger. The bullet struck the safe's door and bounced from there to the store owner's heart, hardly an easy shot to duplicate. He fell over dead beside his wife, who'd had a good, long look at the gang.

Thus the Barrow boys graduated from punks to murderers. Surrender was no longer an option, and getting caught would mean the electric chair.

Waiting for her trial, Bonnie thought dark thoughts about

Clyde and wrote a bitter poem, "Suicide Sal," about a woman whose lover lets her take the rap for his crimes. When her case was indeed dismissed, she went home to her mother, wiser and soberer and swearing to have nothing more to do with Clyde.

Her resolution lasted a week; and then, like a woman drugged, she went off again with the gang. Perhaps a week was long enough to look at the alternatives, the straggle of waitress jobs, the five-cent tips, the hundreds of slabs of pie, thousands of mugs of coffee, stretching ahead through Depression-haunted Dallas under its veil of dust. Perhaps, too, the murder had heightened the drama, and a Clyde under actual threat of execution glowed more brightly than a Clyde who simply broke into gas stations.

The gang circled through the states to the north and west and back to Dallas, always. Clyde loved his family as much as Bonnie loved hers; he had told his sister, "If I have to be away from you all, I might as well be dead." They managed to get home for holidays and birthdays and family occasions, or just for a kiss and a few quick words, meeting in remote woods and fields. At Easter, Bonnie brought a white rabbit for her mother. Once they were ambushed at a rendezvous and shot in the knees escaping, but they couldn't stay away from their families.

Raymond Hamilton, who may not have been quite bright, continued to be a liability. As they cruised through Oklahoma looking for prospects, they passed an open-air dance hall and Raymond, drunk, insisted on stopping to dance. He wandered into the crowd carrying his Mason jar of moonshine. Oklahoma took Prohibition seriously, and the sheriff and his deputy tried to arrest him. Somehow in the scuffle the deputy was shot dead and the sheriff badly wounded. Then, as now, killing law-enforcement officers on the job ratcheted up the "wanted" status. The ill-starred Raymond followed this up by trying to entice a waitress with tales of his glamorous life of crime, but the waitress's boyfriend was a policeman and Raymond went off to stand trial.

The Depression ground on, and earning a living by robbery was more and more like gleaning a field after the harvest. One bank yielded eighty dollars, but the next turned out to have failed some weeks before and left not a dime behind. The gang attracted suspicion by paying their bills in sacks of nickels and pennies scraped from cash registers.

While Bonnie and Clyde were spending Christmas with their families, they enlisted W. D. Jones, a sixteen-year-old who was so dizzied by the honor that he accidentally killed a man whose car they were trying to steal. Body count: four, and soon five, another deputy sheriff.

Clyde's brother Buck got out of prison and his first thought was to see Clyde. The brothers arranged a rendezvous in a rented garage apartment in Joplin, Missouri, and the group settled in for a spell of family life, broken only by a jewelry-store robbery. Buck's wife Blanche hadn't wanted to come for fear Buck would get in further trouble; she whined and played solitaire and talked to her little white dog. Buck and W.D. slept. Clyde kept an anxious eye at the windows. Bonnie cooked pinto beans and cornbread and sang and wrote poetry.

Clyde had fallen into crime as the only work he was familiar with, a career not exactly chosen but set before him as his designated lunch; if there had been other jobs available, he probably wouldn't have considered them. For Bonnie, crime was the epic ballad she was weaving out of her life. It can't have been easy. She must have had deep resources of imagination to keep her story soaring in her mind while living in stolen cars and rancid tourist cabins and abandoned farmhouses, always falling asleep with the possibility of waking to gunfire; trying to make conversation with a series of dim-witted punks. The excitement of the high-speed car chases was buried under days of motionless boredom hiding out, but the romance kept her spirits high. She never complained. She posed for a snapshot, clowning as a thug, a gun in each hand and a cigar between her teeth. Cheerfully she began a poem,

You've read the story of Jesse James
Of how he lived and died
If you're still in need of something to read
Here's the story of Bonnie and Clyde.

(Her strongest literary influence was obviously Robert W. Service, author of such popular works as "The Shooting of Dan McGrew.") Whether she was victim or villainess didn't seem to matter, as long as the stage was hers and the imaginary audience spellbound. The ending she already knew. She and Clyde had sworn never to be taken alive—"They'll only put us in the electric chair, so what's the use?"

The Joplin neighbors had reported their suspicions and the police staked out the garage apartment. When the constable came to the door, Clyde and W.D. fired from upstairs, killing him. Blanche ran in circles screaming while the others ran for the car. Clyde crashed the car through the police barriers and, firing, collected the shrieking Blanche and they tore away, leaving a second policeman to die that night. (One clue to Clyde's escapes was that he tried to steal only Fords, because their tough hides stood up against anything except Browning automatic rifles.)

They'd left plenty of evidence behind. Two rolls of film gave a positive identification of W.D., wanted for various escapades, and Buck's pardon papers put him right where Blanche had feared, incriminated with his brother. The police felt they were making definite progress, but still they couldn't pin down their prey. By this time half the unsolved murders and robberies in the country were blamed on the Barrow Gang and they began to seem like a supernatural force.

Even when unpursued, Clyde gloried in driving as fast as possible or somewhat faster along the dubious roads of the day. He enjoyed abducting witnesses and deputy sheriffs and treating them to terrifying rides before abandoning them; one deputy said he was less frightened by the wild ride than by the wild exhilaration it produced in the gang.

Swooping along a Texas highway with Bonnie and W.D., Clyde came to the site of a former bridge over a ravine. Unable to stop at seventy miles an hour, they flew over the edge and rolled twice on their way down. Bonnie was thrown and pinned under the car, while gas leaked out and then caught fire. Burning, she screamed while the two men tried to lift the car, but it was too heavy. A pair of farmers nearby had seen the accident, and although they couldn't help seeing the fountains of guns spraying out around the car as it rolled, they came to help, and Clyde carried Bonnie to the farmhouse. Her face and arms were only blistered but her right leg was savagely burned from hip to ankle, clear to the bone in places.

There was no question of an ambulance or hospital, and nothing at all for the pain. One of the farmers had slipped away and called the police, but when the sheriff and marshal showed up, Clyde clipped them into their own handcuffs and tied them together with barbed wire. Then the gang drove hell-for-leather to Fort Smith, Arkansas, Bonnie moaning horribly, and checked into a tourist cabin, where she slipped into delirium.

Buck and W.D., in a gallant effort to pay for medical care for her, robbed a bank and a grocery store, and somewhere along their way a town marshal got killed and a posse turned out. It was time to move on, though days of driving were agony for Bonnie. The only medical help was a doctor's bag in one of the cars they stole, with a few basic supplies like hydrogen peroxide.

Why she didn't die of trauma or gangrene or blood-poisoning is a mystery, unless perhaps her scenario rejected an alternate ending. She'd written,

> Some day they'll go down together,
> And they'll bury them side by side.
> To some it'll be grief, to the law a relief,
> But it's death for Bonnie and Clyde.

At one of their clandestine reunions, she told her mother not to leave her in a funeral home when the law gunned them down but to bring her home for a last night. "It's been so long since I was home. I want to lie in the front room with you and Billie and Buster sitting beside me. A long cool, peaceful night together before I leave you." (Best not to even think about Emma Parker, mother to such a bright, loving, pretty daughter so eager for her own destruction, so besotted with what Thomas Mann calls "the voluptuousness of doom.")

Bonnie's condition actually improved and soon they were on the road again, camping out in the woods, crossing state lines, changing license plates, robbing gas stations, and paying their tourist-court bills with bags of nickels.

The law caught up with them in a motel in Missouri, and in the shoot-out Buck was hit twice in the head. Clyde carried him out to the car while Blanche screamed, stuffed him in, and, with W.D. on the running board with a Browning automatic, they drove firing through the assembled police and their vehicles. A bullet smashed a window and Blanche's eyes were pierced with shards of glass.

Resting up in a wooded park in Iowa, Clyde dressed everyone's wounds. Buck looked bad. Clyde had promised their mother that if either of them were dying, they'd be brought back home; he planned to leave for Dallas at daybreak. However, a farmer had found a half-burned sack of Bonnie's stained bandages, and by daybreak the camp was surrounded by every available armed man. Bonnie shouted the alarm, Clyde and W.D. sprayed the woods with Brownings while Bonnie, barely able to stagger, and Blanche tried to get Buck into a car, Clyde jumped in but took a shattering bullet in the left arm and the car swerved and jammed on a tree-stump. As they dragged themselves to the spare car, Bonnie and Buck were hit, W.D. was hit in the chest and face, and the police shot out the car's tires and gas tank. The gang tried to get to the woods on foot; Buck was shot again in the chest and back and collapsed. Running to help him, Clyde was shot in the leg.

The sobbing Blanche refused to leave Buck, so with a promise to come back with another car, the three dragged their wounds toward the river, under fire. Bonnie fainted from pain and somehow Clyde, with one good arm and one good leg, carried her across the river. (If he'd been the hero instead of the villain, he'd have made a fine hero.) Hiding his bleeding comrades in a cornfield, he limped off to steal another car.

The police hauled Buck and Blanche to the hospital where Buck, under heavy guard, died, and so finally did get home to Dallas. The funeral was well-attended, especially by watchful police, but some people swore they saw Clyde there anyway, wearing a dress and bonnet. Blanche, blinded in one eye, got fifteen years as an accessory.

Raymond Hamilton, he of the drinking problem and the nervous trigger finger, wrote to Bonnie and Clyde that he was serving a two-hundred-and-sixty-three-year sentence on a Texas prison farm, and would they please get him out? Ever chivalrous, the two obliged, though Hamilton had bragged to so many people about his coming rescue that half a dozen extra escapees showed up at the getaway car with him. Clyde made room for them all, stuffing four in the trunk, and they shot their way out.

One of the prison guards died of bullet wounds, and the forces of Texas law took it personally. They created a new office, special investigator for the Texas prison system, with particular emphasis on Bonnie and Clyde. They picked Captain Frank Hamer, an ex-Ranger and a cut above the small-town deputies the gang had been running rings around.

Shortly after the breakout, Clyde caught the ungrateful Hamilton with his hand in the money bag from an unusually successful bank job and dismissed him in disgrace. Some of their extra passengers they also dumped, but they kept Henry Methvin, which was a mistake. He was just as nervous as Hamilton, and killed a couple of harmless motorcycle cops in cold blood, not the Barrow Gang's style at all.

The official bloodhounds broke into a trot. Frank Hamer was the first to figure out the circular path of robberies and sightings, always converging in Dallas for holidays. Helpfully, young W. D. Jones, in jail, had supplied a complete list of the usual hideouts and stopovers on the circuit.

In Louisiana, Henry Methvin's father worried about him. He was a drunk who drove a logging truck when he was sober enough to drive, but he was paternal enough not to want his son back on the same prison farm where the guard had been killed. Frank Hamer had a free hand to make deals, and Methvin dealt. Henry had told his father about their prearranged rendezvous point on the road. It turned into a rendezvous with a small army.

Methvin Senior parked his truck by the woods already bristling with police, jacked up the rear, threw the spare on the ground, and hid. Clyde slowed down to inspect the truck as he passed on his way to meet Henry. He and Bonnie just had time to grab their guns before everyone opened fire. The two weren't so much shot as shredded.

In Gibsland, Louisiana, it was the event of the year. The whole population swarmed to the site and marveled, and felt foolish at how young and small the outlaws were who had loomed so huge in the headlines for so long. The scramble for souvenirs was fierce: all the adjacent trees were cut down in search of souvenir bullets. One man was stopped from slicing off and pocketing Clyde's ear. Bonnie was dressed, as she often was, in red, with a crucifix around her neck. She was twenty-three.

A reporter overheard the victorious Frank Hamer saying, "Well, they died with their guns in their hands."

Bonnie would have loved that line. She would have worked it into a poem.

Exiles

Reasonably enough, most expatriates flee small, damp, crowded places in search of space and sunlight. Americans, still with open land to retreat to and Alaska and Florida at the ends of the road, rarely leave, and when they do they go to Paris; but the British and the northern Europeans head, shivering, for the Sahara, Kenya, Brazil, and Australia. They aim for the light like moths. Britons lucky enough to grow up in exile, like the writer Rumer Godden in India and the pioneer bush pilot Beryl Markham in Africa, loved the space and skies of their borrowed countries with a passion. Victorian English traveler Isabella Bird wrote from Colorado, "In our sunless misty climate you do not know the influence which persistent fine weather exercises on the spirits. I have been ten months in almost perpetual sunshine and now a single cloudy day makes me feel quite depressed."

Lady Hester Lucy Stanhope was born in Kent in 1776, eldest child of the third Earl Stanhope, who was an excitable and bad-tempered peer. She left home to live with her uncle, statesman William Pitt, and serve as his secretary and general manager and mix in society; she was said to be witty and beautiful, but wicked of tongue. Pitt left her a nice pension when he died, and in 1810 she wiped the mud of England from her boots forever. She prowled the Middle East in search of the perfect home, and found it on a mountain on the Lebanese coast, among the Druses, many miles from nowhere. Here she set herself up as an absolute ruler over the surrounding districts, where she was revered for her imperious temper and generally believed to be magic, with powers of divination. By all reports, her temper grew worse with age and by the time she died at sixty-three she was a perfect tyrant.

Denmark's weather is similar to England's, and Isak Dinesen left for East Africa in 1913, where she wrestled with her coffee plantation, shot marauding lions, flew over the Great Rift Valley in her lover's plane, and wrote, among other things, *Out of Africa.*

The great sheik Fahad Bey said of Gertrude Bell, "she is only a woman, but she is a mighty and valiant one." High praise, considering a sheik's usual opinion of the fair sex. A tall, commanding redhead, Bell was born in 1868 into a respectable English family and was one of the first women to study at Oxford. England couldn't contain her; she was restless and conquered several unconquerable alps before finding her true home in the deserts of the Middle East.

She traveled in Persia and translated Persian poetry. She studied Arabic; she rode sidesaddle across the Arabian Desert, where the Arabs pronounced her an honorary man. She had a genius for scratching up friendships with sheiks and holy men who rarely deigned to speak to women, and she paid attention to everything she saw. En route to Mesopotamia she stumbled on a sixth-century castle and made scale drawings of it for archaeologists. She met Lawrence of Arabia. Traveling in 1913 from Damascus to the desert of northern Arabia, the Nejd, where no Westerner had trod for twenty years, she was taken prisoner by the emir's uncle in Hayil and was held for nine days before she brazened her way out with pure bluff and fury.

When World War I broke out, the same officials who'd deplored her reckless journeying recognized its value: nobody knew as much as Bell about the routes, the wells, the complicated intertribal relationships, and how the locals felt about the British. She was taken on as an intelligence agent in the Arab Bureau and posted to Cairo, where she renewed her friendship with Lawrence and told him a useful thing or two.

As the only woman political officer in the British Forces, and arrogant at that, she was unpopular with her countrymen, and her views in favor of Arab self-determination clashed with the official views. Even her enemies bowed to her knowledge, though, and when she went to discuss the Arab question at the Paris Peace Conference, her hostile colleague Arnold Wilson admitted that of all their many so-called experts, "not one, except Miss Bell, had any first-hand knowledge of Iraq, or Nejd, or, indeed, of Persia."

In 1921, when Winston Churchill was made Colonial Secretary, he invited thirty-nine men, including Lawrence, and one woman to help him solve the Middle East riddle. Who was to lead the newborn country of Iraq, no longer a chattel of the Ottoman Empire? Bell and Lawrence insisted on Prince Faisal, popular leader in the revolt against the Turks, and Bell managed to persuade the Iraqis that he was the man for the job.

She helped draw up the borders of the new country. After

Faisal took office, she was his political advisor, and came to be known as "the uncrowned queen of Iraq."

Then, with the new government settled in, she felt underemployed. She took up archaeology again, wrote Iraq's antiquities laws, and started its excellent archaeology museum. Still, it wasn't the same as being the most powerful woman in the British Empire. She brooded; perhaps she should have married? She'd had lovers, but no husband, which was probably just as well; it would have been an odd life, being married to "the daughter of the desert," forever waving goodbye to her camel caravan.

When she was fifty-eight and perhaps unendurably bored, she took an overdose of sleeping pills; she was buried in Baghdad with full military honors.

Some exiles find their true spiritual homes in a single leap; others make their way toward paradise in a series of stumbles. The Honorable Jane Digby worked her way man by man toward joyous exile. She was, in rapid succession, Lady Ellenborough, Baroness Venningen, Countess Theotoky, and Mrs. Sheik Abdul Medjuel El Mezrab, and those were only the legal liaisons. Sprinkled among them were any number of lovers, including King Ludwig of Bavaria; his son, King Otho of Greece; an Austrian prince named Schwarzenberg, by whom she had two daughters; the future Napoleon III; and Honoré de Balzac.

She didn't do it for money or social position; she had plenty of those to start with, though with Victoria on the throne, all those divorces didn't sit well with her nice English relatives. She did it for love. Each new man was the love of her life, and every man who saw her fell in love with her. Her first lover wrote when he met her that she was "one of the most lovely women I ever saw, quite fair, blue eyes that would move a saint, and lips that would tempt one to forswear heaven to touch them."

She was always trusting, simple-hearted, and hopeful, but considerably brighter than you might think. She spoke and read nine languages and became the foremost authority on Syrian antiquities; Sir Richard Burton thought her quite the cleverest woman he'd ever met. It's true her children bored her, and she left five of them behind with their various fathers; she quite liked number six, Count Theotoky's son, but he died of a fall when still very young. (She was a splendid horsewoman, and Balzac observed that women who were superb riders were often lacking in *"tendresse."*) She was passionate but never sentimental, and quite undomesticated.

Her various removes and decampments kept pulling her steadily eastward until finally a young Arab lover introduced her to the desert and the black Bedouin tents, and she knew she was home. It had taken her quite a while and she was well into her forties when she met Medjuel, but it was worth the wait. He was dashing and dark and fearless; she loved him, and his tribesmen, and the nomadic life. Galloping around in the blazing desert before the days of sunscreen or Oil of Olay, somehow she kept her transparent English skin, and when she was fifty she looked thirty—and acted twenty. When she accepted Medjuel's marriage proposal, she wrote that she felt fifteen: "Je me croirais quinze ans."

She built a house in Damascus, where they lived a civilized life for six months of the year, and the other six months they roamed the desert in tents. Accepting the Arab customs, she fed and waited on her husband and washed his feet, but she was far from housebroken and rode into battle beside him on the frequent intertribal skirmishes, a crack shot with a rifle at full gallop. (After one fight they disappeared, and her obituaries in newspapers around the world credited her with up to nine husbands, but she galloped back out of the desert again alive and well.)

Quite against all the rules of fiction, theater, and morality, this shameless hussy escaped the wages of sin and lived divinely happy with her sheik for nearly thirty years. Pure happiness kept her young and adventurous and beloved until she died in Damascus of cholera, seventy-four and pretty as a peach.

In looks, heredity, temperament, and destiny, dark Isabelle Eberhardt was bright Jane Digby's perfect opposite. Exile and a brooding Slavic instability ran in her family; many relatives committed suicide and she sometimes tried it herself. Her mother left her husband, a Russian general, took her three children, and legged it for Geneva with the children's Armenian tutor, who'd left his own wife and children behind in Russia. In Geneva she and the tutor had two more children, Augustin and Isabelle, who as they grew up were passionately in love with each other, an unsettling start in life.

Isabelle was tall, slim, and flat-chested, with tilted black eyes and high cheekbones, a style scorned in the 1890s. Feeling unattractive as a girl, she dressed as a boy and cut off her hair. Suburban Geneva was pale and chilly and prim, and Isabelle pined for the burning sands of Algeria and what she called stranger and stronger music. She read all she could find about North Africa, and taught herself Arabic, and when she was eighteen she persuaded her mother to move with her to Bône, on the Algerian coast, where they lived in the Arab quarter and avoided their French colonial compatriots. Here she converted to Islam and followed it with a mystic's zeal, never neglecting the five daily prayers; she wore a burnoose and called herself a man, Si Mahoud.

After her mother died, Isabelle had no money to stay on and she went reluctantly back to Geneva and her ailing father the tutor. Augustin was there too, brooding Slavically. Everyone was miserable and it was all very Chekhovian around the house. As soon as her father died—one biographer suggests she and Augustin poisoned him—she headed for Paris to gather enough money to get back to Africa. Apparently she scrounged a commission from a rich widow to look for the remains of her late husband, an explorer who'd been assassinated somewhere out on the burning sands, so back she went.

Local legends in remote oases suggest that she may indeed have been looking for the vanished fellow, but she was easily distracted and loved wandering for its own sake. She covered incredible chunks of empty territory alone, with only her horse for company, avoiding the French and hobnobbing only with Arabs, sleeping on the dirt floors of huts among the rats or out in the open, happy as only the happy exile can be, drunk on space under skies without end.

She was often drunk on more than space. Absinthe and anisette were forbidden to Moslems, of course, but she didn't seem to feel that this applied to her, or compromised her passionate faith. She used hashish, too, and lots of it. She took dozens, if not hundreds, of casual Arab lovers, summoning them out of the crowds at the market, using and discarding them in true manly fashion, and indeed the Arabs seemed to accept her as a man, or at least honor her disguise. Unworried by any sense of conflict, she spent days at the feet of mystics absorbing religious instruction.

The French colony was scandalized, mostly by the Islamic aspect, and all the more so when she was half killed by a fanatic with a sword who claimed Allah had ordered him to assassinate her. There was a trial. The assassin got twenty years' hard labor, but the victim was clearly a focal point for trouble and they ordered her out of North Africa.

She landed in Marseilles, where she languished in a squalid rented room. She had no money; the French widow had withdrawn her support, exasperated by Si Mahoud's fruitless wanderings. She thought lovingly of suicide, wrote several excellent stories, and ruptured herself laboring as a dock worker.

The only way to get back to North Africa was as the wife of a citizen. She sent for Slimene, an Arab lover she'd kept on hand for quite a while, married him in Marseilles, and returned with him to her Eden, still dressed as Si Mahoud in her trademark high red boots. They must have made an arresting couple; he must have been uncommonly tolerant, or perhaps apathetic. She was fond of him after her fashion, but he can't have seen much of her. Sometimes she vanished into the desert; when in Algiers she was a famous fixture in the cafés, sitting cross-legged on the floor, drinking, smoking *kif,* and talking all night in her strangely grating nasal voice. For laughably small crumbs of money she wrote for the newspaper *L'Akhbar.* (The paper's editor got his hands on her writings after her death, reworked them in the florid style of the time, and published them as his own. Only her journals, having been safely lost for decades, survive in her own clear voice.)

Her great break came when *Dépêché Algérienne* sent her as a war correspondent to cover some rumbles over near the Moroccan border. It was bliss. She hung out with the Legionnaires, drinking and smoking *kif* all night, then sprang into the saddle at dawn to gather her stories. This was the stuff of the legend that would blossom and grow fabulous after her death; she was *La Bonne Nomade, Le Cosaque du Desert.* She was recognized as an authority on the great desert and a confidante of Arab leaders. Having neither European friends nor money for European comforts, she alone knew the Arabs from ground level, sharing their fleas and addictions and diseases. By now she probably had syphilis as well as severe malaria, the price of the taste of space and the right to wander.

Too reckless or too lazy to take care of herself, she lost her teeth. Her health fell apart. She was only twenty-eight but people who knew her at the time said she was a wreck of a woman. Finally she consented to check into a hospital in a small town at the desert's edge, and rented a shack in the ravine below it where she planned to rendezvous with Slimene. Impatient, she defied the doctor and slipped out against orders, down to the shack, just in time for a torrential flash flood that poured down the ravine, carrying everything away.

Slimene escaped. She drowned. Drowning in the Sahara is a rare way to die, but Si Mahoud was always a rarity.

On the other side of the world, in a different desert, lived a totally different sort of exile, a primly dressed Irishwoman named Daisy Bates. Those who have heard of her at all probably read a recent popular book, *Daisy Bates in the Desert,* by Julia Blackburn, a blend of debunkery, fiction, and fantasy that makes her a vain, self-centered, social-climbing liar. Surely it was never meant to be taken as serious history, but it obscures the record, since it's all we can easily learn. Daisy's own works are hard to find; my own copy of her book *The Passing of the Aborigines* finally surfaced in a used-book store in Perth. Daisy herself contributed to the confusion, playing cat-and-mouse with reporters and fudging dates and places and details of her early life.

However you look at her, though, Daisy Bates remains the queen of expatriates. She left misty little Ireland for Australia, and then polite Australian society for the outback and the Aborigines, and there she stayed, in a tent, wearing corsets and high-button boots and recording her neighbors' tales and rituals. It would have been a hundred and twelve in the shade had there been any shade, but she never left off a single layer of petticoat or unbuttoned her high collar, though the naked native women, watching her dress, giggled in wonderment. A loose mix of journalist, government investigator, anthropologist, ombudsman, interpreter, and nurse, she stayed there for half a century, until she was past eighty, and died still struggling to get back there.

Observing the confusion of the records, skeptics have called her "an incorrigible liar" and assume that since she lied about her age, she must also be lying about the Aborigines' burial and circumcision rituals, though the skeptics weren't there themselves, and Bates made and filed elaborate maps and reports for the government, and ninety-four folios of them repose in the national library; she can hardly have invented them all.

In her biography of Bates, published here in 1972, the Australian writer Elizabeth Salter accepts Daisy's own version of her early years: she was born in 1863, or perhaps 1861, to a prosperous and cultivated Irish Protestant family. After her mother died, she lived with her grandmother; after her grandmother died, she lived with her father, who set her to reading Dickens, Scott, Thackeray, and Lytton, and discouraged her passion for science. She was a blue-eyed, chestnut-haired beauty, witty and fond of tennis and hockey, with a fine seat on a horse (or, later, a camel) and a captivating Irish grin. Shortly after her father died, she was diagnosed with lung problems and she set forth for the more wholesome weather of Australia, where she would be a guest of the Bishop of North Queensland.

Here she rode out on explorations and partied with the smart expatriate set. At her first recorded glimpse of the Aborigines, she found them "the queerest-looking mortals, with their long lean legs and arms without an atom of flesh on them, more like spiders than anything human," the usual white settlers' view. In search of the pioneer life, she answered an ad for a governess at a cattle station, and there she met Jack Bates, a wild young horseman and cattle drover, and in what she later called "an error of judgment" she married him, in February of 1885. She was twenty-one. He promptly went off on a six-month cattle drive. When told she was pregnant, she cried, "But I don't want a baby!"

Jack wasn't very bright and they had nothing much in common, but he did teach her a few things about survival in the bush that came in useful later. Their son, Arnold Hamilton Bates, was born August 16, 1886, and his arrival apparently marked the end of their sex life. Poor Arnold; though Daisy was passionately fond of children and other people's children adored her, her son didn't appeal to her. He's been described as dull, withdrawn, and rather lazy, and may have reminded her of his father.

She'd given Jack several thousand pounds she'd inherited so that he could buy them a property, but somehow the money got mislaid. Jack was on the trail much of the time; Daisy and Arnold lived in hotels. When a monetary crisis wiped out the last of her capital, she slipped into depression and a doctor recommended a holiday back in the British Isles. She put Arnold into a boarding school and sailed away, arriving penniless.

Having sold the last of her jewelry, she wangled a job at the prestigious *Review of Reviews* in London, making a pound a week as general office help and occasional writer. Here she met all the best progressive minds of the day, stubbornly holding her own as the lone Tory among the liberals, disapproving of modern notions in general, and the women's movement in particular. (She always did enjoy the proud reactionary stance, clinging to her Victorian garb clear through the age of the flapper and into the blue-jeans era.)

Tony county families took her up, and she was popular among her cousins and connections, who all assumed she was a widow. Jack never wrote to her. Perhaps he couldn't write. She fell in love with the dashing Carrick Hoare and they may have been secretly engaged. Did she mention Jack to him? Perhaps the situation was closing in on her when her bank came up with some unexpected money, and she went guiltily back to Australia and thirteen-year-old Arnold.

Jack was now a hefty beer drinker in his forties, what the snobbish Daisy probably considered "common." Through a friend whose cattle he had saved, they managed to lay claim to 180,000 acres of potential cattle station, with no house and no cattle. Wistfully, Daisy named it Glen Carrick, after her lost love. She enrolled Arnold at the Christian Brothers school in Perth, arranged for him to board with a nice family, and rode off to the northwest and the claim, taking notes for an article to be published in *The Journal of Agriculture*.

She loved every minute—the perils, the bush, the storms, the birds, beetles, and Aborigines. Her life's work had found her.

After the land negotiations were settled, she left Jack and traveled south to Bishop Gibney to report on the Aborigines and insist on joining him on a journey to the Trappist mission.

Here Daisy herself takes up the tale in *The Passing of the Aborigines*, published in Australia in 1944. Its premise is shockingly incorrect: she believes civilization is bad for the natives; those who come in contact with it degenerate and die; assimilation is impossible and segregation the best of the bad answers; and the well-meaning white civilizers are so ignorant of native customs that their interference is always disastrous: "The Australian native can withstand all the reverses of nature, fiendish droughts and sweeping floods, horrors of thirst and enforced starvation, but he cannot withstand civilization." His mind works differently. "Only in God's good time will you begin to understand the riddle of the native mind," she wrote. "It is the study, not of a year or two of field work, but of a whole lifetime."

Civilizers need to believe in the basic goodness of civilization and the duty of the enlightened to bring Christianity, baths, clothing, nutrition, book learning, and employment to those without them. This is really good of us, and many good people have endured great hardship to help the savages, but first we must believe in our essentially superior lives. Daisy was odd for her times in believing that primitive lives were worthy and dignified in themselves and not just a larval form of humanity in need of improvement.

Improvement was fatal. When dragged to the government hospitals they were housed together with members of different totems whose hostile magic worked on them while they slept; they died in droves of whooping cough, measles, flu, terror, grief, and homesickness. The hospitals washed them thoroughly with warm water and soap, so that their skins withered and thinned until they peeled away from the flesh, because, says Daisy, their skins are different and cleanliness is fatal. Many of their ceremonies involved plastering each other with fat and human blood, which was left to wear off in the course of time, along with whatever else had stuck to it. Their bath, a ritual cleansing, consisted of standing in the thick smoke of a greenwood fire, singing the smoke song; Daisy herself was honored with this procedure, perhaps because her friends thought white people smelled just awful (the flavor wasn't great either), though not as bad as half-breeds.

They accepted her. She was fearless and sympathetic and learned a hundred and twenty native languages, but that doesn't quite explain how she was made an honorary member of the Aboriginal world or how, in a patriarchy where women were bartered and rented out by their husbands, allowed to eat only after the dogs had been fed, and killed instantly for violating any of dozens of taboos, Daisy was made an honorary man, privy to male rituals. She found herself a relative to all the scattered tribes and totems all over the country. "Kabbarli," they called her, the Magic Grandmother, more spirit than human. Like so many of history's adventuring women, she must have had some uncommon skill or charm or guardian spirit not easily traced.

Her book is not an autobiography, and she drops herself into it without the usual preamble. We find her working to rehabilitate a tumbledown Trappist mission that was struggling to minister to the natives. She was there to write a report for the London *Times,* or so she says, but ended up doing four months' hard labor grubbing up stumps and repairing wells, while the native women assigned to help her "played with the babies and laughed both with and at me, full of merriment and good feeling. . . . The force of my example failed dismally." In a world where a handful of grubs was food, skin was clothing enough, and a pile of sticks was shelter, work was hard to explain.

On the matter of stocking Glen Carrick with cattle, the facts are a bit muddled. Certainly Daisy worked the great cattle drive, taking 770 head from the West Kimberleys to Central West Australia. The *West Australian* reported, "There is in Perth a cultured, quiet, and somewhat frail looking lady who has just completed one of the most arduous trips that any lady has ever undertaken and has established what must be almost a record in the endurance of the 'weaker' sex." She wrote about it herself, much later, in "3,000 Miles in a Side Saddle." (Of course she rode side-saddle; what else can you do in those skirts?) The head count included 200 for Glen Carrick; the rest apparently were under contract elsewhere. According to her account in *The Passing of the Aborigines,* she ran the drive herself, along with a few hired drovers, for six months of eighteen-hour days in the saddle. Suddenly, fifty pages into her book, she mentions that her twelve-year-old son is riding with her. This is the first the reader has heard of a son. He's mentioned, though namelessly, several more times and then, once the cattle are disposed of, she makes a first-person-singular departure for Perth, to take up "the task to which my life had been dedicated" among the Aborigines. What happened to the boy is apparently nobody's business. Besides, he was fifteen at the time, not twelve, but as a general rule the whistling women make absentminded mothers; sometimes she referred to Arnold as William.

What she doesn't tell us is that Jack was heading the drive, at the point of its bovine triangle, while she and Arnold rode herd back and forth on its broad trailing base. The cattle intended for Glen Carrick were lost on the dreaded Eighty-Mile Beach; she blamed Jack; the trip was a disaster and marked the end of any attempt at married life. Apparently she'd seen marriage only as a necessary part of the pioneer settler's life. Jack went off to manage a cattle station in the Roebuck Plains, dropping out of the picture entirely, and she went to study the Abos, having, she said, "an innate racial affinity with them, since they were Irish at heart." Cheerful, she meant, like herself, with a happy taste for storytelling.

Investigating conditions and collecting data for the government, she spent two years with the Bibbulman, a once-great tribe of the western coastal plains. They were uncircumcised, and the overpowering new waves of the circumcised had driven them out of their homeland. This apparently small distinction was the deep division between the natives of Daisy's time, and among the circumcised the rite was the great manhood initiation. She was allowed to watch and describes it in detail, all its many stages and ceremonies, with quarts of human blood drunk at each step and the leftover blood dried and eaten in chunks. For long periods the initiate is allowed no other food. This is followed by ritual visits far and wide involving more blood-drinking, until years have gone by and the young man, by now no longer so young, is finally adult, freed from dietary taboos, and allowed to take his designated bride or brides. (It's little wonder the Aborigines didn't fancy salaried jobs; ceremonies occupied most of their time.)

Skeptics have questioned that she was actually allowed to watch such sacred proceedings, but she has the minutest details down, and the zoologist E. L. Grant Watson reports that she was with him at a similar ceremony: "They thought we were ghosts," he said.

Dispossessed, and in fatal contact with civilization for seventy years, the Perth-based Bibbulman were demoralized and dying out, many of drink, singing sad songs of their old homeland. Their traditional gathering grounds had been plowed and fenced and their numbers so shrunken they couldn't obey their elaborate marriage and kinship laws, which required supplies of siblings and cousins. Traditions had broken down. Daisy sat by the tribe's deathbed taking notes for the government. After burying the last of them, she set out on a two-year pilgrimage through the southwest, looking for the remnants of the different totems—possum, emu, fish, rain, kangaroo—and finding many of them extinct, others beggars or government pensioners. She nursed measles and tuberculosis patients, spooning gruel into them by the hour, until they learned to enjoy it and refused to get well, and were joined by others from far and wide coming to be sick and pampered, whole huts full of them bedded in filth with their mouths open for gruel.

She records these matters with humor and sense and no trace of condescension. Some things are amusing, all are equally interesting, and she has no disgust or moral outrage. In this area, baby cannibalism is common, and among one group, every woman who had had a baby had killed and eaten it, sharing the meat with her sisters, who returned the favor. Daisy assures us, though, that they rarely killed children who had managed to live for a few months, and were loving and dutiful mothers to the survivors, fattening up their favorites with tasty morsels of infant siblings.

She accepted a government commission at eight shillings a day to record the dialects and customs of the natives, and in 1912, after eight years of research, she went back to Perth to report in to the government. She filled an 800-page volume with comparative reports, but all her research convinced her that the previous fieldwork was faulty, and besides, her tent had spoiled her for city life and she wanted to go on with her work: "I realized that they were passing from us. I must make their passing easier." The government was scandalized by the idea, but consented to send her with a white police escort to help set up her tent. After the escort left, slowly the natives began to creep out of the bush and approach the place, where she stood alone, and when they were close enough, she invited them to join her in a cup of tea, as any Irishwoman would.

She went "wandering from camp to camp, attending to the bodily needs of the scattered flock," learning the prehistoric names of every rock and pool, and the meaning of dreams, and the magical properties of stars and compass points. When she was made a member of the rain totem, they taught her the rain song, a catchy little ditty, and she was overheard singing it to herself in her tent; the cloudburst that followed greatly enhanced her reputation.

In the white world, she was published in scientific journals and invited into distinguished scientific societies. She was picked to organize, lead, and keep peace in a great corroboree for the Perth Carnival; she helped with the body painting and soothed intertotemic tensions.

In the Great Australian Bight she found adults as well as babies on the menu: "The Baduwonga of Boundary Dam drank the blood of those they had killed. The Kaalurwonga, east of the Badu, were a fierce arrogant tribe who pursued fat men, women, and girls and cooked the dead by making a deep hole in the sand, trussing the body and there roasting it, and tossing it about until it cooled sufficient for them to divide it. Another group would cut off hand and foot, and partake of these first, to prevent the ghost from following and spearing them spiritually." But here, too, she was Kabbarli, the Magic Grandmother, and walked without fear. (In any case, she was a wee slip of a woman, hardly worth eating.)

Offhandedly she mentions having sold Glen Carrick, the cattle ranch she'd so painfully tried to stock; she needed the money for supplies for the natives. Then back to the important matters: an invasion threatens, but she defuses the situation, and is delighted to find that the invaders are men of the Wanji-Wanji travel dance, who perform a historical dream-dance as they circle the Aboriginal trade route around the continent, taking perhaps two generations to complete the circuit, performing a dream-dance about the coming of the circumcised people. For two weeks they played three performances a day; no one, including the performers, remembered what the songs and dances meant, and shortly thereafter the tradition petered out for lack of audience.

In a raucous ceremony, Daisy was initiated into the freedom of all the totems, a kind of international passport as friend of the whole Aboriginal world. All the children and the other women were banished miles away while, surrounded by naked men in full paint with spears, Daisy accepted her credentials wearing "a sober European coat and skirt, a sailor hat with a veil, and neat, high-heeled shoes. We must have looked a quaint assembly indeed." Indeed. With many ritual fires, screams, songs, mystical incantations, and more songs, Daisy Bates of Ireland was made the keeper of the sacred male totem-boards and placed in charge of hiding them from white men.

In 1914 she was invited back to civilization to attend a scientific congress in Adelaide. She chose as travel companions Gaura and her fourteenth husband, who had recently purchased her from the thirteenth for two shillings and a tobacco pipe; presently number thirteen also joined the group and traveled along. At the edge of the terrible Nullarbor Plain, four hundred and fifty miles of sun-baked nothing, they sent a last smoke-signal of farewell. The natives never went into the Nullarbor because of the great magic snake Ganba, and white folks didn't like it either. However, Daisy's party rejoiced to find edible birds, ants, snails, and other provender. Daisy, no cook herself, praised the skillful native cuisine that brought out the full flavor of whatever; wombat, cooked for four hours in hot ashes, came out tasting like the most delicious roasted pork, also "a long fat carpet snake called gooma rolled into lengths and roasted." As they traveled along, lurching in the camel buggy, they sang the Wanji-Wanji songs, and Daisy's sweet Irish soprano no doubt drifted across the scorched scrub, singing

Warri wan-gan-ye,
Koogunarri wanji-wanji,
Warri wan-gan-ye.

In Adelaide, she was shocked to find that war had been declared in Europe; she lectured in Melbourne and Sydney; she accepted the same government job in South Australia that she'd been doing in the west; and she climbed back into the camel buggy.

She settled west of Fowler's Bay, among the remnants of groups from all the edges of the Plain, three of them blind and helpless, deserted by their kin and mercilessly teased. She moved these away from the others and "sat down" with them for several years. Most of us strive to maximize the target of our efforts and it seems odd to spend so much time on so few, but Daisy hunted birds and rabbits for them, chopped their firewood, lighted their pipes, and took them for walks hanging to the end of a pole. She was happy there, learning legends, inspecting fossil prints, and studying birds and lizards and native songs. It was a handsome place: "Just to look upon its beauty was an ecstasy . . . the perfect happiness these beautiful open spaces give."

Her charges weren't necessarily worth the effort. One of them, Dowie, was a nasty piece of work. He'd been his parents' pride and joy and they'd given him four baby sisters to eat and rubbed him down with their fat, so he grew big and strong. Grown, he was unquenchably bloodthirsty, eating people not ceremoniously but with gusto. He killed his first four wives shortly after the weddings and shared the meat around; other wives followed, also neighbors. He was mean as a snake and strong as a bull and unwelcome in any society. Then one day, hunting in strange territory full of strange demons, he was caught in a storm of hail and thunder and bad magic that drove him completely mad. He howled and barged around all night slashing things, while the locals cowered. He lost one eye in the storm and another failed through sheer dementia, but he was dangerous even blind, striking out wildly into the darkness, pursued by a ghost.

Daisy nursed and fed him. Often he wandered off and she had to lead him back and put him to bed. Finally he wandered so far afield that when she found him, she had to hoist him naked onto her back and, bent over double and leaning on her digging-stick, carry him back to camp, remembering when she was halfway there that she was still a member of the most exclusive women's club in Perth, which sent her into such uncontrollable giggles she nearly dropped him.

Mercifully he died soon afterward, and she dug his grave with her digging-stick.

The coming of the railroad was ruination for the natives. It drank their water, draining the ancestral watering holes, frightened away the game, and taught them to beg. When Daisy came to Ooldea Siding in 1919 she found derelict natives of all totems camping by the tracks and traveling the line to beg food and tobacco wherever it stopped. White and half-caste hobos mingled with them, and prostitution flourished. With no concept of paternity, when the native women had half-breed babies, they took it as a punishment for eating white man's food and scoured the newborn with charcoal to try to darken it. All, including Daisy, grew dependent on the train, and when a strike shut down service they were in serious trouble for food and water, and Daisy with a camp-full of flu patients. She herself lived on the scantiest of rations: tea, a little porridge, an occasional fire-roasted potato, sometimes a boiled egg. Sometimes native delicacies: witchetty-grubs, she reports, have "a creamy almond flavor" but they're so rich they must be eaten sparingly. (In a life of grueling work in a wicked climate, exposed to countless diseases, she stayed mostly in vigorous health and strength far into old age. So much for the fruits-and-vegetables police.)

Train service was finally restored in time for her to serve her wards a real Christmas dinner, complete with a huge and repulsive plum pudding boiled up in one of her old nightgowns.

Depressing as the track-side camps must have been, she stayed, the only halfway house or buffer between the wild natives and the white man's world along a thousand miles of train track. She nursed her patients—once she had eight down with pneumonia simultaneously—with homemade cough mixtures, oil rubdowns, what food she could get her hands on, and grandmotherly cheer; cheerfulness, not cleanliness, is next to godliness, she maintained. The worst cases she carried into her tent to sleep beside her. She used no white man's medicine because she considered it bad for the black man's system; she dressed wounds with soft white ashes, treated diarrhea with tree gum and constipation with iguana liver, and left her patients in their own sandy or grassy beds. Sometimes they recovered, but often they died of the white man's ailments and the black man's magic; with so many totem groups jumbled together, the danger of alien magic multiplied, and death by magic was common. Daisy cured it with countermagic, drawing the evil out of the afflicted body and burning it off over a fire while she fanned the smoke away from the victim. She grew quite a reputation for witchcraft.

When the Prince of Wales passed through on his Australian tour, she gathered the scattered natives along the track and took them, along with her frailest patients, to Cook Siding, eighty-six miles away, where she coached them in a splendid presentation of native crafts and dances. His Highness was a brick about it, invited Daisy to sit on the dais with him and explain things, and then had a stab at spear-throwing. He left behind a splendid feast of roast sheep and tobacco.

Retreating a mile or so away from the tracks for privacy, Daisy set up her eight-by-ten tent in what would be home for the next sixteen years. Here she put out water and crumbs for the birds, who hung around tamely and sang duets with her, and played with the little lizards the natives called "Kabbarli's dogs," which sat on her lap and caught flies. She sent curious specimens of all sorts to the British Museum.

From all over the Central West, natives came to see her, sometimes journeying for a year or two. Daisy introduced them all to the necessary customs of civilization, including clothes and the white man's taboo against eating people. On their own they learned to beg and to charge train passengers shillings for posing for photographs. "Amongst the hundreds that 'sat down' with me at Ooldea," she writes sadly, "there was not one that ever returned to his own waters and the natural bush life."

To feed her patients she sold off the last of her property, "including my side-saddle and bridle—last relic of a happy past," and when that money was gone she fell back on journalism and begging for donations, since the government stipend was pitifully stingy. She fed only the sick and the helpless, though, sternly sending the able to go forage for their traditional dinners. It was a losing battle, and she knew it, though she wrote that "not an hour of my time was wasted in all those years."

If she sounds noble and selfless, yet another among the legions of self-sacrificing women, she wasn't. Always driven at least as much by curiosity as by compassion, she's just as interested in the hunting strategies of her lizards as in the diseases of the natives. For those blessed or cursed all their lives by curiosity, life can unwind along strange paths.

A great drought gripped the land for eight years, with

scarcely a drop falling and traditional water supplies drying up everywhere (with help from the white man's cattle and voraciously thirsty trains). When the drought spawned an enormous Christmas brush fire, she managed to save thirty-five years worth of notes and manuscripts by burying them deep in the sand. Then the drought broke with a storm so violent she had to hold on to the ridge pole of her tent to keep it from blowing away.

She was seventy-four in 1933 when she was created a Commander of the Order of the British Empire by King George V, but she said "my step was as light and my heart as gay as they had been in youth."

She closes the book as she leaves her camp for civilization, to sort and transcribe her bundles of papers, carrying along the secret sacred totem boards entrusted to her so long before.

Elizabeth Salter's biography fills in the gaps. The villain in her version is A. R. Radcliffe-Brown, leader of a Cambridge anthropological expedition she'd been allowed to join. He considered her an amateur; she considered him "no gentleman." He was a handsome and arrogant young man, and he freely mutilated the only copy of her tremendous work, *A Short Authentic Historical Record of the Habits, Customs, and Languages of the Aboriginal Natives of this State*. She refused to work with him as his collaborator and he took full revenge. He used her work in his own publications and lectures without mentioning her, and rode the momentum into becoming the first Professor of Anthropology at Sydney University. He permanently damaged her credibility and chances of publication. Thanks to him, she was honored as a saint, not a scientist; a curiosity; a "self-ordained Florence Nightingale"; and widely suspected of fraud.

Probably she'd been rude to him at the outset. She often was. She was proud and stubborn as a cat, and when W. G. South, Chief Protector of the Aborigines, came and told her to disperse her little group, she ordered him off the property.

The Passing of the Aborigines was serialized in the newspapers in 1936 as *My Natives and I* and published as a book two years later, but it was only a tiny fraction of her work. She had accumulated a great toppling mass of research over the decades, and now needed time to put it in order and money to live on while she worked. The government offered her two pounds, or about ten dollars, a week, which wasn't enough for survival in Adelaide, so she moved a hundred miles north and lived in a tent again, at Pyap on the Murray, for four years.

The data finally compiled, she hit the road. Still drawing her two pounds a week, this time as "Consultant for Native Affairs," she set up camp at a different stop on the railroad, to work on a children's book of Aboriginal legends and take care of the drifting nomads. The natives there were a thieving, degenerate lot, long out of touch with their traditions and immune to the magic of Kabbarli. She was half blind; unable to read the instructions on the food-ration stamps, she went hungry. People who met her considered her "slightly mental," though still cheerful.

In 1945 the exasperated government sent an ambulance to drag her out of her camp, by force if necessary. Force was necessary. She arrived at the hospital bruised by her brush with the "gangsters" and was admitted with severe malnutrition.

She still worked every day on her writing; she still walked everywhere, ignoring elevators; she still wore the suit she'd bought in 1900. She kept escaping from friends and guardians, still trying to get back to her natives and the red rock roads of the bush. Captured, she was put into a convalescent home. In 1951 she died, age ninety or perhaps ninety-two, and was buried, not at the gravesite she'd picked out by the Nullarbor Plain but in Adelaide's North Road Cemetery.

Suburbia must have seemed the strangest exile of all.

Here we would leave her in peace if it weren't for *Daisy Bates in the Desert*. Blackburn's premise is simple: "Daisy Bates was a liar, of that I am sure." In the next two pages she uses the words "sinister," "frightening," "fierce," "dangerous," "difficult," "disdainful," "reptilian," "misguided," and "demented." Clearly this will not be a worshipful work.

To start with, Blackburn says her whole childhood is a lie and the scholarly, well-traveled, well-to-do Protestant papa was actually a poor Catholic drunk who'd lit out for America, and that Daisy was raised in an orphanage. She came to Australia not as a bishop's guest but as a penniless immigrant. Working as a governess on a cattle station she was married by a Catholic priest to a stockman named Edwin Harry Murrant, later known as "Breaker" Morant and executed for murder in Cape Town by a British firing squad, as seen in the 1980 movie. Immediately after the wedding, Breaker went to jail for stealing pigs and Daisy left him. Less than a year later she married, this time as a Protestant, Jack Bates, making herself a bigamist.

Blackburn is vague about her sources, but in Salter's biography there's a photograph of young Daisy wearing the elaborately ruffled white evening gown in which she was presented to the Duke and Duchess of York in Perth. How a penniless orphan immigrant, or even the wife of an irresponsible cattle drover, could buy such a dress, not to mention meet dukes, is a mystery Blackburn doesn't approach. Cavalierly, she sweeps all the pieces off the board. During the London years, she says, Daisy never worked for the *Review of Reviews* and probably supported herself as a prostitute. There were no bishops, no dashing suitors, no inheritances, no bank deposits, no Glen Carrick, no property or jewelry to sell, no country-house dances, no influential friends. As to where Daisy found money to feed and nurse her wards, since she furiously rejected charity, Blackburn doesn't give a hint. The Blackburn Daisy's only source of revenue had been prostitution, not an easy living in the empty outback, especially when you're over seventy.

Then the author pops into the first person and writes as Daisy, pretentious, paranoid, and obsessively vain, spending much of her time gazing at her naked self in a mirror, even when she's quite old. Her Daisy has monologues, conversations, delusions, sexual fantasies (Blackburn seems much more interested in sex than Daisy was), and scores of dreams, in one of which she eats her son Arnold. Otherwise the narrative is essentially Daisy's own *Passing of the Aborigines*.

In the closing section, Blackburn suggests that Daisy didn't even write the book. Probably a secretary wrote it, though how, all penniless out in the howling desert wastes, she would find and pay a secretary isn't explained.

Daisy Bates in the Desert was published in the United States to critical acclaim. Nobody knew much about its subject, and possibly gave the author credit for inventing her, which, in a sense she did. It's a novelist's privilege.

This wouldn't be worth mentioning, except that as of now it's all we have to remember her by, brave Daisy singing the rain song to herself and taming lizards to keep her spirits up in the wilderness, and it seems a shame.

Wayfarers

The self-exiled believe they've been born in the wrong place and set out to find the right place, the place with their name on it, and pitch a tent there. The travelers believe the whole world has their name on it; they pack only portable tents and gather no moss.

Travelers are overwhelmingly male. The writers and photographers who roam for the *National Geographic* are male. Check any travel anthology and you may find a token Freya Stark piece, but by and large this is man's work, for a goodly handful of reasons.

Most women marry. A woman married to a wandering man waited for him back home, while the children grew older and forgot their father's face, and she was much admired for her patience; any man who paced the battlements and scanned the horizon for his wife's sail or the dust of a lone horsewoman cantering home across the plains would be, if there'd ever been such a man, a fool. Letting her leave in the first place would have made him a laughingstock.

Men have always been sent forth into the world to report on conditions, routes, geography, local products, and prospects for trade or conquest. Who would send a woman? A woman would

117

see the world from a woman's viewpoint, which is unavoidably distorted from the norm. Women and men are different. The excellent travel writer James Morris, for reasons of his own, underwent a sex change in mid-career and took to writing as Jan Morris; he now appears under both names in the anthologies. As Jan, he travels as a woman, and from time to time the reader is startled when someone calls him "madam." Madam? It takes a full minute's struggle to remember that our author is wearing skirts. The book is a man's book; the traveler is looking through a man's eyes and asking a man's questions. There's more to gender than genitals.

Men notice men and the works of men. We can read a long and satisfying travel book by an adventuring man and come away feeling that the only life-forms in the entire country are the adult human male and the animals used for military transport.

Women notice marriage customs, goats, chickens, cooking pots, and whether the natives beat their donkeys, whether the children are friendly or the babies covered with sores and the cows half-starved. They watch the women pounding grain; they get to hear the old stories the old women tell. Trivial stuff. When a man carries letters of introduction, he gets interviews with prime ministers; a woman with letters gets to spend a few days with a local family and sit at the kitchen table.

Often it's her only chance to speak to the natives. The local men are out and about and available, but how can a lone female stranger, unless she carries credentials from the *New York Times* itself, introduce herself and strike up a conversation? Even in civilized countries a woman traveling alone is suspect, and in some places she's assumed to be a prostitute. She can't march into the tavern, the club, or the headman's hut and ask questions of strange men.

Historically, lack of money kept women where they belonged.

Through most of recorded time it was rare for a woman to be in charge of more than grocery money, and even rarer for her male relatives to hand her a sack-full so she could wander off unsupervised. The traveling women of record are unmarried; their parents died and left no one to oversee their allowance.

A man without money could do odd jobs for his fare or his lodgings; he could ship as a deckhand, or help with the harvest or drive cattle to the railhead, pocket the money, and move on. A woman without money could hardly get out of sight of her house. With luck, once home again, either sex could write a book about it to defray expenses, but that never helped with the initial outlay, and the notion of traveling solely in order to get paid for writing about it is a recent one. The women's books were buried under the avalanche of men's adventures; the whole world read Sir Richard Burton's *Wanderings in West Africa,* but who remembers Mary Kingsley's far more entertaining *Travels in West Africa?*

Then there's the conquering instinct, travel based on challenge, followed by boast. See, there is the desert never crossed, the South Pole not yet trodden, the sea so far unsailed in a dinghy, the earth not yet circled in a manned balloon: a man takes such things personally. They're the glove thrown in the face that must be answered by a duel. Women lack this response; when an obstacle draws its line in the sand and dares them, they tend to shrug and go around it.

Another drawback to feminine travel is time. It could be argued that the airplane has condensed the world something marvelous, but that isn't travel, more a sort of instant relocation: you are here, and then you are there. To find out what "there" is you must move slowly, by mule, bicycle, Jeep, canoe, camel, or afoot. This involves unpredictable masses of time, and the risk of not getting home when you said you would.

Traditionally, men have kissed their families goodbye and disappeared for the South China Sea or the goldfields for years with scarcely a backward glance. For a woman over age twenty, a week or two is all she thinks she can spare from her accustomed world. Even if she has neither job nor children, what will become of her house and garden without her, and will her cat starve and her friends forget her? Her heart drags its feet. Like Lot's wife, she looks over her shoulder.

Only a handful of the strong and lighthearted simply walk out of their doors and vanish. Sometimes they're on a quest. Sometimes they're just trotting ahead of the long yellow dogs of domestic boredom that seize you by the heels if you linger. It takes a brave woman with a fine indifference to public opinion, because a wandering man is a hero's hymn to freedom, but a wandering woman feels criminally irresponsible. Deep in our hearts we all know that a man's purposes may lie over the hills and far away, but a woman's lie under her roof, or at least no more than an hour away in case someone needs her. Running away from home, a rite of passage for a boy, is wickedness in a girl; the Prodigal Son's sister would have been pursued and forcibly returned to her duty, with a good beating thrown in. The bone of restlessness is bred out of her, or withers after adolescence. Usually.

We think of the Victorian age, the second half of the nineteenth century, as a stuffy, repressive, indoor world of horsehair sofas and prudery, but a number of eccentric, adventurous women sprang out of it blazing like comets. Not married women, of course; marriage closed off all other possible lives, but women who'd evaded domesticity broke through the parlor walls and made news. In America, they fought and spied in the Civil War and sheltered runaway slaves. They headed west and galloped through the prairie grass with the wind in their faces, singing new songs. In England, as soon as their parents died, spinsters booked passage on steamers into the unknown. Perhaps knowing that a woman, however prim, stood at the helm of Empire worked in their hearts like yeast.

Isabella Bird wrote *Englishwoman in America* (1856), *Six Months in the Sandwich Islands* (1875), *A Lady's Life in the Rocky Mountains* (1879), *Unbeaten Tracks in Japan* (1880), *The Golden Chersonese* (1883), *Journeys in Persia and Kurdistan* (1891), *Among the Tibetans* (1894), *Korea and Her Neighbors* (1898), *The Yangtse Valley and Beyond* (1899), and *Chinese Pictures* (1900). She had to. England made her sick. She was a dutiful person who felt that traveling just for the fun of it was sinful; but whenever she went home, she became a chronic invalid, sleepless and in constant pain. Whenever she left it, her health was wondrously restored.

She'd been a sickly child and the doctor wanted her outdoors, so her clergyman father took her with him while riding around Yorkshire on parish business. (Like so many lady adventurers, she was a splendid rider, traditional mark of the unmaternal and undomesticated.) At eighteen, she had a spinal tumor removed and the doctor sent her to the Scottish Highlands to convalesce. Roaming and trekking, she felt better immediately, and sold her first magazine article about the trip. Home again, she relapsed into back pain and headaches, and the doctor, after the amiable custom of doctors then, prescribed a sea voyage.

She traveled happily over six thousand miles of Canada and the United States and came home and wrote a book about it, but a year after it was published she was deep in the grip of the homeland sickness again. She went back to America, this time with the excuse of gathering material for her father's book on evangelism, but he died shortly after she got home and the book idea died with him.

She vowed to settle down. She and her mother and sister moved to Edinburgh, where she busied herself with good works and articles on religious matters and got sicker and sicker. Her mother died and left the sisters with a very modest income, but still Isabella did penance by staying home, dosing the pain and insomnia with laudanum and chlorodyne to no avail.

Her doctor, clearly a sensible chap, ordered another sea voyage, and this time she found herself in Hawaii, then called the Sandwich Islands. In 1873, before tourists, it was quite a different place, and Bird was in heaven with the light, the warmth, the empty open spaces, the freedom. Most important, she discovered the Mexican saddle and what she called "my Hawaiian riding costume."

With a bad back, she'd been grounded because she couldn't ride sidesaddle, and indeed it's a wonder the strongest back in the world could gallop over the countryside with its lower half at right angles to its top. The riding dress in Hawaii consisted of a fitted jacket and modest ankle-length skirt over "full Turkish trousers gathered into frills falling over the boots—a thoroughly serviceable and feminine costume for mountaineering and other rough traveling." Thus skirted and trousered, she could ride astride causing only occasional scandal. Her suit was red plaid, supplemented by a big hat and spurs, and it companioned her over many a rough mile before falling into tatters past mending.

The Hawaiian visit, scheduled for three weeks, expanded to seven months. The former invalid climbed Mauna Loa, at 13,650 feet the world's top volcano. It was a ferocious scramble, "clambering up acclivities so steep that the pack horse rolled backwards and my cat-like mule fell twice"; and she loved it, arriving at the top "serene in the eternal solitudes." (Solitude was always a high priority, and it may be that the sight of too many people back home was as bad for her as the dark and the damp cold. She was a claustrophobe and not all that fond of the human race anyway.)

She seems to have left Hawaii, finally, simply because she was too happy there and having too much fun. As noted, she was a dutiful soul, and her clergyman papa probably disapproved of excessive pleasure. She set forth for America again, this time to the Rockies.

A Lady's Life in the Rocky Mountains is a collection of letters she wrote to her sister, but they read more like installments of a book in progress, which they were. It's hard to believe her stay-at-home sister was riveted by the lists of measurements, precise recordings of mileage, temperature, elevation, acreage, bushels per acre, price per bushel, and the height and diameter of trees. She tells her sister that sheep-shearers get six and a half cents per head for inferior sheep and seven and a half for the better ones, and can shear sixty to eighty a day; she walks the length of her train so her sister can know its makeup, car by car, and exact length (seven hundred feet).

The facts are interspersed with bursts of eloquence. Sample: "The sunset has passed through every stage of beauty, through every glory of color, through riot and triumph, through pathos and tenderness, into a long, dreamy, painless rest, succeeded by the profound solemnity of the moonlight and a stillness broken only by the night cries of beasts in the aromatic forests." This was the way a well-brought-up woman of the day was expected to write, and it was much admired. But make no mistake, she was not some simpering poetizer; Bird, as soon as she got away from home, was tough. She could round up cattle; she could kill intrusive rattlesnakes with a kitchen knife. She could catch and saddle a horse and ride it for twelve or fifteen hours through deep snowdrifts, up and down ice-glazed slopes, into the ink-dark night where she couldn't see her horse's ears in front of her, socks and boots frozen to her feet, picking ice-crystals out of her frozen eyes, and praising the skies and mountains all the way.

She's a pushover for the scenery of the American West but finds the inhabitants and their works unworthy of it. Sacramento is "very repulsive"; Cheyenne "detestable"; Truckee smells so bad it makes her ill; "no place could be more unattractive" than Colorado Springs; Denver is a "braggart city"; Boulder "a hideous collection of frame houses"; the small settlement towns are "altogether revolting." American government and laws are feeble and corrupt and administered by scoundrels and churls. American children are, like their parents, "cankered by greed and selfishness" and shrewdly dishonest, brought up as they are in an atmosphere of "greed, godlessness, and frequently of profanity." The godly don't come off any better, though, and the Mormon women are "ugly and their shapeless blue dresses hideous." The scattered, isolated settlers are shabby and feckless; sometimes their boots don't match and their bridles are patched with rope. Feeling as she does about the settlers, you'd think she'd sympathize with the Indians, but she says, "The Americans will never solve the Indian problem till the Indian is extinct. . . . The only difference between the savage and the civilized Indian is that the latter carries firearms and gets drunk on whisky."

The handful of people she approves of have freshly arrived British accents. Like most good English travelers, however disloyally she may have left the dismal shores of home for foreign sun and foreign landscapes, she never commits the ultimate disloyalty of approving of the people, especially not those who'd committed the base ingratitude of the American Revolution and richly deserve the degradation into which they've fallen since.

Once she gets clear of the natives, the Rockies are all "brilliancy of sky and atmosphere, that blaze of sunshine and universal glitter." She rhapsodizes over sunrises and sunsets as if she'd never seen either before, and perhaps, living in coal-burning Britain during the Industrial Revolution, she hadn't. Writing of *The Golden Chersonese* a reviewer said, "Not the least noteworthy among Miss Bird's gifts is a heaven-sent faculty for having adventures. . . . Things turn out as if by special inspiration. She trusts to fortune, to what ought to happen, and it does happen." She wants to find a guide and make her way to Estes Park and climb Longs Peak, and of course she does.

Estes Park was an unsurveyed chunk of land, reached only on horseback and inhabited only by seasonal hunters and trappers, that seems to have covered what is now Rocky Mountain National Park and its surrounding ski resorts in northern Colorado. Isabella gives it three exclamation points in her letter to her sister: "the very place I have been seeking, but in everything it exceeds all my dreams." Some of her euphoria rubs off on the notorious trapper and ruffian Mountain Jim Nugent.

Mountain Jim's shanty sits at the entrance to Estes and he's the first person she meets there. He was what was called a "colorful character," so colorful he starred fictionally in many a western tale, and in real life had been a famous scout and enthusiastic fighter in the frontier Indian wars. Apparently he suffered from bouts of depression and drink, or perhaps just temper tantrums, known locally as his "ugly fits," when it was safest to avoid him, but when he, son of a British officer, spoke to Isabella, his voice was pure English and she was enchanted to find such a "refined" accent in "a complete child of the mountains." Even his looks are exotic: a grizzly bear has gouged out one of his eyes and disfigured that side of his face, but his brow is "magnificently formed," his curls golden, and his profile nobleness itself. In short, an irresistible mix of wilderness and culture. Isabella, though she never says so, is in love.

Naturally there were no inns or hotels, but the scattered hunters and trappers "kept travelers" at the usual inn rates, expecting a bit of a hand with the chores as well. She bunks in a Welsh settler's cabin and explores Estes Park on horseback, sometimes with Jim as a guide, always with joy, "gaining health every hour." Longs Peak beckons. She finds it far superior in personality to Pikes Peak and flatters its height as 14,700 feet, though it seems to have shrunk slightly since. It had first been climbed five years before, and she won't rest till she's been up there too.

Jim, obviously captivated by our ladylike daredevil, takes her up, and has to literally haul her like a sack of flour the last steep bit of the way, and lower her tied to a lariat on the way down, but it's worth the cold and the bruises. She waxes downright idolatrous: "no sort of description within my powers could enable another to realize the glorious sublimity, the majestic solitude, and the unspeakable awfulness and fascination. . . ." It doesn't hurt that Jim's there too. He recites poetry, he regrets his misspent youth, their conversation in the wilderness is cultured and polite, and if passionate undercurrents quivered around their campfire, Isabella did not write about them to her sister. After all, she was past forty, a Victorian antique. Still, it would have made quite a Katharine Hepburn movie.

Winter is already on the wind and she wants to see more of Colorado. After a three-day delay when snow blocked the door and piled up on the floor, she hopped on her Indian pony, Birdie, and set forth alone, following the most rudimentary and sometimes illusory trails on an eight-hundred-mile ramble to see the sights. "It is a splendid life for health and enjoyment. All my luggage being in a pack, and my conveyance being a horse, we can go anywhere where we can get food and shelter." Snow melts on the plains but piles up in the passes; it's nine below zero when she and Birdie stagger through the drifts on the Arkansas Divide. The ice is worse, and the pony falls down over and over, though miraculously neither of them breaks a leg. Resourceful Isabella takes a pair of heavy socks from her pack and pulls them over Birdie's front feet, which works fine until the socks fall apart.

She's grown quite a reputation in the western newspapers, and when she stops for the night people know who she is. When she wants to go to Green Lake, she's told that no one's been able to get through for five weeks, but she sends to the livery stable for a horse anyway. The stable sends back to say, "If it's the English lady traveling in the mountains, she can have a horse, but not anyone else." She goes, of course. The sunset up there is sublime.

She runs out of money. The Denver banks, being in trouble themselves, refuse to cash her notes, and when she's down to twenty-six cents, she has no choice but to go back and cadge off her friends in Estes Park, that "grand, solitary, uplifted, sublime, remote, beast-haunted lair," with the added pleasures of Mountain Jim. Riding in after dark, he's the first person she meets, and he takes her to her former quarters, but her hosts, like most in the area, have left for the winter, leaving two young hunters in their cabin. She moves in with them for a month, waiting for money, helping with the livestock.

Winter has set in and food is a problem, particularly tea; like others of her kind, she considers tea at least three of the four basic food groups, and anxiously counts the remaining days of it. Storms come. "I melted a tin of water for washing by the fire, but it was frozen hard before I could use it. My hair, which was thoroughly wet with the thawed snow of yesterday, is frozen in plaits. . . . In my unchinked room the mercury is one degree below zero." Between storms, Mountain Jim visits, and takes her on long rides, and tells her the story of his life. ("My soul dissolved in pity for his dark, lost, self-ruined life . . . a man of great abilities, real genius, singular gifts. . . .")

She and one of the young hunters go to visit him in his den so he can vet her newspaper piece on climbing Longs Peak. "The interior of the den was frightful, yet among his black and hideous surroundings the grace of his manner and the genius of his conversation were only more apparent." She read him the piece and he wept with emotion, this monster that all Western mothers threatened their naughty children with. It's a powerful juju when a writer can reduce a handsome one-man audience to tears with her words, and a good thing Isabella was old enough to have some sense or she'd have moved right into his hut.

When the money finally comes through, she resolves to leave, reluctantly, since there's no way she can live there forever. Jim escorts her through the drifts and across the frozen rivers down to the plains. At their last rest house, in the evening, he recites to her some poems he has written. (She doesn't tell us the subject matter, but certainly she'd been much on his mind.) She urges him to give up drinking; they muse on what might have been, but it is now too late, too late.

She never saw him again. She later wrote, "He is a man whom any woman might love but whom no sane woman would marry," and she was right, of course. He was shot and killed in a land dispute the following year.

At home, she gathered the letters she'd written and published *A Lady's Life,* then fell ill again and set out for Japan. Her travels had barely begun.

Marianne North, traveling painter of exotic flowers, was, like many an adventuring lady, her father's pet. She called him "for nearly forty years my one friend and companion," which must have been rather hard on her mother and older brother. She was born in 1830 in Hastings, England. Her adored father was a Member of Parliament, with considerable free time to travel, and he took his daughter along.

As a girl, she was unburdened by lessons and she and her father rode together and she painted pictures of flowers, a virtuous occupation. Around the time she was born, *Gardener's Magazine* opined that, "to be able to draw flowers botanically . . . is one of the most useful accomplishments of your ladies of leisure living in the country." Useful for what, it doesn't say, and certainly nobody expected a nice girl like Marianne to take it to such extremes, spending fifteen years alone in canoes or on camelback looking for more flowers to paint.

After her mother died, she and her father traveled through Europe as far as Constantinople and were planning to climb some alps when Mr. North took ill. He died as soon as she got him home.

She was shattered. Without him, home was no longer home. She decided to make "painting from nature the master of my life," a curious choice of words. She doesn't explain why she picked flower-painting; her sister said her real talent was for music. Maybe she was continuing her father's journeys for him, tracking down native plants from continent to continent in his shadowy company. Maybe she just wanted to travel.

She spoke only English. "I had not the gift of tongues," she excuses herself blithely. In the glory days of the British Empire, if you had connections in London, you automatically had connections all over the world, in Borneo and Brazil as well as Bombay. Homesick colonials were delighted to see a new English face, and a well-connected woman with letters of introduction could circle the globe speaking English. Marianne was welcomed everywhere. She was attractive, with fair skin and blond hair in the stern arrangement of the day and strong, placid Saxon features. She seems easily pleased, and her memoir rings with delighted laughter at fresh discoveries. Friends blossomed in her footsteps. "Kind people" took care of her, and then passed her on to other kind people. In the nineteenth century, hospitality was an obligation and visiting was a kind of art form, and she was clearly an artist at it. In Brazil a man and his daughter, on the strength of five minutes' acquaintance, invited her to spend a fortnight with them; she stayed for eight months, using their home as a base for her jungle ramblings.

Tropical plants were what she'd determined to paint so, being misinformed about the nature of the Americas, she sailed for Massachusetts. Undismayed by the latitude, she loved the United States and the funny accents of the natives; she met the poet Longfellow and found him kind, and concealed her horror at his lunch table when he served her "cold tea with lumps of ice in it."

Presumably still in search of tropical plants, she went to Canada, where she painted Niagara Falls, though its portraits were already in oversupply. She traveled to Ohio and upstate New York and Manhattan and Newark, painting all the way. In Washington, the secretary of state took her to the White House, where she thought the Grants were cozy and homey, though the president did drink tea at dinner. (Nobody told her he was restraining himself from stronger stuff.)

Finally getting her bearings, she found Jamaica, this time with no letters to smooth the way, but "a young Cuban engineer appeared from the moon or elsewhere, hunted up my luggage, paid my carriage and porters (for I had only American money) and saw me safe to the inn." It was always like that. She rented a house, but so many people, including the governor, begged her to stay with them that she gave up the house and traveled from host to host on borrowed horses.

After a brief stop back in England, she headed for Brazil. Daily she rode into the jungle on muleback, sometimes on week-long treks through deep mud among snakes, mosquitoes, and spiders as big as sparrows, and daily she painted pictures of plants, fruits, and flowers. This would be unremarkable in a passionate artist with a talent burning to express itself, or in a dedicated botanist inspired to record, like Audubon with his birds, or in a mystic in love with wild places, but Marianne North was none of the above. She had taken only a few lessons in watercolors and none in botany. She attacked her task with no sort of system, simply painting whatever she saw. She never considered selling her pictures; she didn't need money. Her technique improved over time, as anyone's would with all that practice, but in her memoir she never mentions the artist's dissatisfactions or triumphs; she might have been making muffins instead of pictures for all she seems to care. Painting was simply her passport to the world.

In Rio, she dropped in on the emperor, a friend of a friend of her father's, and liked him very much. Then she touched base briefly in England, but it was too cold, so she went to Tenerife, and from there to California, where she wandered and painted in Yosemite before shipping out for Japan, which was "most attractive." Though the country was still closed to Europeans, the Mikado specially invited her to stay and paint. Unfortunately the winter was cold and gave her rheumatic fever, so she went to Hong Kong, where Commodore Parish took care of her and sent her off to Saigon. In Singapore, she stayed two weeks at Government House and "screamed with delight" at finding wild pitcher plants.

With letters to the Rajah and Rani of Sarawak, she had a

grand time in Borneo. His Highness sent her to his mountain farm with a cook, a soldier, and a coop full of chickens, and she stayed till she'd eaten all the chickens. The soldier proved useful on her canoe trips, with his "fine long sword to decapitate the leeches which stuck to me by the way . . . a most enjoyable day."

North was a splendid Briton. If she ever had a moment's doubt or anxiety, she certainly isn't going to tell us, and very likely she didn't. Closely followed through the forest by a huge black ape, she wonders only what it thinks of her. Nineteenth-century British confidence was a marvel, and her father must have packed her well with it.

On to Java, "one magnificent garden of luxuriance." Dinner with the kind governor-general produced letters of introduction to officials all over the country, who put her up and passed her on; native chiefs escorted her to the next native chief, who broke out still more tea and biscuits. Everyone begged her to stay forever.

In Ceylon, the bedroom the governor gave her had been most recently occupied by the Prince of Wales, and the governor himself checked to make sure the sheets had been changed. There were many elephants. Then from Ceylon she went by way of Aden, Naples, Rome, and Cannes to London, in February of 1877. In September she sailed for India.

She'd always found foreign religions slightly sinister and the temple at Madura was a shock, "full of darkness and uncanniness, with monkeys, elephants, bulls and cows, parrots, and every kind of strange person inside it. The god and goddess lived in dark central stalls to which no unbeliever is allowed entrance; but two small black elephants with illuminated faces, painted fresh in red and white every morning, were admitted into that 'holy of holies.'" She's clearly miffed; the English weren't used to being turned away at the door, even the door to heathenish rituals.

Stage by stage she escaped the welcoming arms of compatriots and reached Tanjore, where she stayed with kind Dr. Burnell; the kind Princess of Tanjore put a tent up for her, with guards on duty, so she could paint the temple in comfort. Traveling by cabin boat, bullock cart, dugout canoe, and steamer, she made her way on to Bombay, where she moved into Government House. And always she painted. Her unconvincing plants and trees still seemed to be molded from industrial rubber, but her landscapes were less depressing; the bold daylight of India looks cheerful after the turgid jungles.

She traveled in India for a year and a half, hosted by kind generals and judges, governors and princes and maharajahs. Once in a flood she was stranded on a small island in the swiftly rising waters, surrounded by natives who sat down patiently to await their fate. She found a sunken boat full of water and made them haul it up and empty it, "getting into one of those rages which are sometimes necessary when dealing with semi-savages," and off they floated.

She painted Mount Everest. She painted Kanchenjunga. She painted the Taj Mahal. Having no further excuse to stay, she went home, where many kind friends and the damp chill of an English March awaited her.

Kind General M'Murdo staged an exhibition of her paintings and the admission shillings paid for two-thirds of her travel expenses. "The remaining third," she wrote, "I thought well spent in the saving of fatigue and boredom at home."

She began negotiations to build a gallery at Kew Gardens, at her own expense, to house her oeuvre, but then a friend took her to visit Charles Darwin, in her eyes "the greatest man living." Darwin told her to go paint in Australia, so she packed up and left at once. She'd been home for a whole year.

In Australia the inns were full of fleas, but as usual she was never in them long; kind local dignitaries rescued her and took her to their homes and then passed her on to others. Sometimes she branched out from flora to fauna but her heart wasn't in it and the most charitable thing to call her koala bears is "nonrepresentational." Wherever she went she forged out into the bush alone, armed only with a paintbrush and a fine disregard of ordinary precautions; apparently she didn't quite believe in such hazards as venomous snakes. Perhaps Britons of her day, striding through their far-flung world, felt that foreign dangers simply wouldn't have the impudence to strike them.

She stayed with the governors of Tasmania and New Zealand, but the weather was too cold. She acquired three tiny opossum-mice and headed for San Francisco.

After paying respects to the fast-vanishing redwood trees, she took train for New York, complete with the energetic opossum-mice, "a great delight to my fellow-travelers." Los Angeles ("did not attract me"), St. Louis ("a monstrous city"), Cincinnati ("looked grand on its hill in the sunset"), Washington ("a bad dinner"), Philadelphia ("a noble city, perhaps the finest in America"), New York, and home, reaching Liverpool in June 1881.

The pavilion at Kew was finished and she settled in to catalog her paintings for it. It made a fine summation of her life's work; she was fifty-two and growing rather deaf; rheumatism bothered her; some people would have called it a day. No, the obsession wasn't finished with her yet. She looked at the collection and realized she hadn't done Africa.

Kind friends met her at Cape Town and lent her a pony cart. She visited an ostrich farm at hatching time but as usual found it no more astonishing than anything else; she might have grown up on an ostrich farm. She was pleased at seeing "genuine savages" near Port Elizabeth wearing red drapery and feathers and metal rings on their arms and legs. She hadn't expected to find such quaint reminders of the pre-Empire world, not so close to civilization, practically in the British living room, and she wondered if they could be quite real. (She doesn't paint them, of course; people weren't her forte.)

After less than a year in Africa she went home, but three months later she was in the Seychelles Islands in the Indian Ocean. Here "nutmegs, cinnamon, and cloves were all growing luxuriantly, but the people are too lazy to pick them." She was still a stalwart traveler, scrambling up mountains and sliding down gorges, but long-distance journeys were a problem, since all the boats were "full of dried fish and natives (equally unpleasant at close quarters)."

Then, without warning, she cracked up. She was staying peacefully with friends, painting the views, when nameless people started playing tricks on her. "I thought that they would rob and even murder me. God knows the truth. Doctors say my nerves broke down. . . ." This woman who scoffed at crocodiles and cannibals sewed her money into her clothes and barricaded the door and windows; she heard threatening voices day and night, though nobody else heard them. In her memoir, she makes it clear that she doesn't believe the doctors. She believes in the disembodied assassins. Shattered nerves and delusions would have been shamefully sissy and completely un-British. Genuine threats of murder were dignified, imaginary ones embarrassing.

The voices pursued her home to England and then fell silent while she arranged her paintings at Kew.

Daunted as always by the prospect of an English winter, in November she sailed for Chile to paint the *Araucaria imbricata* tree. Halfway there, she writes, "my nerves gave way again (if they were nerves!) and the torture has continued more or less ever since." She really was a trouper, though. The terrors in her head were the only ones that bothered her. As she set forth to track down the *Araucaria*, people warned her she'd be eaten by pumas or Indians, but "as usual, I found when I got nearer the spot that all difficulties vanished."

The tree duly painted, she left Chile, pausing in Lima to recover her "nerves," which she still puts in skeptical quotation marks. Too ill to go to Mexico as planned, she was forced back to "the fatigue and boredom at home."

She rented a house in Gloucestershire, accompanied only by "my enemies, the so-called 'nerves.'" She started a garden, and kind visitors brought her plants for it. Here the last of the well-traveled Tasmanian mice, Sir Henry, died and was buried. After a long bout of liver disease, North joined him.

She'd called herself a "commonplace person," and she was. Geniuses are expected to rip off their ties to the ordinary and escape their ordained place in the world, but North's mind could be described as bland and her talent as adequate. Her passion for her father had kept her unmarried beyond the usual marriage age, but by every custom of her class and kind she should have stayed home and painted her own sweet peas, joined the Garden Club, lent her pretty voice to the church choir, and dropped two lumps of sugar into her tea each day at four. Maybe, with a suitable companion, spent a few winter weeks in the south of France on the Promenade des Anglais.

She chose adventure. She was blinkered by British complacency, but she was brave, with the placid courage of the unimaginative. She worked with pigheaded diligence under frightful conditions. Her gallery at Kew holds 832 oil paintings; Vermeer, who worked comfortably in a studio and never had to haul his equipment up cliffs or through flooded rapids, left us only forty-two.

Four plants were named for her, not a great scientific legacy, considering the length of her journeys, but perhaps that wasn't the point. Perhaps there was no point; perhaps she simply found England a crashing bore. In any case, she thought up something exciting to do with her life and did it, a remarkable achievement for a woman so very unremarkable.

When she gathered up her dripping skirts and waded back to where she'd tied her canoe, Mary Kingsley found a hippopotamus looming over it. The hippo, for all it looks like a bathtub toy, ranks high among Africa's most dangerous creatures, but Kingsley says, "I scratched him behind the ear with my umbrella and we parted on good terms." Yes, she carried an umbrella. She slogged through the swamps and jungles dressed, like Daisy Bates, as an impeccable Victorian Englishwoman, though often caked with mud or chin-deep in slimy mangrove swamps, in corset and high collar and black skirts. The outfit, she insisted, was highly practical, since when she fell into a pit dug for game its ample skirts padded her against the sharpened stakes at the bottom. Perhaps it also deterred the cannibals she grew so fond of; to the nakeds' eye, she can't have looked much like dinner.

As a general rule, the male writing of his travels wants the reader to understand the dangers he has passed and his skill and courage in conquering them. Lacking life-threatening encounters, he can make several pages out of fleas in his bedding or flies in his porridge. Women take the opposite path and laugh their perils off a little too lightly; blizzard and avalanche, charging rhino and hostile tribesmen trip amusingly by. This forestalls the reader who might say, "Serves you right. A woman had no business being there in the first place." Or maybe the voyagers really did find the coiled cobra delightful, being such a fine change from groceries and gossip, tea parties and frocks and the lives their mothers led.

A crocodile, Mary Kingsley tells us, "chose to get his front paws over the stern of my canoe, and endeavored to improve our acquaintance. I had to retire to the bows, to keep the balance right, and fetch him a clip on the snout with a paddle, when he withdrew. . . ." He was, she notes, quite a small crocodile, about eight feet long, "only a pushing young creature who had not learnt manners." (Up close, crocodiles give off "a strong, musky smell," similar to the smell of the larger boa constrictors.)

She not only laughs at her perils, she laughs at her own courage: "I behave exquisitely, and am quite lost in admiration of my own conduct, and busily deciding in my own mind whether I shall wear one of those plain ring halos, or a solid plate one, à la Cimabue." No man would have written that line. Or: "I can confidently say that I am not afraid of any wild animal—until I see it—and then, well, I will yield to nobody in terror." Her terror, luckily, manifests itself in prudence, and she sits very still for twenty minutes just three feet from a leopard, both of them pinned among some rocks by a tornado. The leopard, she reports, "lashed the ground with his tail and . . . swore, softly but repeatedly and profoundly" at the weather.

Had Hemingway read Kingsley? Poor man, I hope not; she had twice his cojones and she wasn't even armed: "I do not think it ladylike to go shooting things with a gun."

There she is on the cover of her book, billowing sleeves and a black collar up to her chin, hair slicked back under a tidy hat, every inch a lady, or perhaps the mistress of a select, severe boarding school, but if you look closely at the primly sealed lips, you can see that she's struggling not to giggle at the photographer.

Mary Kingsley was born in 1862 and, like Marianne North, adored her traveling father. The Honorable Mr. North, however, was a highly respectable fellow; Dr. Kingsley was not. He took no interest in doctoring to support his family and much preferred wandering in exotic lands for a year or two at a stretch, mooching off the rich. Mary observed that he persuaded himself that "because he had a wife and family it was his dire and awful duty to go and hunt grizzly bears in a Red Indian infested district." Kept home with an invalid mother and tightly confined to house and garden, Mary waited for him, and listened raptly when he did blow in for a visit. Like Marianne North, she was pressed into service organizing and writing up his travel notes, but that was pretty much the extent of her education.

She nursed her sick mother until she died; she nursed her sick father until he died; and then her brother announced that he didn't feel so well himself and she'd better stay home and nurse him. Finally, all duties discharged, age thirty, she took her five hundred pounds a year and headed for West Africa, with a commission from the British Museum to collect snakes, fish, beetles, rocks, worms, and whatever else looked interesting. She told people she wanted to finish the work her father had planned on African religious fetishes; it's not clear just what work, if any, he'd actually done, but that was her story and her passport.

For three years, afoot and by canoe and occasional sailboat, she covered great swaths of West Africa, and loved it. "If you do fall under its spell," she wrote, "it takes all the color out of other kinds of living." Thanks to her lack of a sound Victorian education, her writing is fresh and natural and prances on the page like breathless letters from a happy friend. In keeping with the reticence of the day, she tells us nothing about her childhood traumas, depressions, fears, dreams, and disappointments; for those interested in her sex life, she says only, in a letter, "I know nothing myself of love. . . . I have never been in love, nor has anyone ever been in love with me." Unlikely, but we must take it or leave it. Those were different days.

Being female, she tells us about local hair styles, clothing, marriage customs, fetishes, fishing baskets, cooking pots, witchcraft, and food ("a good snake, properly cooked, is one of the best meats one gets out here, far and away better than the African fowl"). Some of the tribes are lazy cooks, and she speaks with feeling of a certain monotonous manioc preparation, found under different names in different areas but always tasting like "bad paste with a dash of vinegar"; it drives the men to drink, she says. Other tribes produce a creative and delicious cuisine, for which she gives recipes. One, for meat or fish, involves seasoning with the prepared kernels of a certain wild mango, then layering the meat with red pepper and odeaka cheese, wrapping it in plantain leaves, and cooking it slowly over embers. This makes boa constrictor and hippopotamus particularly delicious, but alas, no seasoning can mask the musky taste of crocodile.

Echoing Daisy, she deplores the ignorance of the various European administrators in dealing with the African natives and thinks it's absurd to suppose Christianity answers all problems: "Though it may be possible to convert Africans *en masse* into practical Christians it is quite impossible to convert Europeans *en masse* to it." The floppy Mother Hubbards the missionaries put on the women are not just hideous, they're dangerous, and catch fire when the wearer cooks dinner. The church's hard line against polygamy is narrow-minded; in a world where women do all the work indoors and out, no one wife can cope with it all, and if she's sensible she insists on at least two co-wives. The alternative is slavery, and such men as keep slaves to do the work can live like good Christians with only one wife.

The colonial administrators considered all the natives basically the same and basically childlike, which they weren't in the least; their apparent simplicity is, she says, because none of their many languages were adequate to express the acuteness and subtlety of their thoughts. Tribal distinctions were lost on the colonials. "Unless you live alone among the natives," she snaps, "you never get to know them," and an Igalwa and a Bubi are as different in their lives as a Londoner and a Laplander. In the tribal hierarchy, the M'ponge, Igalwas, and Ajumba sat at the top; their women scorned to marry into lesser groups. And all the tribes looked down on the Fan (or Faung), and the Fan looked down on them.

Only Mary Kingsley could love the Fan. They gave new resonance to the word "savages." They were feared and avoided by black and white alike; traders dispatched into their areas were routinely eaten; their employers, respectful of the danger and expense of investigating, wrote off their deaths to "disease." The Fan weren't fussy; they also ate neighbors, relatives, and citizens of other Fan villages with which they had quarrels or blood feuds, meaning all of them. Other groups practiced a ritual sacrificial cannibalism from time to time, but for the Fan it was just food; they sat right down and ate what they wanted, cut the rest into chunks, and smoked it for later. Sometimes they bought slaves to be fattened for the table.

Kingsley stepped where no white foot had stepped before. She made friends by trading cloth and chewing tobacco with the Fan in exchange for rubber and ivory she didn't need or want, and when her trade goods ran out she sold them her clothes, because "these Fans, when a trader has no more goods to sell them, are liable to start trade all over again by killing him, and taking back their ivory and rubber and keeping it until another trader comes along." The clothes sold well, and she enjoyed seeing one of her white blouses "worn by a brawny warrior in conjunction with nothing else but red paint and a bunch of leopard tails." Stocking-tops were good to pull over the head, with the rest trailing in the breeze.

Spending the night in a Fan hut deep in the French Congo, she was bothered by a smell even fiercer than most and traced it to a bag hanging from the roof, its mouth neatly tied up. "I then shook its contents out in my hat, for fear of losing anything of value. They were a human hand, three big toes, four eyes, two ears, and other portions of the human frame. The hand was fresh, the others only so-so, and shriveled. . . . The Fans will eat their fellow friendly tribesfolk, yet they like to keep a little something belonging to them as a memento." She replaced the keepsakes, hung up the bag, and went back to sleep. (Her hat, presumably, she put on in the morning; it's not as if she had a spare.)

The coastal tribes had been a dull and lethargic lot, their numbers dwindling from sheer inertia, but something in the Fan spoke to Kingsley, just as the Aborigines seemed to Daisy Bates like fellow Irishmen. Their faces were bright and expressive; they were restless, active, quarrelsome, and "full of fire, temper, intelligence, and go." (Perhaps it was the high-protein diet; in India Marianne North had found the vegetarians vapid compared to the meat-eaters.) They traveled with her as she went collecting, and showed her how to manage the fifteen-foot long-tailed native canoe; she was always proud of her seamanship, and particularly pleased with this feat.

With several very reluctant natives and no equipment, she climbed the great Peak of Cameroon, 13,760 feet, through howling tornadoes, sleet-filled downpours, flooded torrents, and sheets of lightning, and when she finally struggled to the top, the fog was so thick she couldn't see the view she'd come to look at. However, except for cold and sunburn, she enjoyed it hugely.

She did her own collecting, saying she didn't want anyone's blood, black or white, on her head. Armed only with a machete, she hacked her way through the vine-covered fallen trees, beset by scorpions and elephant ticks, in search of beetles, and fetched back venomous snakes thrashing in a cleft stick. From time to time a case of her hard-won specimens would be lost forever in flooded rapids or murky lakes. She wallowed through swamps looking for fish and came out covered with leeches, "a frill of them around our necks like astrakhan collars. . . . I was quite faint from loss of blood." Traveling without creature comforts through the White Man's Grave, surrounded by endemic, epidemic, and parasitic diseases, her own pleasure and enthusiasm must have kept her incredibly healthy; in her three years' journeying she complains only of one nasty cold, caught on the chilly slopes of Mount Cameroon.

She was having the time of her life. But the collecting was only a sideline to what she'd come to do, and her investigations of religion and ritual make a wondrous gallery of ghost stories. Some may seem familiar to us now, but it was fresh news to anthropologists at the time.

Native legal tangles were mind-boggling, and she reports on such matters as the rental due when the grandchildren of a slave are married to free men who aren't their owners, but only leasing them, so to speak, from the heirs of their late grandmother's original owner. In a world without written words, all matters were solved by endless arguments that might last for weeks and entangle themselves in the ever-present problems of witchcraft.

Witchcraft, she writes, "has killed and still kills more men and women than the slave trade," running a close second to smallpox. There were no natural or accidental deaths; all was malevolent, and the leopard who has eaten someone's baby is no ordinary leopard but a vengeful spirit. A dead man's widows and slaves are immediately suspect; as in Western witch-hunts, anyone who survives the investigative tortures is guilty and dies by ritual tortures. Some talismans are powerful against witchcraft, such as the treasured human eyeball, preferably a white man's, but any talisman's power can be stolen away at any time by witches, living or dead.

The air is thick with loose souls and most of them are dangerous, a condition complicated by the fact that inanimate objects also have souls, so that the ghost of a deceased spear may skewer the passerby on a certain path at a certain hour. Some souls have their uses, though; among the Yoruba, a boy doesn't become officially adult until he has killed a man, after which the victim's soul serves him as his disembodied slave. Still, even slave souls couldn't quite be trusted, and one king kept a captive spirit so demanding that every Tuesday, to keep it tractable, he had to sacrifice a human victim to it, amid dancing and festivities.

"I confess that the more I know of the West Coast Africans, the more I like them," she writes. She does think them fools for "their power of believing in things," but she feels the same way about her own credulous countrymen.

She sailed back for her second visit home in 1895, but there are no farewells and the book ends abruptly. She obviously means to come back; everywhere her writings are seeded with future plans: "So far my information is second-hand"; "I do not yet know"; "I have not yet sufficient evidence"; "[the forests] in which, so far, I can do little more than look at the pictures, although now I am busily learning the alphabet of their language so that I may some day read what the pictures mean."

Among her collections, she brought back to England one quite new fish, which was named after her, one quite new snake, a lizard the British Museum had been wanting for ten years, a great wealth of new information on West Africa, and many unpopular opinions about its governance. She wrote *Travels in West Africa,* published in 1897 and an immediate hit, then *West African Studies,* with more details on trade and native skills and even more unpopular criticisms of the colonial governments and the missionaries. She went about lecturing, no doubt shivering all the way in the chilly English fog and raising eyebrows and hackles with her tales, and was consulted, though privately, by important people in charge of colonies. This delayed her return to the natives and their forests until the Boer War broke out in South Africa.

In 1900 she went to Cape Town and volunteered her services nursing Boer prisoners in a hellish camp infested with typhoid and dysentery. She caught the fever, died, and was buried at sea. She was only thirty-seven, which seems unfair. We as well as she have been cheated out of many further merry adventures and curious lore.

Wherever the travelers went, they wrote up their journals, faithfully, at night, by whatever light could be arranged, shielding the page from downpours or defrosting the ink bottle over the fire, beset by fleas or bedbugs, rattlesnakes or hostile natives. Before National Geographic specials on television, this was how the civilized world learned about the rest of the world; before camcorders, this was the record the wayfarers brought back or mailed home and shared around.

As the twentieth century progressed, if that's the right word, "travel writing" became a recognized career and the writing was the purpose of the trip; many men and a few women journeyed in order to write and sell a book or magazine pieces to finance another journey. Of the women, Freya Stark is probably the best known. She didn't set forth until she was forty but she made up for lost time, starting in Persia with *The Valleys of the Assassins,* in 1934. She served during the war with the British Ministry of Information in Aden, Baghdad, and Cairo, then resumed her travels along untrodden ways for a total of two dozen books, and in 1974 was made Dame Commander of the British Empire. She died in Italy at the age of a hundred, though the miles might be more to the point than the years.

Perhaps the most engaging of modern travel writers is the Irishwoman Dervla Murphy, who broke the most basic rule of female travel—all travel, all adventures—by having herself a baby and taking it along.

Murphy was born with itchy feet, and her preferred transportation was the one-speed bicycle. Since paving hadn't yet been discovered in most of the places she went, and in the snow-choked high mountain passes she had to carry the thing over many a steep mile, it seems less convenient than even feet, but she always considered it the best way to travel. For her tenth birthday she'd been given a bike and a world atlas, and the connection between them seemed immediately obvious.

From the time she left school at fifteen to care for the traditional invalid mother until she was in her thirties she was caged up at home; but when her mother finally died she took off like a shot for India, making notes all the way for her 1965 book, *Full Tilt—Dunkirk to Delhi by Bicycle.* It was January of the worst winter in eighty years and her plans hadn't included quite such deep snow; she spent less time on her bike than it spent on her shoulders, but on she went whistling, with a spare shirt, plenty of books, brandy, cigarettes, and a loaded .25 in her saddlebag.

(This last came in handy when she was attacked by wild dogs, or perhaps wolves, near Belgrade and had to fight her way out, and again when a six-foot "scantily clad" Kurd tried to rape her in an inn.) Frequently soaked through in the bitter cold, she forestalled pneumonia with "lots of rum." She slept on the ground or the floor of a tea shop or police station, she bathed in any available body of water, with or without an audience, and she ate and drank anything offered, including swigs from a dirty beer bottle being handed around an obviously tubercular gathering.

Like her wayfaring sisters before her, Murphy laughs at her perils and takes thoughtless risks that would horrify a more sensible traveler. Without guide or equipment she scales the tallest mountains, pausing often for cigarette breaks and a swig of brandy. When ghastly accidents befall her, she chalks them cheerfully up to her own stupidity, or her inability to read a map. In addition to a faulty sense of direction, she's accident-prone: when she rests herself on a convenient rock it turns out to be a cactus, and she earns the distinction of having her ribs broken in five widely separated countries. At the most terrifying points in all her journeys, she sits down and laughs and laughs at the sheer awfulness of it.

Like others, she found Iran a nightmarish den of thieves where nothing gets done without bribery. She was robbed over and over. An armed police officer threw her into a cell and tried to rape her; she kneed him in the groin and escaped, only to be stoned in the next village. Most people assumed she was a man, since no woman would wander around alone like that, but they stoned her anyway.

After Iran, everything about Afghanistan was pure joy. Instead of stealing her clothes or demanding bribes, the people were insulted when she offered money. The world's best-looking people, she exults, though with the world's worst roads; she pushed her bike most of the way, but even so it got torn to ribbons. She's endlessly charmed and delighted, even by the scorpions, even though she gets three ribs broken by a rifle butt during a brouhaha on a bus; and when she takes a nap on a mountainside, she wakes to find a filthy old nomad has pitched a tent over her to keep off the sun.

The people are interesting, intelligent, lively, elegant, and primitive. Wherever she goes, Murphy, like Bates and Kingsley, praises the primitive and deplores the progress that meddling Europeans leave in their colonial wake. She feels that most progress, including literacy, is a mistake in the long run, like the proud presence of indoor flush toilets installed where no water system supplies them and nobody plans to tackle the technology involved, but everyone uses them anyway. (Unlike the Victorians, she's outspoken about bathroom matters and clears up many nagging questions in the reader's mind.)

Like Isabella Bird, she glories in mountain scenery, sunrise and sunset, perilous chasms, snowy peaks, and no sign of human life except, perhaps, ten thousand feet below and ten miles away, a cluster of abandoned stone huts. She throws herself into the village life everywhere and cheers at the local polo game, played on a mile-long pitch with teams of up to a hundred horsemen competing to spear a dead sheep from the ground and drop it into a hole. She drinks hot sheep's milk for breakfast and dips her hands into the communal pot of food and finds boiled clover the most delicious of vegetables.

Pakistan was a letdown, as any place would have been, and hot. Since she always tries out the native customs, she quickly gets addicted to chewing the stimulant betel nuts, which stain her teeth. She learns the satisfaction of hunting down body lice and crushing them between her fingers. The people smell awful; in close quarters, downright lethal. Once, on a nice evening walk, she comes across a reasonably fresh corpse with its head bashed in, but refrains from meddling in the matter; the tribesmen, she notes, go heavily armed and are "much addicted to murdering each other but they're amiable to me."

The food depends on ghee, a form of butter cured, she says, for two years in a lightly processed sheepskin, the same being used also to ferment a winelike substance that tastes like dead sheep. Food here is hard to come by and even harder to eat, and much of the country she travels through is so remote that the natives scatter terrified at their first sight of a bicycle. Hers is the first bike ever to cross the Babusar Pass, but was ignominiously carried most of the way. (The first Jeep to cross it, she reports, was welcomed by the villagers with bundles of new-cut grass to refresh it after the journey.)

India smells even worse than Pakistan and, like North and Kingsley, Murphy finds vegetarian peoples weedy and apathetic. The Punjab is boring, the natives are even stupider than the Iranians, and their principal occupation is squatting beside fresh cow-patties waiting for the sun to dry them so they can be gathered for fuel. Somebody steals her bike lamp.

We can see her struggling to maintain the curious and equable eye of the traveler, but it's clear that Afghanistan was a hard act to follow, and the emotional high there has dropped her into boredom, unable to do justice to India.

Apologetically, she went back later.

First, though, she decided to have a child.

Traveling women, unlike traveling men, should give up in advance any thought of the home and children of normal life, but Murphy splurged and treated herself to Rachel, and bought

149

an abandoned marketplace in her home village of Lismore, roofing over the old stone stalls to make the rooms of a home. For nearly five years she confined herself to merely European journeys, just to keep in fighting trim, and then she packed up a change of underwear, Band-Aids, vitamin pills, and a copy of *Squirrel Nutkin,* and set off with Rachel to revisit India the hard way, a plan that would horrify most women and any man, and write *On a Shoestring to Coorg.*

As usual she had nothing much in mind except to wander and look and listen, and they head south from Bombay and fetch up in Coorg, "an infinite turmoil of blue mountains," expatriot hippies (it's 1974), friendly natives, a beach to camp out on, and interesting food and drink. (She draws the line only at Coke, Pepsi, and a particularly nasty rice-coconut bread.) Her first priority is a liquor store, and she's pleased when the hippies point her to one that never closes. The Sikkimese ragi beer is so unexpectedly potent she has to break off a journal entry unfinished. Feni is a local spirit made from cashew nuts, deadly when mixed with beer. For breakfast every morning she drinks a liter of palm-toddy beer (at two and a half pence), "most refreshing" even though the bottle's neck is often choked with dead ants. She invents a popular cocktail of arak, honey, and lime juice, called "MCC," for Murphy's Coorg Cocktail, and visitors come from far and wide to sample it. Standing all night on a jam-packed train she keeps her spirits up with a bottle of rum.

She never actually says that penny-pinching travel with a small child can drive a person to drink, and presents her Rachel as a sturdy, curious, sociable, and amiable companion, but mothers among her readers must suppose she was just as often as tired, reluctant, and uncooperative as anybody's five-year-old, however sturdy. Murphy is trying to defy a basic point of history, that the young keep women home and only the childless woman wanders, but she does admit that "one is a much less lighthearted traveler with a foal at foot," a message that might be posted on many a refrigerator door and inscribed on many a tombstone.

At that, she might seem dangerously lighthearted to some. When Rachel disappears, she assumes she's made some new friends and gone off with them; when she herself is laid up with an infected ant bite and desperate for privacy, she sends the little girl off alone into a forest infested with seven different kinds of venomous snakes. (If they'd been in America, she'd be jailed for reckless endangerment of a minor and Rachel would be in a foster home.)

With a foal at foot, she was forced to take buses and trains, squeezed into third class: "Beyond a doubt, one has to walk or cycle really to appreciate the flavor of a place. Bus journeys are all very well in their way but they are not true traveling." Whenever possible she parks Rachel with newfound friends and sets off on foot to climb the solitary mountains, poking her nose into places so remote that the natives have never seen even a picture of a white person and flee in alarm. She charms her way into the full range of Coorg activities—weddings, christenings, funerals, cremations, pilgrimages, harvest ceremonies, family reunions, prayers, and prodigious drinking bouts.

When Rachel steps on a dead fish with four-inch spines, Murphy cures her with infusions of seawater. When she gets an infected foot, Murphy operates with a boiled safety pin ("a truly terrifying mess"), then carries her piggyback while she recovers. While swimming, which she does everywhere she goes, Murphy is robbed of all her money. (No surprise; it happens often.) On a train journey, they both fall desperately ill with brucellosis and spend two days and two nights unvisited in a little travelers' hut by the train station until Rachel persuades a rickshaw-wallah to carry a note; the doctor comes and doses them till Murphy's well enough to be moved to a hospital.

As soon as they can totter, they go wandering in the Periyar game sanctuary, accompanied only by elephants, gaur, snakes, and signs of leopards. Murphy always finds guides intrusive nuisances.

In spite of all, Coorg is so beautiful, the light so intoxicating (remember she was Irish), the people so kind that she would like to stay forever. She felt the same about Afghanistan, and Tibet, and parts of Ethiopia. Even the most footloose woman sometimes gets her ankles seized by the feminine urge to stay.

The next year, when Rachel was six, they trekked for three months in midwinter through the Karakorum mountains, the smallest of which stands 18,000 feet, dodging disasters and living mostly on dried apricots. Of this, she wrote *Where the Indus Is Young,* which Jan Morris in *the Times* called "Altogether the most appallingly fascinating travel book I have ever read."

When Rachel was nine, they took a mule named Juana down along the top of the Andes, loosely following Francisco Pizarro's route in conquering Peru. Juana was an excellent companion, intrepid and just as nice as Jock, the mule who'd taken Murphy through Ethiopia in the sixties. Without a map, and with only a feeling that she ought to try to keep the valley on her left, Murphy leads them into crisis after crisis, into cul-de-sacs at 16,000 feet surrounded by sheer cliffs and long drops, with no room to turn around, no choice but to fling themselves down the cliff and hope to land unbroken in yet another cul-de-sac. After a trying day in a blizzard in the high Andes, Rachel says, "Do you know what you're like? You're like one of those Spartan mothers who left babies out all night on the mountains to see if they were worth the raising."

A wicked drought has left no food to be bought in the villages and only, to Murphy's dismay, a single bottle of beer in the only bar they find. The basic male travel writer moves through such remote defiles with a retinue of hired help behind carrying on their heads, or their camels, or llamas, or canoes, canned soup, soap, shaving cream, brandy, tea, sleeping bags, novels, assorted guns, tinned salmon, trade goods, antibiotics, extra clothes, and Fortnam and Mason's marmalade, with a photographer bringing up the rear; but Murphy is a minimalist, though it comes close to killing her, and possibly her child, more than once, and she needs room in her backpack for fifty pounds of books, since she does her homework on the road.

Fodder for the mule involves bribes, barter, wheedling, and borderline theft, while a stale biscuit and a canned sardine make the human dinner after a long day's hiking and climbing. She chews coca. Sometimes they're lucky with a local delicacy such as roast guinea pig ("Here one would eat one's grandmother even if she weren't very well cooked"), but most of the time they're hungry.

Still, life has its moments. After a local feast day, Murphy writes "yesterday was spent in a haze of nameless alcohol," and dimly remembers dancing in the square with the campesinos, even though she can't dance and never could. Rachel's presence hasn't slowed her down much, but the reader can feel that her concentration on the place is diluted and a section of her mind screened off for Rachel. No mother with a child in tow can ever forget the child, even in sleep. Even dancing with the campesinos.

Locals refuse to believe she's a woman: "I could see their point. By now I look scarcely human, never mind feminine, with hideously bloodshot eyes (dust and wind), a dirt-and-sun-blackened face, thick cracked lips and hair like a gorilla's mane.

Add to that my Peruvian army boots, bulging bush shirt, ragged jeans, broad shoulders, and deep voice—it's no wonder I'm addressed more often than not as 'senor.'"

Still, at forty-seven, dirty, half-starved, and tailed by a nine-year-old, she hasn't lost the joy and sometimes longs to turn somersaults, "A recurring temptation, sometimes given in to, when the beauty of a landscape goes to my head."

When Rachel was fourteen, they went to Madagascar. Nobody should have to travel with a fourteen-year-old. Rachel has lost her cheerful curiosity, hates hiking with a backpack and sleeping on the ground, and longs only to go snorkeling on the west coast, toward which they pick their way.

Madagascar smells sometimes of jasmine, sometimes of "shit, piss, and rotting fish," but Murphy as always takes it as it comes, except when sleeping in close quarters with close-packed, unusually pungent bodies. The food is basically sticky, unsalted rice and raw eggs, sometimes with an extra treat such as baked cat, canned zebu, or a prized recipe in which fish, entrails and all, is carefully rotted till it reeks, then fried and served whole and ungutted. (Rachel sulks and subsists on the peanuts and glucose tablets they brought along.) When Murphy inquired what lemur tastes like, they said it was delicious and tastes like cat, apparently a standard comparison, like chicken with Americans.

The country, which has been compared in form, color, consistency, and sterility to a brick, is an ecological ruin that seems to be facing starvation. As soon as the French colonials left, their telephone poles, roads, schools, radio transmitters, and trucks broke down and were left to decay; imports vanished, and the people reverted, apparently happily, to subsistence farming among the wreckage of colonial days. Their religion is an elaborate system of charms, superstitions, ancestor worship, and taboos that resisted Christianity; babies born on unlucky days were formerly put out to be trampled by zebu; in some areas the sun-dried heart and eyes of a human fetus are still a potent charm.

This is fine with Murphy, who thinks all progress is poison. The babies are the most beautiful in the world and the people are proud, dignified, and cheerful in spite of their hard lives. All she objects to is the scarcity of food and drink, the empty beer bottles on the shelves of shops displayed as a reminder of former days. She buys something called wine, but can't swallow it. In Nepal she once sampled a local raki that struck her blind for twenty-four hours; in Madagascar she drinks something name-less that's even worse. Then she finds a tipple she likes, and drinks deeply of it until learning that it's made from the sap of the Man-Eating Tree and killed many a French colonial and is even now giving her gout.

From time to time she looks wistfully at the mountain ranges and wishes she could walk aimlessly in them for months and months, but no, there's always Rachel. They're beginning to snap at each other.

The natives assure her that there's no way they can get south through the mountains, so of course they go anyway, in a howl-ing gale. When they finally reach the west coast, the sea's too rough for Rachel's snorkeling, and besides, the resort town's beach, running along under the beachfront hotels, is also the town's toilet.

On their next-to-last day they both get horribly sick; Murphy checks their urine and diagnoses hepatitis. Just the same, she takes away with her the magic pinch of red Madagascar dirt that ensures your return. Next time, presumably, alone.

When Rachel was eighteen, they traveled through Cameroon with a horse named Egbert, but eighteen is practically human.

Then Murphy went back to her solitary rambles, having done her best to prove you can have it both ways. The last I heard, she was just back from riding a bicycle all over South Africa.

Renegades

She was, according to West Virginia State Historian Virgil Lewis, "a maid with fair complexion, hazel eyes, a perfectly developed form, a sweet disposition, a mind strong and vigorous, softened by the rudiments of an education obtained in the schools of Liverpool."

He doesn't say how he knows, writing over a hundred years later in 1891, since the only contemporary glimpse of "Mad Ann" Bailey is an undated head-and-shoulders drawing from the Ohio Historical Society. She has an intimidating, rock-solid, broad-boned skull with hooded eyes and a tangle of uncombed shoulder-length hair; she seems to have been built like a tank and nothing in even the most whitewashed bones of her recorded history suggests a sweet disposition, but proper hero ines follow certain rules.

West Virginia was still Virginia then, and Virginians are famous for fondling their history, but books of Virginian history five inches thick, mentioning surely every resident there since Jamestown, don't mention Ann Bailey. She was not a nice lady. Virgil Lewis so admired her courage, though, that he contrived to write her biography by leaving out the rough stuff and mak-

157

ing up much of the rest. Like Dr. Lossing, in his *Eminent Americans,* he was selective with heroines, and approved only those with the "complete union of strength, courage, love, devotion, meekness and shrewdness which fitted them for the often terrible ordeals through which they had to pass." The "meekness" clause gave him a problem, and since he had no use for any woman who has "ingloriously stained her hands in human blood," he has to leave out a lot.

A different source says Bailey "killed more than one person's share of Indians," but doesn't specify how many constituted a fair share. A contemporary is on record as saying she "halways carried a haxe and a haugur and could chop as well as hany man," but passes over the question of just what, or whom, she was chopping.

She was born in Liverpool, England, around 1742, daughter of a soldier in Queen Anne's wars who named her after the monarch. When she was nineteen or so her parents died and she went to Virginia. Lewis says she came to the wild frontier to stay with the Bell family, friends or perhaps relatives, but others say she was an indentured servant. (Lewis is giving her a leg up socially, but there was nothing reprehensible in coming across indentured, your passage to be paid by your new employers, for a girl who wanted to see the world beyond Liverpool.)

In 1765, in the remote Indian-inhabited wilds near the settlement of Staunton, she met and married Richard Trotter, described by Lewis as one of nature's noblemen, and became, he tells us, a "devoted wife" in a cabin in a clearing. Two years later she produced a son, William. In '74, an Indian uprising in the wind, the governor came to muster an army at Staunton; Ann was foremost among the recruiters. No doubt she urged her husband forth, and Trotter dutifully marched away through the trackless forest to Ohio, where the Indians disposed of him and a number of his comrades.

Ann, a widow at thirty-two, vowed bloody vengeance. Lewis calls her zeal "patriotism and heroism combined," but it may have been plain rage, or a naturally warlike spirit inherited from her father, who fought at Blenheim, or perhaps being a devoted wife looking after William in a humble cabin had driven her round the bend. (At seven, William had no siblings, an unusual state of affairs at the time.) She parked the child on a neighbor lady and as far as we know didn't give him another thought for decades. She was busy. A splendid rider and a crack shot with a rifle, she prowled the western border from Roanoke to the Potomac urging recruitment against both the "savages" and, as the Revolution lumbered onto the scene, the British. She was an arresting sight, too, "clad," says Lewis, "in buckskin pants, with petticoat, heavy brogan shoes, a man's coat and hat, a belt about her waist in which was worn the hunting-knife, and with a rifle on her shoulder." A different source adds a tomahawk to her arsenal, on top of the previously mentioned tools. The petticoat must have been an entertaining touch.

The Revolution was won but the Indian skirmishes went on. Ann, who knew every deer track and Indian trail in the Alleghenies, carried military messages over uncharted distances, often sleeping on the ground beside her horse, rifle within reach.

She was forty-three when she met and married the frontier ranger John Bailey, who took her along when he went to garrison a new fort where Charleston, West Virginia, now stands. The fort's commander used her as a messenger, scout, and spy. The bridegroom can't have seen her often.

In the fall of '91 the fort got news of Indians gathering in strength nearby, preparing for an attack, and when the commander checked his supplies he found they were almost out of gunpowder. Surrender and a lingering, unpleasant death seemed inevitable; the nearest gunpowder was a hundred tough miles away at Lewisburg. The commander called for volunteers to gallop off to get it. Silence fell. The soldiers dropped their eyes and shuffled their feet. Presently the firm voice of Ann Bailey, who was now forty-nine, spoke up: "I will go," she said.

They gave her their best horse and she took off into the darkness surrounded by Indians. She rode straight through, making Sheridan's famous later ride to Winchester look like a canter around the park, and got the powder. Lewisburg gave her an extra horse to carry it and back she galloped, dodging Indians and arriving in the very nick to save the fort.

A later footnote is supplied by one Charles Robb of the U.S. Army, stationed thereabouts in 1861, who was moved to poesy by the tale. Like Lewis, he needs to pretty her up a bit, and instead of milling around improperly amongst the soldiers, he has her tucked decently away in a "ladies' hall," where she hears rumors of the desperate situation and volunteers.

> *Her step was firm, her features fine,*
> *Of Mortal mould the most divine.*

Robb insists that before leaving she whispered in her husband's ear and pressed his hand, but since the husband was definitely among the nonvolunteers we can only imagine what she whispered. Then she bursts out to startle the Indians:

> *But—lo! A lady fair and bright*
> *And seated on a charger light,*
> *Bold and free as one immortal,*
> *Bounded o'er the op'ning portal.*

The savages give chase but she eludes them, and then a slavering panther, and then a ravening wolf, and some more Indians, towering mountains, and a raging torrent.

The succor thus so nobly sought
To Charleston Fort was timely brought;
Whilst Justice, on the scroll of fame,
In letters bold, engraved her name.

A rousing fine epic of the sort the nineteenth century could dash off before breakfast, but nobody ever hauled it into the schoolroom beside Sheridan's and Paul Revere's much tamer romps.

The fort voted her the sorely taxed horse she'd ridden; she named him Liverpool and he was her main companion in the years to come. At some unrecorded point her husband, the cowardly worm, died; she probably wasn't around at the time. She embraced the nomadic life, sleeping in the woods or in settlers' cabins in her travels; a cave on the Kanawha River was still in Lewis's time called Ann Bailey's Cave. As Lewis puts it, "She was a stranger to fear, and while men were still subjected to garrison duty in the border stockade forts, she boldly sallied forth into the wilderness as if to challenge the ferocity of wild beasts and the vengeance of savage men." He chalks this up to her "ardent love for humanity." Well, maybe. He and others make a fuss over the medical skills she brought to the scattered settlers, perhaps not noticing that on all frontiers everywhere, every adult needs to know how to deliver a baby, set a broken bone, and dose a fever.

She skirmished often and gladly with the Indians in her travels and grew a reputation among them as being supernaturally bulletproof; they called her "The Great White Squaw" and she passed into their legends. Even after the Indian threat had finally been subdued, and the remaining hostile Indians relocated, she continued to ride restlessly over her wilderness territory. She ran a delivery service from Staunton out to the faraway outliers, peddled some trade goods—coffee, tools, pocket knives—and drove hogs and cattle hither and yon as needed.

Troubled by rumors that she drank and used bad language, Lewis inquired of survivors and descendants. One of them remembered as a little girl stumbling upon Ann and the fort commander arguing, a bottle of brandy in use between them (so much for the "ladies' hall"), but nobody said she was a lush, and if she swore (it's unlikely she didn't), the children who grew up to testify refused to remember.

At seventy-five she was still roving the wilderness, famous enough to be welcomed, even in the towns, in spite of her clothes—the petticoat must have been fairly bedraggled, what with years of sleeping in caves and hollow logs.

William, the abandoned son, now married and prosperous, suddenly reappears in the tale. His filial feelings must have been fairly dim, but perhaps Ann's admirers put pressure on him to take charge. Her own maternal feelings hadn't improved any, either, and she raised hell when he dragged her up north of the Ohio River to live with him. (His wife's views can only be imagined.) Almost immediately she moved out of his house and built herself "with her own hands a pen of fence-rails which she covered and thatched with straw, and in it she attempted to live." William hauled her back inside; she was still locally famous, and you can't have your famous elderly mother living under a pile of rails. She said she'd stay only if he built her a separate cabin near his house so she could live alone. He did. His wife may have helped to persuade him.

The town of Gallipolis was only nine miles away, and she regularly walked or paddled her canoe in to visit around, roam-

ing the streets with her rifle and bragging about her marksman-
ship and developing what Lewis delicately calls "many eccentricities," which he declines to detail. He's still determined to
make her respectable in spite of her best efforts, and he insists
that the night she died she had gathered her dear little grandchildren in her humble cabin and told them stories before dying in
her sleep.

She was eighty-three, having thumbed her nose at everyone
and played hide-and-seek with death for most of her life, and a
fine wild life it was, too, brandishing its tomahawk so rudely
behind the biographer's back.

In a modern work, *Ghosts of Virginia,* L. B. Taylor, Jr., attempts
to round up the multitudinous wraiths of the Old Dominion. He
interviewed one B. B. Strum, who teaches at Radford University
and used to see Ann's ghost often, back when he was at summer
camp: "She was riding a pale horse, and she was always sighted
out towards Lake Moomaw. She seemed to be calling for her son
William."

I doubt it.

By order of the mayor of Cascade, Montana, Mary Fields was
the only woman not a prostitute allowed to drink in the local
bar, but it's hard to believe that being forbidden would have
stopped her for a minute. "Stagecoach Mary" was a steamroller.
At six feet and two hundred pounds, she could lick any two men
in Montana Territory. She had a standing bet that she could
knock any man out cold with a single punch, and it's not known
that anyone collected.

She was born a slave in Tennessee in 1832 and served as maid
and friend to a woman who became an Ursuline sister, Mother
Amadeus. After Emancipation she went in search of adventure

163

and found a job in Mississippi, working on the steamboat *Robert E. Lee.* She was on board for its famous race against the *Natchez,* and a grand wild ride it was, too; she told the tale all her life.

Her old friend Mother Amadeus was transferred to a fledgling convent dropped in the wilds of Montana to convert the heathen, where she came down with pneumonia and sent for Mary. Mary went west. The Montana of the 1880s was clearly her spiritual home and her character expanded to fill the wide-open spaces and inspire folklore.

When she'd nursed her friend back to health, she stayed on to work at the convent, surely the oddest employee of any religious institution ever, in men's clothes with an apron over them, a pair of six-shooters and a shotgun, smoking vile homemade cigars, provoking fistfights, and cursing freely. Though nominally a Catholic, she easily fended off the sisters' efforts to civilize her.

As an employee, though, she gave every satisfaction. She picked up visitors from the train station, drove the wagon to fetch supplies from faraway towns, washed the convent's clothes and linens, tended the hundreds of chickens and the vegetable gardens, chopped wood, dug latrines, and tackled simple stonework and carpentry. In her free time, she polished her reputation for brawling. The town apparently cherished her for peculiarities that would have horrified the East and landed her in jail; the West loved its oddballs. The newspaper crowed that she had broken more noses than anyone else in central Montana. Whenever she decided she was having a birthday, the town closed the school and threw her a party.

Some of the tales probably didn't shrink in the telling. There was the night when, coming home with a load of supplies, she was attacked by a pack of wolves and her horses bolted and overturned the wagon. All night she kept the wolves at bay with revolvers and rifle and then, at daybreak, got home triumphant with the cargo. Presumably she'd righted the wagon and reloaded it single-handed. Those of us who have never tried to set an overturned freight wagon back on its wheels can only give her the benefit of a serious doubt.

She worked for the Ursulines for ten years. Then one of the hired hands at the mission complained that she was earning nine dollars a month while he made only seven, and she was a mere woman, and a black one to boot, and couldn't possibly be worth that much. He complained loudly in the saloons. He wrote a protest to the bishop. Mary was annoyed.

One day when he went out to clean the latrine, she followed him, meaning to shoot him and tip his body into it, but she missed. He fired back. The two of them emptied their six-guns at each other, neither scoring a direct hit, but one of Mary's bullets ricocheted off a stone wall and scored for his left buttock. More significantly, other bullets penetrated the bishop's laundry, hanging on the line to dry, and ruined two fine new shirts. (You'd think a bishop could hire someone to wash his clothes at home, but apparently he sent them to the convent.)

This was the last straw. The bishop, not having had the sisters' chance to know and cherish Mary, ordered the convent to fire her. Mary traveled to Helena to protest, but his shirts had been shipped clear from Boston and the bishop was adamant.

Out of work, she tried running a restaurant in Cascade, but it closed down promptly. (Her credit policy was generous to the point of bankruptcy.) Then Mother Amadeus pulled strings and got her a mail route. Some say the convent bought her a wagon and a team of horses; some say she covered her circuit with a mule named Moses. Some say she only carried mail and packages between the town and the convent; some say she delivered unfailingly throughout central Montana and her services were invaluable in smoothing the land-claim process and advancing settlement. Needless to say, wherever she was, she made her appointed rounds through snow and rain and heat and gloom of night and came to be called "Stagecoach Mary."

The terrain was wild and rugged and the weather fierce. She stuck it out for eight years before, at age seventy, she decided to give herself a rest. She settled in town and opened a modest laundry service in her little house, leaving herself plenty of time to hang out in the saloon, where it was said that though she was a crack shot with a rifle, her aim at the spittoon was faulty.

She was hardly decrepit yet, though. When she spotted a fellow on the street with a two-dollar overdue laundry bill, she hustled straight out of the bar, chased him down, and knocked him flat with a single punch. That, she said, settled his bill.

She mellowed a bit. Always fond of children, she was a popular surrogate mother to the young of Cascade, and when she was paid to take care of them, spent the money on treats and candy for them. One small boy, visiting from nearby Dearborn, remembered her lovingly and later, when he was world famous as Gary Cooper, wrote a story about her for *Ebony* magazine.

She also adopted the town baseball team, defended its honor with her fists, and decorated the players with buttonhole bouquets for each game and more lavish bouquets for home runs. The town, in return, seems to have adopted her. When the hotel changed hands, one of the conditions of the deal was that Mary Fields get her meals there free for the rest of her life. When her house burned down, the townsfolk built her a new one.

When she died at eighty of liver failure, everyone turned out to lament. Probably Cascade felt a bit hollow at its center, without its local treasure. Probably the saloon seemed strangely quiet and bland, its stories flabby and its whiskey savorless, with Stagecoach Mary gone.

Belle Starr the Bandit Queen, the Petticoat Terror of the Plains, the Female Jesse James, was born Myra Maybelle Shirley, and if she'd stayed that way, people probably wouldn't have heard as much about her. As Belle Starr, her name kindled freelance journalists, dime novelists, balladeers, scores of gullible biographers, screenwriters, and the front page of the *New York Times* into a towering inferno of invention.

She was just what the East wanted to hear about the West in the 1880s, with the Civil War over and life bogged down in respectability. She was just what the West wanted, too. Any raw, newly settled country, like Ann Bailey's Virginia in the eighteenth century, and the West in the nineteenth, needs more than farmers and blacksmiths. It needs its own stories, and heroes and villains and ghosts. *The Legend of Sleepy Hollow* couldn't be uprooted and moved to the Rockies, any more than Stagecoach Mary would have been admired for breaking noses in Boston. Sometimes, in their haste to fill the vacuum, people elevated third-rate punks like Billy the Kid to legendary heights. With Belle, they inflated a rather run-of-the-mill horsethief into exotic villainry.

They said she had lovers beyond counting; they said she rode at the head of her own murderous band of cutthroat brigands. Some said she was a Cherokee, a "maroon Amazon" whose "dread name struck terror to the hearts"; others that she read Homer in the original for recreation. She was either "phenomenally beautiful" or "bony and flat-chested" with "a mean mouth." It was said that she was "a generous friend"; it was said that "a more cruel human never walked the deck of a pirate ship," and that she had strangled a man at age fifteen with her little white hands and killed three more before she was eighteen. Each new chronicler had to pile the tale deeper than the one before, so that by the time we dig down to the actual woman, the reality seems strangely dowdy.

She wasn't as beautiful as the role called for—the ravishing Gene Tierney played her in a 1941 movie and the billowy Jane Russell in another in 1952—but in her early photographs she's nice enough looking, with a fresh, frank, open face and a prettily sculpted mouth. She was born around 1848 in southwest Missouri, where her father had given up farming and opened a successful hotel and livery stable. The family was respectable, intellectual, and musical, with a library and a piano, and little Myra Maybelle went to the Carthage Female Academy, where she studied Greek, Latin, Hebrew, and music. A classmate says she was "small and dark, bright, intelligent . . . but of a fierce nature and would fight anyone." Her brother taught her to ride and shoot; like all good rebels, she was splendid and fearless on horseback.

It's a long step from the Female Academy and the parlor piano to Petticoat Terror of the Plains. The easy explanation is that she took up with the wrong man, which she did. The wrong man has been a decisive, usually irrevocable, career move for many a girl. Sometimes she's been misled, sometimes she's driven by a missionary's zeal to reform the poor fellow, but sometimes, as with Bonnie Parker, he's her ticket to ride into a wilder scenario and take advantage of historical or geographical openings for madder music and stronger wine.

During the Civil War, Missouri was divided in its loyalties, mustering two separate armies that waged a miniature civil war of their own. The town of Carthage, including John Shirley's hotel, burned down in the process, and the family, Confederate sympathizers, headed for Texas, young Myra driving one of the wagons.

In Dallas, John Shirley took up farming again, and sometimes Myra went to the local school, where her quick temper made her unpopular. Dallas in the 1860s was a booming, brawling entertainment center full of saloons and gambling halls and carpetbaggers and partying cattlemen. Outlaws like Jesse James and the Younger Brothers were prospering and a number of biographers insist that Myra had a fling with the infamous Cole Younger, resulting in her daughter, Pearl, when she was fifteen. Some say she was married to him.

Glenn Shirley, in a 1982 biography, has trudged heroically through actual court records and contemporary local newspapers and brought back the unglamourous facts. Myra married Jim Reed, son of family friends from back in Missouri who'd also come to Texas. She was eighteen and he was twenty, and they lived with her family for a while, then went back to the Reeds' old place in Missouri. Two years later she had a baby, named Rosie Lee but called Pearl. Myra adored her. While the chroniclers have her roistering through Dallas dance halls, gambling and galloping around town on a fire-breathing steed firing her pistols at the sky, the real Myra was living with her mother-in-law, taking care of her baby, and attending Bethel Baptist Church in Rich Hill, Missouri.

It was her husband who was having fun. Bored with farming, he'd taken up gambling and traveling around with his racehorses and hanging out with bad hats like Cole Younger, Frank James, and a towering, murderous-looking Cherokee named Tom Starr, head of the notorious Starr clan that caused so much grief to respectable Cherokees. He had eight sons, nucleus of a gang whose horse-stealing and whiskey-smuggling were punctuated with murders.

Jim Reed, in his portrait a mild-looking man with close-set eyes and male-pattern baldness, embraced the outlaw life. During a discussion about a horse, his brother was killed, so Jim killed the killer and then lit out with Myra and Pearl for Los Angeles. There he got a job in a gambling house and Myra had another baby, a boy they called Eddie. When he got spotted passing counterfeit money and the authorities found he was wanted for murder, he left in haste, and Myra took the children back to her family in Texas. Jim joined them there, brooding, and moodily killed some more people.

We don't know much about this first husband, this nondescript son of God-fearing Missouri farmers, but he seems to have become addicted to crime with lightning speed, sliding from horseracing to serial murder like a man possessed. He did have one lucky break, when he and a couple of others robbed a man named Grayson over in the Creek Nation of some $30,000 in gold. The feature writers and biographers naturally put Myra in on the job, and had her flush with her share of the loot, swanking it up in Dallas gambling dens wearing velvet skirts and ostrich plumes and a necklace of rattlesnake rattles. Alas, according to the accounts of the time and the victim's own report, she was nowhere near the scene and certainly never got rich from it, since Jim promptly gambled away his share and then ran off with a young girl to San Antonio, pausing on his way to rob a stagecoach carrying United States mail, which much increased the price on his head.

He was finally trapped in a farmhouse. Inspired by the reward, a man named Morris pulled a gun and ordered him to surrender; Jim ducked under a table and hoisted it up between himself and Morris and was on his way out the door in a crouch when Morris fired through the table and killed him. It was August, and this unsavory fellow rotted quickly: the drayman hired to haul the corpse to potters' field was so sickened by the smell that he dumped it by the side of the road and fled.

The romancers pack his widow's next few years with excitement—holdups, arrests, elopements, jails, bank robberies, and a gang of outlaws who were all her lovers, making her "Queen of the Desperadoes." In bleak fact, all we know is a sad little letter to her Reed in-laws a year after Jim died. She's plagued by nerves and headaches and grieved by her father's death. A brother is on the run from the law. The farm is unprofitable and unsellable and her mother is about to leave it and take Eddie with her. The only bright note is Pearl, who "has the reputation of being the prettiest little girl in Dallas."

Of course, not everyone writes the truth to their in-laws, but no records support the exotic tales of her other activities. Her next authenticated sighting is in 1879 in Galena, Kansas, where a former sheriff whose father had owned a hotel there told an interviewer she was "a mighty good-looking woman, well educated, quietly dressed—not tough like the newspapers made out." (Her contemporaries often seem more impressed with her book-reading than her crimes; probably it was a much rarer talent in the area.) Another remembered her as "always well-behaved." At some point she may have had a brief affair with Bruce Younger, a relative of the famous brothers; in one yarn, she forced him at gunpoint to marry her, after which he galloped off and she never saw him again.

If you've been married to an outlaw, you're likely to have outlaw friends, and she took up again with the Starr clan, especially old Tom's son Sam. Sam was three-quarters Cherokee, proudly illiterate, and an imposing, broad-shouldered figure with his hair held back in a red ribbon, riveting eyes, and the granite face of a picture-book Indian. They were married in 1880 and Myra Maybelle became Belle Starr.

171

Taking Pearl, they settled on Sam's allotment at Youngers' Bend, an elbow in the South Canadian River, deep in Starr country, where the Youngers and Jameses had often rendezvoused. It was prime strategic real estate, reached only by a steep, narrow, rock-cluttered cleft in the cliffs by the river; the cliffs themselves were pocked with hidden caves for sentries. Their cabin faced a meadow that intruders would have to cross in plain sight, and if this didn't deter a posse, old Tom Starr's reputation probably would.

Belle went through a flurry of domesticity, arranging her books and covering the walls with flowered white calico, apparently hoping for a quiet, outlaw-free life. Jesse James, however, knew the way and dropped in to visit for several weeks. Others followed. Presently Belle was running a retreat home for so many desperadoes, she had to throw up a couple of guest cabins and outfit a handy cave for extra sleeping quarters. And before long, it seems, she was dabbling in outlawry herself.

Like her guests, Belle may have smuggled whiskey into the wild towns where Indians drank illegally in the back rooms and she may well have fenced some stolen horses. She was rumored to have set up trading stations where horses acquired from points north could be swapped for those picked up to the south, to be sold far from where their owners and brands were known. Horses were a terrible temptation, especially out where they roamed the open range miles from the owner's eye. They were valuable, easily sold in a brisk market, easy to transport, and couldn't be buried or locked in a safe like gold. Indeed, horse-stealing was so easy that it came to be regarded as morally wrong, contemptible, sleazy, and cowardly, compared to, say, train robbery. "Nothing lower," people said, "than a horse-thief."

Belle was known to have a way with horses. Perhaps, like

stray dogs, they simply followed her home. In 1882, she and Sam were charged at Fort Smith with stealing a horse from a man named Crane and another from a man named Campbell. It was her first arrest and she took it hard, fighting her captors tooth and claw, sabotaging the long wagon trip, and trying to kill a guard with his own pistol. She wound up traveling in chains. At the trial, a reporter noted that "a devil-may-care expression rested on her countenance. . . ." She was found guilty on two counts and Sam on one; he got a year and she two six-month sentences at the House of Corrections in Detroit.

Pearl, now in her teens, was sent to live with respectable friends who owned a hotel. Belle wrote her a bravely cheering letter beginning, "My Dear Little One— It is useless to attempt to conceal my trouble from you and though you are nothing but a child I have confidence that my darling will bear with fortitude what I now write." She promises that "never again will I be placed in such humiliating circumstances and that in the future your tender little heart shall never more ache, or a blush be called to your cheek on your mother's account." The House of Corrections—apparently a model institution for its, or any, time—has "beautiful grounds, with fountains and everything nice. There I can have my education renewed, and I stand sadly in need of it. Sam will have to attend school and I think it the best thing ever happened to him." When she gets out, she promises, life will be lovely, she will break and train Pearl's horse for her, little Eddie shall be borrowed back from his grandmother so they can all be together and "be as gay and happy as the birds." She ends, "But you must devote your time to your studies. Bye bye, sweet baby mine."

As previously noted, weaving responsible motherhood and the criminal career together has never been easy. Belle did keep her word, though, and whether or not Pearl blushed for her, she served no more jail time, quite a feat considering the scores of murders and robberies she's credited with. Her hopes for Sam's schooling came to nothing—he staunchly scorned the white man's book-learning—but she herself apparently had a pleasant time in Detroit, spending much of her sentence discussing literature with the prison matron and teaching French and music to the warden's children. Everyone was impressed by her ladylike language.

After nine months, she and Sam were released, picked up Pearl, and went back to Youngers' Bend. Old Tom Starr had had the place looked after and all was well, except that the three cats they'd left behind had increased themselves to twenty-five, as cats will. Pearl did the cooking, Belle helped Sam with a bit of farming. What they did in the evenings is a mystery. Belle must have been grateful for Pearl's company; she obviously loved Sam, defended him fiercely against insult and nursed his gunshot wounds, but he looks like a man who could survive on two or three words a week. It's one of the odder marriages in the annals.

Belle cut a dashing, imperious figure in the area, always well-mounted and sporting elegantly decorated boots and side saddle, but she had lost her looks. The fresh, open face of her earlier photos was now mannish, harsh, and raddled, a not-uncommon effect of western life at the time. Her jawline sagged. Old-timers interviewed later about her enterprises told wild tales of her fearsome gang that no marshal dared follow into Belle Starr Canyon, of her heavy gambling in Fort Smith, piano playing in saloons, and galloping her horse down the sidewalks. Somehow, though, she stayed out of the local papers and off the police blotter.

Sam got in trouble for holding up the U.S. Mail and robbing a store and post office of government money; he went into

174

hiding nearby, among his fierce relatives. Then Belle was accused of horse stealing. The indictment said she did "feloniously steal, take and carry away of the goods and chattels of Albert McCarty, a white man and not an Indian, one horse, of the value of seventy-five dollars." In the meantime, Sam and some others allegedly marched into someone's house and ransacked it and made off with forty dollars, to which they added a neighbor's pistol and another neighbor's horse. Most of the victims couldn't identify any of the robbers, but one young woman insisted Belle was among them, dressed like a man and brandishing a pair of six-shooters.

An Indian posse of seven men raided the Starr place but everyone escaped easily, Sam jumping his horse off a twenty-foot bluff and swimming the river. Belle pulled a revolver on one of the posse but he took it away from her and kept it for a souvenir. A second raid succeeded, though, and served a warrant on her. To keep Sam from ambushing and killing the posse, she and Pearl rode off with them peaceably.

She hired some lawyers and rounded up half a dozen witnesses to swear she was at a dance at the time. Out on bail, she was a star attraction on the Fort Smith streets. She gave an interview to a reporter from the *Dallas Morning News,* and the reporter reported her as "a dashing horsewoman, and exceedingly graceful in the saddle . . . well-formed, a dark brunette, with bright and intelligent black eyes." For some reason she took offense at the piece when she saw it, and at the trial she spotted the reporter in the courtroom, a small, bespectacled fellow, grabbed him by the scruff of the neck, hauled him over the railing, and whacked him with her riding whip.

None of the prosecution witnesses could identify her and the young woman who thought she'd seen her changed her story. Belle went free. She went free on the matter of McCarty's horse, too, but back home she found Sam holed up at his brother's, badly wounded by the Indian police. They'd spotted him riding Belle's favorite mare, Venus, through a cornfield and policeman Frank West fired, killing the mare and shooting Sam in the head. He lay bleeding and unconscious while two of the officers went to borrow a wagon to haul him away. While they were gone, Sam came to, leaped up and snatched one of the guards' guns from its holster and held them both at bay while he leaped onto one of their horses and rode away, swearing they'd pay for killing Belle's mare.

Belle talked him into surrendering to the U.S. marshal, since his only federal charge was the old post-office robbery, and the feds would be easier on him than the Indian police, who had grudges against the Starr clan and some cruel and unusual punishments available. He surrendered in Fort Smith. While they were waiting there, the town threw a splendid fair, and Belle was its main attraction in a wild riding and shooting performance, leaping on and off her horse at a gallop while shattering clay pigeons.

Sam's trial was held over till late in the winter. To cheer everyone up, he and Belle took Eddie and Pearl to the annual Christmas dance at an old friend's house. The party spilled outdoors, where a huge heap of logs blazed away in the evening chill. Frank West, killer of Venus the mare, showed up and warmed his hands at the fire. Inside, Belle was playing the organ when a friend came in and told her. She called to Sam to "go down and get the son-of-a-bitch," and then struck up a tune for the second dance.

Sam marched out and accosted Frank West. Words were exchanged, then Sam drew his revolver and fired; West, mortally wounded, fired back before he fell. Both died on the spot. With the blazing logs in the background and the dance tunes floating out into the night air, no screenwriter could have improved upon the occasion.

Under Cherokee law, the widowed Belle was no longer a Cherokee but an "intruder" and couldn't legally stay on her Indian property. Quickly she enlisted a much younger man, a protégé of old Tom Starr's, Bill July, sometimes called July Starr, to move in with her and proclaimed it a common-law marriage. July was no Sam Starr—he was called "a common horse-thief" and, worse, a coward who ran away from fights—but then, Belle was no longer much of a belle.

Pearl was now nineteen and Eddie seventeen, and they objected to July. She was having trouble with them anyway. Eddie kept getting into scrapes. One night he quietly borrowed Belle's favorite horse to go to a party and brought it back worse for wear; she hauled him out of bed and whipped him bloody with her riding crop. She whipped him often, and he came to hate her.

Pearl fell in love with a man Belle considered too poor to be suitable, so she broke off their engagement by treachery, sending Pearl away and then writing to the young man in Pearl's name, saying she had married another. The suitor was so despondent he promptly married someone else. When Pearl came back, she and her ex-fiancé had one last tender farewell meeting, after which she was pregnant. Belle was furious. She offered to get Pearl an abortion, but Pearl was afraid.

Perhaps it's just as well that most of the willful, independent women either went childless or doorstepped their offspring on friends and relations. As mothers, they could be tender enough while the children were little but went forehead-to-forehead with them at adolescence, like George Sand with her Solange. These aren't mothers who compromise gracefully in the inevitable clash of wills. Pearl was banished to her grandmother's.

Belle had spread the word that Youngers' Bend was no longer

an outlaw hideout and she seemed to be calming down and gaining a reputation as a kind and helpful neighbor, but Eddie and July would keep stealing horses. Eddie was forbidden to pick up his mother's mail at the post office in the general store, but when he threatened the store owner at gunpoint, he got it anyway. Belle found out and marched him down to the store, made him apologize to the owner, then snatched a bullwhip off the wall and whipped him long and hard, in public. He left home and never saw her again.

A man named Edgar Watson, a white settler from Arkansas, wanted to rent some farmland from Belle, but she got to chatting with his wife and learned he was wanted for murder in Florida. Since she was under threat of eviction if she harbored fugitives, she turned him down. He brooded.

Returning from a journey, Belle stopped off to visit a friend. Edgar Watson saw her from the friend's porch and slipped out of sight. She visited and went on her way, munching a piece of cornbread. Watson apparently waited at the fence corner and when she came within range he shot her in the back with buckshot and then, after she fell, emptied the other barrel into her face. Her horse came home still wearing her decorated side saddle. She was buried with her favorite revolver, the one she called "my baby," in her hand.

The front page of the *New York Times* cried out that she was "the most desperate woman that ever figured on the borders. . . . She had been arrested for murder and robbery a score of times, but always managed to escape." The tail-spinners rejoiced and took wing.

Watson was tried but got off because too many others— Eddie and July, for instance—had their own motives. He went back to Florida, where he seems to have killed an extraordinary number of other people before being shot down by police.

And the offspring of the Bandit Queen? Eddie served serious time for larceny and later reformed, became a deputy marshal, and was killed trying to make an arrest. After a brief marriage, Pearl, once her mother's adored, went to work in a brothel and later opened one of her own. She had some more children, and got thrown in the Fort Smith jail so often for alcoholic and moral lapses that she was banished from the town, not too easy to do in such a time and place. Maybe they were right, those thousands of years of mothers patiently behaving themselves.

Belle, though, was just beginning to come into her glory. However she may have served her children, in her many gaudy guises she has served her public well for over a hundred years, though as far as we know, that wasn't what she meant to do. What she did have in mind we can't possibly imagine, or what her options were, raised with music and books by upright folks as she was. Apparently we have all the facts, but the reasons are elusive. Perhaps, as in a western movie of the 1950s, she might have taught school, given piano lessons, married the sheriff instead of the outlaw, civilized the local desperadoes, and ushered her children respectably into the world.

Somehow, it wasn't in the cards. Or the stars. Or the genes. Or wherever our fates reside.

Grandstanders

Very little girls, if they were pretty and nicely dressed, could always cry "Look at me! Watch me! Look what I can do!" and indulgent uncles or nannies might smile or even applaud, but as soon as the little girls got to be ten or twelve, they were scolded for it, and told to sit down and be quiet and act like ladies. Visibility, for a girl, was indelicate and annoyed the menfolk. In all proper female hearts, "Look at me!" was folded away to fester, or allowed out loose only when they entered the ballroom in the fullness of their beauty on the arm of a famous man, an option not open to all.

With a little extra encouragement, though, especially from a doting father, a girl could grow up and grow old without ever leaving the spotlight at center stage.

Belle Boyd's ghost appears often around the scenes of her brief glory, near Winchester and Front Royal, Virginia, where, according to witnesses, "she rushes with messages to a ghostly army commanded by Stonewall Jackson." (How helpful of it to explain its errand as it gallops soundlessly by, lest people think it's just off to the store for a packet of hatpins.)

Boyd is usually referred to as a "beautiful Confederate spy," because it's traditional that lady spies be beautiful. In photographs, she's handsome but certainly not beautiful, not by the styles of the times, with cheekbones, a long jaw, and a strong nose and chin, but Southern girls learned early how to charm the beholder anyway, and she was definitely a fair-skinned strawberry blonde, which helps. One historian says, "The fact is, Belle was one of those girls who don't have to be pretty. She had a way with men . . . a situation most convenient for a lady spy." Everyone agrees she had a certain something; it may have been what we now call "self-esteem" (formerly "narcissism"). In a world of sweet-spoken, self-effacing women, she was a bombshell of cockiness, and her memoir sends the reader reeling from the onslaught of pure ego.

She came by it early. Her parents, by the evidence, simply doted on her. She was always their eye-apple, with "only child" written all over her, so it comes as a shock to learn she had seven younger siblings; obviously by the time they came along she had firmly preempted the family limelight and her parents' full attention. Her siblings simply aren't part of the story and her confidante and crony wasn't a sister but her young personal slave, Eliza Corsey.

She was born in the village of Martinsburg in what was then still Virginia, to a prosperous and sociable family. When she was eleven, her parents, in a rare repressive mood, told her she was too young to join in a dinner party they were giving for distinguished guests. As the gracious gathering prepared to rise from the table, they were alarmed by a tremendous clatter, the door burst open, and Belle plunged in on horseback, prancing and cavorting around the china and glassware. "Well, my horse is old enough, isn't he?" she cried. Her father was rushing to deal out justice when the very important guest of honor stopped him, saying, "Surely so high a spirit should not be thoughtlessly quelled by severe punishment."

It never was. Belle got away with murder.

In an effort to quiet her down, her parents sent her to Mount Washington Female College, near Baltimore, and after graduating she made her debut and, escorted by her mother and Eliza, spent a dazzling debutante winter in Washington—"pre-eminently brilliant," she called it—impressed by senators, flitting among the night life, and hobnobbing with important people in a city shortly to be rocked by Southerners resigning and going home. The war was on its way; she was back in Martinsburg just in time for her seventeenth birthday and Virginia's secession.

Her father, who was forty-four, declined a commission, a gentlemanly gesture of the time, and enlisted as a private. He was stationed down the road at Harpers Ferry, at least until his regiment retreated before the Union advance, back through Martinsburg; in northern Virginia, the Civil War was always just a short walk away. In the first of dozens of takings and retakings, Martinsburg was occupied by Union troops.

A general celebration on the Fourth of July led the troops to drink, and one of the Union men spread the word that Belle's bedroom was decorated with Confederate flags. Whooping, a group broke into the Boyd house and stormed upstairs to destroy them. The slave girl Eliza, always a quick thinker, had beaten them to it and the flags were nowhere to be found. Disappointed, the men decided to raise a Union flag over the house. Belle's mother, no shrinking violet herself, said, according to Belle, "Men, every member of my household will die before that flag shall be raised over us."

One of the soldiers cursed her "in language as offensive as it was possible to conceive," and Belle drew her pistol and shot him dead.

The officer in charge of the occupying forces came with his staff and interrogated the household, then promptly acquitted Belle and posted protective sentries around the house. (This odd clemency may have come from Washington's efforts at appeasement as it tried to keep the border states from leaving. On the other hand, it may just be Belle getting away with it as usual.) Later she wrote that she recalled the event "without one shadow of remorse."

Sentry duty is lonely and the Boyd sentries promptly succumbed to Belle's charms and prattled away about troop movements and plans. A novice spy, she wrote it all down in plain English, signed her name, and sent it by messenger, usually Eliza, to the Confederates. She was caught within a week.

At Union headquarters a furious colonel read her the Article of War calling for the death penalty in such cases. She tossed her head at him, unimpressed. He dismissed her with a warning, and she stalked out determined to take up spying in earnest.

To keep her out of trouble, her family sent her south to an aunt and uncle in Front Royal. Here the wounded came streaming in after First Manassas (a Southern victory thanks to clever espionage by Betty Duvall and Rose Greenhow). Belle worked long hours in the foul and bloody emergency hospital until her health broke down and she had to go back to Martinsburg to rest. (This is by her own account; it would be rude to suppose that the unsung and unglamorous hospital chores simply didn't appeal to her.)

Visiting her father in camp at Manassas, she got herself made a courier and an official member of the Confederate Intelligence Service, work better suited to her talents than washing bandages. A certain Colonel Ashby would put on civilian clothes and visit the Union camps as a veterinarian and, while dosing the horses, eavesdrop on the talk of the soldiery; apparently in those days soldiers talked about troop movements instead of women, beer, and the lousy food, as it has been in recent armies. Belle carried Ashby's tidbits to General Beauregard and General Jackson. Her horse, Fleeter, was trained to kneel down and keep a low profile in the woods, though Belle always had trouble keeping her own profile down and collected a dangerous lot of publicity for her pranks. She took up petty theft on the side, pocketing Federal pistols, ammunition, and medical supplies, especially quinine for the malaria victims.

One day when she was out riding, brazenly unchaperoned, with two young officers, her horse shied and bolted away past the Union sentries, behind Union lines. Brassy as always, she rode up to the commanding officer and told him she was his prisoner and pleaded winsomely for her release. The gallant officer replied, "We are exceedingly proud of our beautiful captive, but of course we cannot think of detaining you. May we have the honor of escorting you beyond our lines and restoring you to the custody of your friends? I suppose there is no fear of those cowardly rebels taking us prisoner?"

Belle smiled. Two officers escorted her back to Confederate ground, where her friends were hiding in some bushes. "Here are two prisoners that I have brought you," she sang out. And to the officers, "Here are two of the 'cowardly rebels' whom you hoped there was no danger of meeting."

Her friends took the poor fellows to Confederate headquarters, where the commanding officer promptly released them. It was ungentlemanly of Belle, after such courteous treatment, and certainly it accomplished nothing, but it was one of those gestures she never even tried to resist.

Since those days, America's wars have been fought in other

people's backyards, but in that claustrophobic conflict a skittish horse could land you in enemy territory. Recent spies have been forced to journey to Moscow or Baghdad; Belle didn't even need to leave town. The townsfolk of northern Virginia never knew, when they woke up in the morning, which flag would be flying; Winchester changed hands nearly a hundred times, Martinsburg sometimes three times a day. Through this constantly shifting battleground, Belle managed to wheedle travel passes from both sides, flirting her way past checkpoints, and dancing as gaily with either army. She had a talent for talk that few could resist; even women remarked on the charm of her conversation, though she much preferred talking to men. (Regrettably, today in the countryside all around her home town, word persists that she was generous with more than her conversation; generous to a fault, you might say. If so, no doubt she felt it was a gallant sacrifice for the Cause.)

She and her mother went to Front Royal to visit her aunt and uncle at their hotel there. It was occupied by Union troops, so they stayed in a cottage on the grounds and Belle partied with the occupying forces and learned a thing or two. Hearing of a top-level meeting to be held in the hotel drawing room, she squirreled herself into an upstairs closet with, for some reason, a hole bored in the floor, over the meeting room, and was rewarded with word of a trap being laid for Stonewall Jackson. She saddled a horse and rode through the night, passing sentry lines with false travel passes. No Yankee sentry seemed to wonder why an eighteen-year-old girl was galloping around occupied territory in wartime at two in the morning. Perhaps they were half asleep. She delivered the news to Colonel Ashby in Strasburg, rode the fifteen miles back again, past sentries now completely asleep, and was safe in bed by sunrise and highly pleased with herself. Stonewall evaded the trap.

Seldom has a girl been so happily employed or so temperamentally suited to her job.

Back in Winchester, she got word of a new move against Stonewall, with Union troops converging on him from all over the Shenandoah Valley and the bridges of Front Royal to be burned. She decided he should strike first and decisively, while the occupying troops were still in chaos and the reinforcements not yet arrived. She wrote him a note, but none of the ardent Confederates she approached would try to deliver it. Tossing her curls, she went herself, on foot, through the beginning crossfire, dodging bullets that zipped harmlessly through her clothes, and a fine target she made, too, in a blue dress with a ruffled white apron and a white sunbonnet. A shell exploded beside her and she threw herself on the ground as the fragments whizzed past. Back on her feet, she ran on toward the Confederates: "I shall never run again as I ran on that, to me, memorable day. Hope, fear, the love of life, and my determination to serve my country to the last, conspired to fill my heart with more than feminine courage, and to lend preternatural strength and swiftness to my limbs. I often marvel, and even shudder, when I reflect how I cleared the fields, and bounded over the fences with the agility of a deer."

Stonewall rode forward to join his aide on a hilltop. The aide recognized Belle racing toward them, and thought "she was just the girl to dare to do this thing." He rode up to her, and she gasped out that the entire force should press onward and capture the bridges before they were burned. She described the positions of the Union guns and the whereabouts of the Union forces with, as one officer put it, "the precision of a staff officer making a report, and it was true to the letter." Stonewall ordered a full charge, Front Royal was taken, the bridges were saved.

Afterward he sent her a note: "Miss Belle Boyd, I thank you, for myself and for my army, for the immense service that you rendered your country today. Hastily I am your friend, T. J. Jackson C.S.A."

The triumph was brief, of course, and presently he abandoned the town and the Union troops came back, but the whole war was like that.

Belle invited a couple of alleged rebels to dinner—paroled prisoners, they said they were, on their way back south. She gave one a letter to carry to Stonewall, full of information about Union troop movements. An old black servant called her aside and said she happened to know the man was no Confederate but a Yankee spy. Belle paid no attention.

As every theatergoer knows, when the trusty old family retainer delivers a warning, you ignore it at your peril, but Belle had floated through life on the wings of luck for so long that she took them for granted. The man was indeed a Yankee spy, sent specifically to trap her. She was arrested on the particular and personal order of Secretary of War Stanton, and a Detective Cridge of the Secret Service came for her, and searched her room, including, to her outrage, her clothes. Once again, Eliza had been quick off the mark and gathered the most damaging documents and burned them in the kitchen stove, but this time it wasn't enough.

A spiteful young local woman wrote, "Belle Boyd was taken prisoner and sent off in a carriage with an escort of fifty cavalry men today. I hope she has succeeded in making herself sufficiently notorious now."

Belle says the escort was four hundred and fifty, with a hundred more added after Winchester; Cridge was understandably worried about a daredevil rescue attempt by Ashby's cavalry.

With a regiment of armed and mounted soldiers to guard a single teenaged girl, she may have been frightened, but she was almost certainly gratified too.

At Martinsburg, where she wasn't allowed to visit her family, she and her guards took a train at two in the morning, which must have been rather a dismal moment, but happily a good crowd waited at the Washington station to see the famous spy before she was taken to the Old Capitol Prison. Belle marched in with her head held high, no doubt admiring her own proud spirit; a stagestruck sense of your life as drama can carry you whistling through the rough spots.

The Old Capitol Prison was no Andersonville. It had been the national Capitol building, and Belle's cell had been a congressional committee room, hardly a dungeon. The inmates were a high-class lot of spies and blockade-runners and political suspects, and she was the only woman in the place. Her merriment and saucy back-chat quickly made her the prison pet and the others slipped her candy and flowers; admirers outside the walls sent in streams of delicacies to vary the prison diet. The morning newspapers arrived with her breakfast, always full of delightful coverage of herself. The Provost Marshal of the District of Columbia wrote, "Belle Boyd was a lively, spirited young lady, full of caprices, and a genuine rebel. In person she was tall, with light hair and blue eyes. . . . It was her dashing manner . . . and air of joyous recklessness which made her interesting."

Sometimes she sang. She sang "Dixie" and "Maryland, My Maryland" and other Southern anthems, and many a diarist recalls the tears that sprang to the eyes of strong men on both sides, listening to the singing spy. She even scratched up a romance with a Confederate officer diagonally across the hall; they sent each other notes fastened to a large marble rolled back and forth.

188

Carl Sandburg wrote that there was no reason on earth she shouldn't have been summarily shot instead. As usual, she'd landed on her feet.

After less than a month, she and some other rebels were exchanged and sent to Richmond, while cheering crowds thronged the streets to bid her goodbye. Her fellow prisoners clubbed together to buy her a gold and diamond watch as a remembrance. In Richmond, she was greeted as a hero; the Richmond Blues company lined up and presented arms and the city band serenaded her hotel room. She bought a lot of new clothes and fell into the embrace of the cream of society.

Wherever she went, she was "the Virginia heroine." She was made a captain and an honorary aide to Stonewall Jackson, entitling her to a handsome Confederate riding habit with a captain's insignia; she dressed it up with gold lace and a plumed hat. She was, we're told, "a splendid and reckless rider," and on horseback in uniform she looked every inch the heroine.

While the Confederates were briefly holding Martinsburg, she made her way home to see her mother, who was pregnant and sickly. Virginia had split; Martinsburg was now in West Virginia, to the irritation of many citizens, and Belle was technically living in enemy territory. When the Union retook the town, she was placed under house arrest and Captain Stevenson of the 1st New York Regiment came to talk with her. He told her a widespread rumor credited her with leading Stuart's column in his ride around McClellan, and on another raid in Maryland. In his report, he calls her a colonel, and says she admitted she often rode with Stuart at the head of his cavalry. An inscribed gold watch from his officers bore her out.

It's hard to tell how much of this is strictly true. In any case, she was considered a threat, and presently arrested and sent to Carroll Prison, next door to the Old Capitol but not as nice. Her father went with her, holding her hand, and stayed in Washington trying to help. (Belle's parents spent a lot of time escorting her in her travels. We aren't told whether the seven younger siblings ever needed them while they were off with Belle.)

She had the best room in Carroll, but even so it was hot and smelly. Again, she sang. She sent messages to well-wishers outside by tossing them from the window in a split rubber ball. She always dressed in her prettiest clothes, and sometimes, to while away the time, she fastened a Confederate flag to a stick and brandished it from the window like Barbara Frietchie until it was confiscated. She talked back to her jailers. Sometimes she was allowed to walk outside, under heavy guard, but this attracted such crowds it was discontinued. She helped in a prison break by distracting the superintendent. And always the Southern newspapers arrived to cheer her up: "Had I been a queen, or a reigning princess, my every movement could not have been more faithfully chronicled at this period of my imprisonment. . . . Thus, from the force of circumstances, and not through any desire of my own, I became a celebrity."

And all this time her doting father stayed in Washington, pulling such strings as he could, far from his ailing wife, newborn daughter, and all those other children. When finally she was released to be "banished" to the South, he died, stricken, apparently, by the thought of his beloved Belle alone and in exile. He died with hallucinations of Belle by his bedside.

News of his death waited for her in Richmond, along with a heroine's welcome. To recover her health, she embarked on a long series of pleasant visits all around the South, staying with generous hosts in a land where the grueling last days of the war hadn't dampened the hospitality; indeed, in her memoir, Belle barely mentions the war in any larger, nonpersonal sense. The whole ghastly mess might have been laid on as backdrop for the stirring story of Belle.

Still concerned by her health, she resolved to go to Europe. Perhaps she would carry dispatches; she could waltz around the capital cities as an advocate for the Southern cause. She wrote to Jefferson Davis. He agreed, and sent her five hundred dollars in gold "as bearer of dispatches for the Dept. of State."

Southern ports were under an efficient blockade, cutting them off from the world, except for the daring of a few blockade-runners carrying cotton to England and returning with arms and medicines. On one of these, the *Greyhound,* flying a British flag, she sailed under a "Captain Henry," an alias. (She called herself "Mrs. Lewis," but somehow everyone knew who she was any-way. She may have told them herself. How could the dashing and famous Belle Boyd pretend for long to be boring Mrs. Lewis?)

They crept off to sea with the lights out, but the Yankees spotted them and gave chase, firing. Henry surrendered; Belle burned all her dispatches and letters of introduction, making the five hundred dollars a total loss to the impoverished Confeder-acy. They were boarded by insolent and abusive Yankees, whom Belle of course bravely defied.

The prize-master, young Lieutenant Hardinge, came aboard, and he was "made of other stuff than his comrades," gallant, and good-looking, too. He told Belle to consider herself a pas-senger, not a prisoner, and they sailed north. The next evening, Belle, Henry, and Hardinge sat together on deck. Henry sang; Hardinge recited Shakespeare. (The Civil War was in many odd ways civil indeed, and a gentleman remained a gentleman.) When Henry went on the bridge, Hardinge proposed to Belle, having known her for the better part of two days. She demurred, as any lady should.

They stopped briefly in New York, which small-town Belle found breathtakingly beautiful, "unequaled in the world." With Henry and Hardinge, she went to the theater and shopped in chic stores and was quite eaten with envy: "Though the war raged within a short distance, its horrors had little influence on the butterflies of the Empire City," she wrote bitterly.

At sea again, Hardinge again proposed, so nobly that she couldn't help but accept him, privately resolving to win him over to the Southern cause. Love, however, didn't stop her from getting him in serious trouble: in Boston, she distracted him while Henry made a daring daylight escape. A U.S. marshal came aboard and the ship was searched, but "Captain Henry" was gone, hiding in Boston before making off for Canada. Belle wrote: "I was laughing in my sleeve, saying to myself, 'Again I have got the better of the Yankees!'"

Belle, though technically a prisoner, went ashore in Boston and enjoyed herself enormously there. Hardinge went to Washington to try to arrange her release, and for his pains got himself arrested for complicity in Henry's escape, though not before Belle got permission to go to Canada, with the stipulation that she'd be shot if she ever showed up in the United States again. In Canada, she pulled a few strings of her own, probably involving blackmail; she knew a few choice tidbits about Washington dignitaries. Hardinge was released, and the lovers met again in London and were married in St. James Church, Picadilly, with glorious newspaper coverage. Everyone came. Some say the Prince of Wales was there.

After a week of wedded bliss, Hardinge sailed for America, for reasons unclear, and was promptly arrested in Baltimore as a deserter. He spent five months in assorted prisons. Meanwhile, in London, Belle wrote her memoir, *Belle Boyd in Camp and Prison,* and then fired off a letter to Abraham Lincoln: "I think it

would be well for you and me to come to some definite understanding," she says crisply. She has, she explains, written her
"personal narrative" for publication and it was chock-full of
"atrocious circumstances respecting your government . . . which
would open the eyes of Europe." However, if Lincoln will
release her husband, she won't publish what she knows.

Hardinge was released. He was released quite abruptly, without explanation, immediately after the letter hit the presidential
desk, and when it surfaced, in 1947, it wasn't in the official files.
It was in the sealed Lincoln papers.

Not everyone could have successfully blackmailed Abraham
Lincoln. Not everyone would even have thought of it.

What happened next to poor Hardinge, nobody knows. He
emerged from prison weakened, wearing only a blanket and one
boot, and was seen in the neighborhood, trying to get to Washington and from there to England. He had a prison journal that
found its way to Belle, but we don't know whether he accompanied it, or ever got to London. He vanished. Belle's otherwise
copious account simply doesn't mention how. Her biographers
naturally assume she was too grief-stricken to discuss it, but
after all, they'd been married for only a week, and before that
they'd hardly known each other. Belle was pregnant and broke,
and her main concern, like most people's, was herself.

She took her manuscript to a London publisher, minus the
scandalous Washington gossip, and he was as charmed by her as
by her story. *Belle Boyd in Camp and Prison* was published in London in 1865, and shortly afterward in America, but it was no
long-term guarantee of income. By now she had a daughter,
Grace. What should she do? Why, theater, what else? Hard to
imagine a different choice of career, with the war over and the
bottom fallen out of the espionage market.

After a brief stint in English regional theaters, she took the child and went back to America, taking advantage of President Johnson's amnesty, and toured around. While playing in New Orleans, she captivated a former Union officer, now a sales representative traveling in tea and coffee. They married and had several children and somehow stayed married for fifteen years. There are rumors, though, of time spent in an insane asylum in California, as respectable motherhood drove still another former maverick mad.

In 1884 they were divorced, and a few weeks later she married a penniless actor seventeen years younger than she was and returned joyfully to the stage to support the family. She was a great hit in both North and South doing dramatic monologues about her life as a spy, reliving the glory days.

When she died of a heart attack in 1900, on tour in Wisconsin, she was fifty-six, but everyone says that, like so many wayward women, she looked much younger. Perhaps after all it's the quiet life that breeds gray hair and wrinkles.

Unsurprisingly, the look-at-me factor has always been strongest in the performing arts; Belle Boyd was destined at birth for a stage career and her espionage merely laid its groundwork and gave her its dramatic excuse. Performing artists are required to do interesting things; who would pay good money to watch a respectable housewife?

In 1784, the French opera singer Marie Elisabeth Thible was the first woman to go up in a balloon, rising majestically from Lyon over an admiring crowd that included King Gustav III of Sweden; later she posed dressed as Minerva for publicity pictures of the event. The silent-movie star Pola Negri blackened her eyes like a raccoon and had her white Rolls-Royce upholstered in white velvet. Zsa Zsa Gabor was romantically linked in rumor with Conrad Hilton, Nicky Hilton, Mustafa Kemal Atatürk, John F. Kennedy, Ali Khan, Henry Kissinger, and Mario Lanza. ("I am a marvelous housekeeper," she said. "Every time I leave a man I keep his house.") Tallulah Bankhead's drinking and affairs with both sexes were legendary and her parties fetched police like ants to a picnic, reporters hot on their heels.

For decades, heavy drinking and its attendant music of breaking glass and police sirens kept the names in the news. Then drinking came to seem vulgar and lower-class; the drugs that replaced it were more exotic but not as much fun headline-wise unless the party ended in a fatal overdose. The famous had to fall back on sex and its corollaries, bitter divorces, illegitimate children by the busload, and lawsuits galore, but after the sexual revolution of the seventies put sex within the reach of any suburban matron, it lost its clout in the tabloids. Back in 1950, Ingrid Bergman had a child out of wedlock and the whole world was rocked; as late as 1963 Elizabeth Taylor's affair with Richard Burton broke up their marriages and made her more famous than God. Today, who would notice? Posing naked for magazine covers is scarcely worth comment. As of this moment, a well-known television actress is arranging to give birth for the cameras and run the event on prime time television. It's hard to imagine what next, short of murder, would seize our jaded attention. Grandstanding has fallen on hard times. Gone are the days when a girl could make a name for herself just by posing in transparent draperies.

Transparency could be justified in prudish times by giving it an exotic background, foreign and therefore vaguely educational: oriental for Mata Hari, Greek for Isadora Duncan, Spanish for Lola Montez.

Montez was actually Marie Dolores Eliza Rosanna Gilbert, born in 1818 in Ireland, daughter of a Scottish army officer.

First, at eighteen, she ran off with a Captain James, then left him, edited her name, and took up what she called Spanish dancing, along with a series of lovers, rising socially with each. (She even managed to have an affair with Franz Liszt, the man George Sand said loved "no one but God and the Holy Virgin.") Billed as "the belle Andalusian" (no mention of her native Limerick), she was rumored to have danced nude for select Spanish grandees; she was rumored to have been the centerpiece of a Turkish harem. The perfection of her bosom was internationally famous. So was her temper. Wagner called her "demonic and heartless" and she carried a horsewhip and used it freely on hotel staff, German policemen, and newspaper editors. Still, when not irked, she was fine cheerful company.

Montez was more than just a pretty face. She worked her way into the bed and heart of King Ludwig of Bavaria, who made her a countess and built her a palace and somehow let her become de facto king; she hired and fired cabinet ministers and conferred privately with Bismarck. Apparently she was quite a good ruler for the time and place, but the revolutions of 1848 tore through and deposed her, like many another in that turbulent year. Chin high, she stalked out alone into the roiling mob that howled for her blood, hopped into the waiting carriage without a backward glance, and set off for America and the lecture circuit there.

Probably Montez considered her "Spanish dancing" simply a means to an end; she may not have convinced herself it was either Spanish or dancing. Isadora Duncan was nothing if not sincere about hers. "My Art," she wrote, "is just an effort to express the truth of my Being in gesture and movement." A healthy ego is essential to successful grandstanding; many of us wouldn't think of offering a roomful of strangers the truth of our Being—some of us aren't even sure what it is—and Isadora's inner Being was inseparable from more outer Being than was usually exposed a hundred years ago. Those with no sympathy for modern dance might consider her Art basically an excuse to take her clothes off in public, but then she was always misunderstood by the bourgeois philistine.

She was born and raised in California, a state that produces more than its share of healthy egos, and her talent was obvious early. Shortly after birth, she tells us, "placed in a baby jumper in the center of the table, I was the amusement of the entire family and friends, dancing to any music that was played." Early applause is dangerous stuff. By the time she was six, she was teaching dance as self-expression to the neighborhood children; at ten she had so many pupils she dropped out of school.

Her teaching method was a bit shapeless. She calls it a new system of dancing, but admits that she was "teaching any pretty thing that came into my head," and encouraged her pupils to fling themselves around while she read aloud from Longfellow. A brief attempt at formal ballet lessons was a failure; that wasn't what *she* considered dancing, and standing on one's toes was ugly and unnatural. Dancing should be natural. Everywhere she went around town, she danced her way naturally along the streets.

The whole family was high-minded like that. Her absent father was a poet; her mother taught piano to support them and in the evenings played classical music and read aloud from Shelley and Shakespeare. The rest of the time the four children did whatever they pleased and had many hair-raising adventures— "Of all the family I was the most courageous," Isadora freely admits. When she was twelve, she and her siblings took their act on a tour up and down the California coast, and it was a hit.

197

Still, the San Francisco area was stifling and limited, and presently she persuaded her mother to take her to Chicago. They had twenty-five dollars to live on while Isadora auditioned sweetly in her little white tunic, but no takers. Penniless, they were thrown out of their room, their clothes impounded. She sold the lace collar of her tunic and spent the money on a room and a box of tomatoes. Her mother took to fainting from hunger. Finally a theater manager told her he'd reconsider if she'd lose the sweet little tunic and the Mendelssohn and come back with something zippier. What to do? She marched into the Marshall Field's department store and told the manager she needed fabric for a costume and would pay him back when she got the job.

Perhaps stunned by her nerve, he gave it to her, and her mother sat up all night, fainting occasionally, sewing frills. She got the job: fifty dollars a week, to be paid in advance. At the end of the week she quit, disgusted at having "to amuse the public with something which was against my ideals."

New York was just as bad. They traveled there on borrowed money with the offer of a small part in a play, but the part was appallingly unworthy, and besides, she was unrecognizable in her costume. How express one's Being if nobody knows whose Being it is? The part of the First Fairy in *A Midsummer Night's Dream* was even worse: she had to wear wings. The whole family moved into a one-room studio, propping their five mattresses against the wall by day so Isadora could dance.

Her sister Elizabeth took in some dance pupils; her brother Augustin went on tour with a road company; Isadora landed a part in *The Geisha,* but unfortunately it involved singing in a quartet. Since she couldn't carry a tune, she just stood there looking soulful, but even that was too degrading. She told the producer she "could no longer stand the imbecility of the things that went on in his theater," and besides, "What's the good of having me here, with my genius, when you make no use of me?" He marched off and she never saw him again. *His* loss.

She met a nice young composer and gave a couple of concerts with him, which led to performances on the posh lawns of Newport for the likes of Mrs. Astor. High society applauded, but they were utter philistines and "hadn't any of them the slightest understanding of what I was doing." Just when things seemed darkest, the building they were living in burned down and destroyed all their belongings and they found themselves penniless yet again. Inspired, Isadora realized they must go to London, where she'd be appreciated.

In her own words, "I was never able to understand, then or later on, why, if one wanted to do a thing, one should not do it. For I have never waited to do as I wished. This has frequently brought me to disaster and calamity, but at least I have had the satisfaction of getting my own way."

She went door to door all over New York offering the ladies of society a chance to finance her genius, and was amazed at their foolishness in offering such small sums. She collected only three hundred dollars, not enough for proper fare, so the family had to cross on a cattle boat. London, however, was a delight. Those with ample self-esteem rarely worry about survival, so instead of looking for work they all spent weeks sightseeing until they were "awakened from our tourist dream by an irate landlady asking for her bill to be paid." They ignored her, of course, until, coming home from the National Gallery one day, they found the door locked with their luggage inside. Writing many years later, Isadora was still fuming at the pettiness of it.

They had six shillings. They lived on benches in Green Park and in the British Museum, eating penny buns. Then Isadora picked a newspaper out of the trash and noticed that a woman she'd danced for in New York had taken a house in London. She dashed right over and got a job dancing at the lady's next party, while her mother played the piano and her sister recited Theocritus. It was all "slightly above the heads of the well-fed audience," but more engagements followed. After the brush with the landlady, Isadora knew "we could never again occupy so bourgeois a home as lodging," so they rented a house in Kensington Square, with a key to the square's gardens.

In the gardens late one night, she and her brother Raymond were flitting about dancing, which should by rights have got them taken into custody or at least evicted, but instead the great actress Mrs. Patrick Campbell passed by and asked them where on earth they came from. Isadora said, "not from the earth at all, but from the moon," which so enchanted the star that she took them under her wing.

Fame followed at once; fortune would have too if Isadora hadn't spent it faster than it came in. The Prince of Wales called her a Gainsborough beauty. Poets and painters worshiped her. Every man in London sighed for love of her and she dazzled the brightest lights of the theater scene, dining with Henry Irving and Ellen Terry and dancing for Beerbohm Tree. Alas, though, as before, "theatre managers were unable to understand my art."

The Duncans moved on to Paris, where she and Raymond began each day by dancing in the Luxembourg Gardens. Inspired by Greek vases in the Louvre, she took to dancing in the nude or in transparent tunics, with bare feet and flowers in her hair, whenever the spirit moved her. People dropped in to her studio for a visit and she immediately broke into dance, followed by hours of lecture on its true meaning, "the central spring of all movement, the crater of motor power . . . the mirror of vision" that would prove classical ballet hopelessly wrong-headed because it focused on mechanical movements and not the Soul's Spiritual Vision. Countesses and princesses paid attention.

At her French debut, she danced before "all who counted in Parisian life," and they, too, adored her. (From time to time she flung herself passionately on various men, trying to lose her virginity, but she says she inspired such religious awe in her admirers that they shrank from deflowering her.) She had "found the key which opened for me the hearts and minds of the intellectual and artistic elite of Paris," but this butters no parsnips and, with the artistic way she threw money around, she and her mother were desperately poor and chilly in their drafty studio. Her long-suffering mother was often ill, and no wonder, but Isadora maintained her standards and angrily rejected an offer of a thousand marks a night to dance in a Berlin music hall. She would dance only in an opera house, a worthy "Temple of Music."

Leaving her mother to freeze and starve in Paris, she went off with the dancer Loie Fuller to Germany and then to Hungary. In Budapest she danced for a month in a theater; she worried at first that she might be seen by philistines, but it turned out "an indescribable triumph." One night she improvised to the "Blue Danube" and "the whole audience sprang to their feet in such a delirium of enthusiasm that I had to repeat the waltz many times before they would behave less like mad people." After that Hungary was hers; everywhere she went, always dressed all in white, she was greeted "like some young visiting goddess."

To cap it off, she found a handsome Hungarian actor less inhibited than her French worshipers and they fell into each other's arms in utter bliss. Sex was everything she'd hoped it would be. Apparently there was a misunderstanding, though, because the actor started taking her around to look at apartments and seemed to assume they'd marry and she'd devote herself to his, not her, career. She promptly signed a contract to dance her way through Germany. She'd always sworn she would never lower herself to the "degrading state" of marriage.

Being sensitive and high-strung, she was completely prostrated by the breakup of the affair and had to convalesce luxuriously in spas, attended by doctors, before she went on to captivate all Germany. People ran amok with excitement at the very sight of her; fans unharnessed the horses from her carriage and pulled it through the streets themselves; fans gathered at the enormous plate-glass window of a restaurant to watch her eat and pressed against it so eagerly they broke it in, but no one was seriously injured. Newspapers carried nothing but interviews with Isadora. In Berlin, the audience mobbed the stage and refused to leave the building. "Holy Isadora," they called her. In Munich, the Grand Duke Ferdinand invited her to stay at his villa, causing a gratifying scandal.

For an uplifting spiritual rest, she repaired to Italy and Greece with her family, reciting Homer all the way. In Greece, she and Raymond felt wonderfully appropriate traipsing around in the tunics and sandals of the Ancients, to the bemusement of the moderns, and wept and trembled with delight at everything they found. This was their spiritual home; they must stay here forever, and build a temple to themselves. In the temple they would dance for the sunrise every morning and spend the rest of the day converting the local shepherds back to Greek gods and tunics and dancing. The Duncans of California would single-handedly restore Greece to its Pagan glory.

To this end they bought a hilltop far from the city or the nearest water supply, Raymond drew up a romantic design, and soon cartloads of stone were toiling expensively up the hill. They invited a local priest to sanctify the cornerstones; he sacrificed a black rooster for the occasion and all the neighbors showed up and drank too much raki. Isadora recruited some small local boys to sing the choruses of Aeschylus while she danced, and their winding processions through the countryside astonished all observers.

The temple was half built before they realized how inconvenient it would be without water; desperate attempts to dig a well produced nothing but dust. Besides, all the money was gone. Isadora took ten of the boys, pursued by their mothers' lamentations, to enlighten Vienna with Greek culture.

It didn't work. Nobody wanted Aeschylus, they wanted the "Blue Danube." Every morning she and her sister Elizabeth took the boys for a walk in the Tiergarten, all dressed as ancient Greeks. One day the Kaiserin was riding by and saw them; she and her horse both shied in terror and she fell off. The boys, unappreciative of their opportunity, took to talking back, escaping at night to hang out with low-life, and singing off-key. Isadora sent them back to Greece.

The Greek moment apparently past, she flung herself into German philosophy, ransacking Immanuel Kant's *Critique of Pure Reason* for dance inspiration, her inner being "ravished" by Nietzsche's *Zarathustra*. (With no grim memories of education, those who drop out of school early often overdo it in later life.) Wagner gave her hysterics of pure joy; she stayed with his widow in Bayreuth, admired by the cream of royalty and the arts.

Another lover appeared, inspiring what she called "a superhuman love." She was so taken with this fellow that his mere presence across the room caused her to groan and cry out in "wild flights of ecstasy and fainting bliss." Unfortunately he wasn't much for actual sex and besides, he was married, though his wife didn't appreciate him and perhaps didn't even faint with bliss when she saw him.

King Ferdinand of Bulgaria took to visiting her, always at midnight, causing comment, though she swears it was perfectly chaste. Cosima Wagner persuaded her to dance in *Tannhäuser,* which she did, in "my transparent tunic, showing every part of my dancing body" including "my beautiful legs" and "satiny skin." She and the widow agreed the composer would have wanted it that way.

She pined away for the blissful lover until rescued by an invitation, in January of 1905, to dance in Russia; her reception in St. Petersburg cheered her right up, and she flitted through its snowy streets in her little white tunic and sandals, which must have impressed the locals almost as much as her dancing. She met the great Pavlova, and the great Diaghilev, and the great Stanislavsky, who later wrote, "I, a newly baptized disciple of the great artist, ran to the footlights to applaud. . . . I never missed a single one of the Duncan concerts." He tried to pry her secrets out of her, but the resulting prattle about placing a motor in her soul was disappointing; he must have supposed some sort of method and discipline lay behind her raptures. He was also apparently startled when she flung herself on him in a fit of passion; he grabbed his hat and rushed out into the street. Still, for all her romantic twaddle, she must have had something. Nobody impresses the greatest stars of ballet-obsessed Imperial Russia just by leaping around half naked waving her arms.

It may have been an instinctive sense of timing that led her to keep leaving countries at the very pinnacle of her success. Then again, she may just have been easily bored. She suddenly decided that Berlin was the very place to start her dancing school and persuaded her family to buy a huge house there and furnish it with forty dear little student beds and many inspiring works of art. She advertised for students and took them on rather haphazardly; one gentleman showed up with a four-year-old wrapped in a shawl, handed it to her, and vanished forever. Berlin still loved her. She was the "Gottliche Isadora," and word went around that the sick and the lame, brought into the theater on stretchers, recovered at the very sight of her.

Love struck again. This time it was the English set designer Gordon Craig, son of Ellen Terry, and his "white, lithe, gleaming body." Once again she got some proper sex, though she calls it "the meeting of twin souls," and holed up for two weeks with him in his studio, making love on the floor, while her mother canvassed the hospitals and police stations wringing her hands. The scandal went public and the lady patrons of the school, shocked, withdrew their support. And Isadora was pregnant. Her mother wanted her to marry, not understanding that "I was against marriage with every intelligent force of my being . . . especially for artists."

Mrs. Duncan had had enough. Her health had collapsed with self-sacrifice and hardship and perhaps, more recently, loneliness; there's no hint that Isadora was sharing the delights of international society with her, now that her piano-playing and sewing weren't required. In her memoir, Isadora blames her decline on the years of virtue she devoted to her children when she should have been having affairs instead. Mrs. Duncan went back to the United States and Isadora doesn't seem to have given her another thought for many years.

She had more important matters on hand. Craig was being difficult. His self-esteem was even healthier than Isadora's and he felt his career should come first; she should stay home and nurture him. She was enchanted by her pregnancy, the "divine message that sang in all my being"—what masterpiece wouldn't want to have copies made?—but he was afraid it would interfere with his work.

After a Scandinavian tour she took herself off to a little house on the North Sea, a hundred miles from the nearest town, to listen to the divine message alone, or at least with only a live-in nurse and a friend. Unfortunately the local doctor was experienced only with "peasant women" and so couldn't appreciate that, as she puts it, "the more refined the nerves, the more sensitive the brain, the more all this tends to suffering." Besides, she grew disgusted with the sheer ordinariness of the experience, such as any ordinary woman might have. Also "my lovely body bulged under my astonished gaze."

It was a tough labor; even decades later she's outraged at pains she compares to the tortures of the Spanish Inquisition and to being pinned under a railway train. Back in Berlin, Craig named the baby Deirdre and Isadora, broke again, accepted an invitation to go dance in St. Petersburg, leaving the baby with a nurse. She was still torn about Craig: How could she marry him and give up her Art? How could she not marry him and pine jealously? The answer arrived in the person of a charming young wastrel without a brain in his head. She invited him to come with her on the Russian tour and he brought along eighteen trunks full of clothes. The meeting of twin souls had been stressful; sex for its own sake made a peaceful restorative. She recommends it

Her dream of a dance school had grown to include at least a thousand pupils who would perform to Beethoven's Ninth Symphony (as chorus, of course; she had no mind to train another great soloist, since who needs two?). She scoured the world for a government enlightened enough to support the scheme, but in the meantime, she'd spent all her money again and accepted a six-month American tour with the famous Charles Frohman—"a great manager, but he failed to realize that my Art was not of a theatrical nature" and appealed only to the enlightened.

She was right; nobody came. She tore up her contract but stayed on: she'd been trying unsuccessfully to seduce sculptor George Grey Barnard and hated to leave the job unfinished.

Luckily she met the conductor Walter Damrosch, who set her up with his orchestra at the Metropolitan Opera House, where the enlightened came and did indeed appreciate her. After that she made a joyful tour, including Washington, D.C., where the religious community rose in protest against her state of undress. President Teddy Roosevelt came to a matinee, though, and wrote, "What harm can these ministers find in Isadora's dances? She seems to me as innocent as a child dancing through the garden in the morning sunshine and picking the beautiful flowers of her fantasy."

Rather reluctantly she went back to Europe and was hurt because, after six months, her daughter wept with alarm at the sight of the strange lady. Maybe motherhood wasn't so grand after all. "It would be infinitely more admirable to be able to love all children," she comments.

Broke again, she cast around for a millionaire to finance her school. Her prayers were promptly answered in the person of a tall, blond, handsome, and incredibly rich gentleman she calls her "Lohengrin," thereafter referring to him as "L." (In real life he was Paris Singer, heir to the almost limitless sewing-machine fortune, but we'll go on calling him L.) Off they went on his yacht and again the sex was great: "I came to life in a new and exhilarating manner which I had never known before," she writes, rejuvenated and astonished as she always was with each fresh affair. As she put it, "My life has known but two motives— Love and Art—and often Love destroyed Art, and often the imperious call of Art put a tragic end to Love." (Sometimes the imperious call of alternative lovers had a hand in it too, but an artist must follow her Muse.)

With a few brief interludes to fill dancing contracts, her idyll with L. wandered through pleasant places. During a visit to Venice, she had a sort of vision of an angel in the Cathedral of

San Marco and presently found out she was pregnant again, probably by the angel. After a tour with Maestro Damrosch in America, where the philistines were shocked by the lovers traveling together and by her obvious pregnancy, they wintered in Egypt on L.'s yacht, taking Deirdre, a Steinway, and a pianist. Here her soul "traveled back, through the Mists of the Past to the Gates of Eternity." The baby was a boy, named Patrick, and distinctly resembled the angel.

L. wanted her to marry him and tried to bribe her by taking her to his palatial estate in Devonshire, an exact copy of Versailles except for the fourteen-car garage, but it rained, the dinner parties were boring, and Isadora was reconfirmed in her distaste for domesticity. She lit out on another American tour. By this time she was making love, glorious, free Pagan love, to pretty much anyone who asked. "After a performance, in my tunic, I was so lovely. Why should this loveliness not be enjoyed?" And enjoyed it was. When she got back to Paris, the son she'd left in a cradle was running around and talking and, like his sister before him, hadn't a clue who she was.

She bought a house at Neuilly, near Paris, and furnished it as she did all her homes, to be a perfect backdrop for her loveliness, including, always, a plethora of blue curtains. Blue curtains were her trademark, the expression of her soul and "a never-failing inspiration." Here one night she gave a costume party for tout Paris, and L. caught her on a divan with an artistic luminary and had a fit, most unreasonably, as this was one of the few men she *hadn't* slept with. L. stormed off to Egypt with another woman. Isadora took the children to Versailles, with the Queen of Naples along for company. Deirdre, she's decided, will be a great dancer and Patrick a great composer, and between them ensure her immortality.

After four months' separation, L. asked her to bring the kids and meet him for lunch in Paris; she was anxious to have him back since, after all, he'd bought land in Paris for a theater for her. After lunch the children and their nurse were on their way back to Neuilly when all three of them were killed in an automobile accident.

Isadora was shattered. Being of an artistic temperament, she suffered far more than the rest of us would have and the ugliness of modern funeral customs made it even harder to bear. (It would be nice to think that her grief was sharpened by guilt at having seen so little of them during their short lives, but Isadora's Being was, if not actually remorseless, remarkably remorse-free.) Her brother Augustin took her to Corfu to recover and L. joined her there, anxious to help, but her unrestrained mourning was too much for him and he left abruptly. Then her brother Raymond dragged her off to help him in his work for Albanian refugees, and she decided henceforth to live only for others, as a token of which self-sacrifice she cut off her lovely hair and threw it in the sea. Quite soon, though, she recognized that a refugee camp is no place for an artist and sailed for Constantinople, and from there to Geneva, and then to Paris, and then Italy. One day, while walking along the sands, she saw her dead children and ran after them; they evaporated into mist and she fell down weeping. Who should come along at that very moment but a handsome young man who was clearly a reincarnation of a Michelangelo figure in the Sistine Chapel, perhaps of Michelangelo himself? He turned out to be engaged, but their brief fling cheered her up enormously.

Like any good grandstander, she managed her loss by dramatizing it. At Christmas she went to Rome to think noble thoughts about antiquity and "Sometimes I lifted my arms to this sky and danced along—a tragic figure between the rows of tombs." Once you turn into a tragic figure, you're well on the way to recovery. Like Belle Boyd, she was always half actor, half audience. (It was, perhaps, a mercy that the lost children were still very young, not yet ripe for rebellion, and she was spared the future outrage of Patrick deciding to be a stockbroker and Deirdre a housewife.)

L. completed her cure by buying a huge hotel at Bellevue with room for the thousand pupils who would replace her own children in cementing her immortality. She turned it into a "Temple of Dance of the Future." It was going to transform the very nature of humanity and a better world would be born. Here she entertained other sensitive artists—Rodin came often to sketch—and taught according to her poetical methods: "My powers of teaching seemed indeed to border on the marvelous." Everything was going well except the course of history.

In July 1914, she began to be haunted by psychic premonitions. She was pregnant, though she doesn't say by whom; Michelangelo's ghost? In August the baby was born and died almost immediately, frightened, she believed, by the impending war. Worse, mankind's hope, the Temple of the Dance, became a war hospital. It was all most provoking, since Art is greater than life and war was caused merely by the deplorable custom of eating meat; vegetarians like Isadora never quarrel.

Convalescing at Deauville, she felt sicker and sicker until she consulted a doctor, who threw his arms around her and said all she needed was love. He was right, and his attentions cured her miraculously, though they couldn't stop the war. L. moved her school to New York and she had to follow, back to the land of the philistines. Though he rented the Century Theater for her and she covered it with blue curtains and put on *Oedipus,* playing the chorus single-handed, Americans were as insensitive as ever, and now they were dancing to jazz, "the barbarous yaps and cries of the Negro orchestra." She had to take the pupils to Italy, and then to Geneva, before setting out on her South American tour, where a handsome young man taught her the tango; jazz was barbaric but the sexiness of the tango spoke to her inner being.

Back in New York, L. bailed her out of her usual financial straits and rented the Metropolitan Opera House for her, inviting all the artists, actors, and musicians in New York to a free performance. The remains of her school came over. For some reason the parents of the younger pupils had tracked them down and reclaimed them, leaving only the six oldest, whose parents by now had probably forgotten them. (L. bought Madison Square Garden as a suitable home for her school, but Isadora thought it wasn't quite right, so he canceled the deal.)

After a triumphant performance at the Metropolitan, where she danced the Marseillaise and the Marche Slav in celebration of the Russian Revolution, L. hosted a reception for her at Sherry's and presented her with a fabulously expensive diamond necklace. Unfortunately too much champagne inspired her to teach the Apache tango to a beautiful young boy and L. had finally had enough. Why this was the last straw, after years of cuckoldry, is a mystery, but he stamped out, leaving her with the bills.

She pawned the necklace and sold her ermine coat and an immense emerald she had lying around and accepted a contract to dance in California.

In San Francisco she had lunch with her long-lost mother. Apparently it was not a joyous reunion. Mother, Isadora writes, looked old, a condition brought about by her life of unnatural, soul-starving chastity and too much interest in her children. This is the last we hear of Mrs. Duncan. Besides, San Francisco refused to underwrite a school for her. America was, as always, disappointing, misled as it was by the "inane coquetry of the ballet," the "sensuous convulsions of the Negro," and the "so-called bodily culture of Swedish gymnastics." Americans ought to express themselves "with great strides, leaps and bounds, with lifted forehead and far-spread arms. . . ." They refused to do so and she went back to Paris, in the heart of a war she seems not to have noticed, to live on borrowed money.

Once again love came to the rescue, in the person of a pianist she calls her Archangel. (Few of her lovers were mere Earthlings.) They spent the summer in bed together in Cap Ferrat and then, back in Paris, she sold the wreck that had been the beautiful Bellevue and bought a house in the Rue de la Pompe. Here, when they weren't in bed, she and the Archangel gave Liszt recitals and spent "holy hours, our united souls borne up by the mysterious force which possessed us."

The Archangel turned out mortal after all and fell in love and ran off with one of the pretty pupils. Being Isadora's lover must have been fairly exhausting work, spiritually as well as physically.

She sank into jealous despair, but not for long. An invitation came from Moscow, saying in effect, "The Russian Government alone can understand you. Come to us: we will make your school." She was instantly filled with zeal at the prospect of uplifting the Russian proletariat; the common man, she felt, had always been grateful and eager for her enlightenment, unlike the stuffy, insensitive bourgeois. She who had been so happy to dance for the imperial nobility was even happier to dance on their graves, and off she went to enter "the ideal domain of Communism. . . . Henceforth to be a comrade among comrades."

The year was 1921, and here she ends her autobiography. And here we ought to leave her, too, since her last six years were rather downhill. The school that was to have made her immortal and ennobled the world's soul never materialized, and by now not many outside the dance world would remember her at all if she hadn't died so memorably.

She was in Nice at the time, and though her book gives us no personal dates, she was fifty-one. A gentleman friend was driving her in his sporty Bugatti when her long, glamorous, soulful scarf floated forth so gracefully it got tangled in the rear wheel and choked her to death.

Lifelong grandstanders should go out with a flourish. They owe it to their audience. Lawrence of Arabia did irreparable damage to his reputation by dying in rural England, under the name of Shaw, cracking up his motorcycle on some prosaic errand.

Mata Hari did better. Born Margaretha Geertruida Zelle in Holland in 1876, daughter of a hat-shop proprietor, she married, had a couple of children, divorced her philandering husband and, in 1905, following Montez's road to fame, she reinvented herself as Mata Hari, exotic dancer, daughter of an Oriental prince and a baroness. It's unfair to compare her dancing to Isadora's, since she really didn't know or care much about dance, but she draped herself in veils and posed in what she claimed were authentic Far-Eastern posturings. Paris loved it. She was a hit all over Europe. She also slept with any military officer, of any nationality, that she could get her hands on; apparently she never looked at a civilian, but officers inspired her. As theater work fell off during World War I, she began accepting money from her dates. For a rumored one million francs, she agreed to spy for the French, and she was accused of making a similar deal with the Germans. She liked to live well, and that costs money; she was arrested in the bar of the Plaza Athenée, still one of the most celebrity-haunted hotels in Paris, where today a single room for a night would set you back 2,740 francs.

She was tried in France in 1917 for espionage, on rather shaky grounds. The records are still sealed, but whatever the evidence, she was sentenced to death.

The night before, she slept like a baby and had to be shaken awake. She wrote a couple of letters and then dressed carefully in her prettiest things, a silk kimono, filmy black stockings, high-heeled slippers tied with silk ribbons, and a fur-trimmed black velvet coat. Topping this with a beribboned floppy black hat, she pulled on her kid gloves and said, "I am ready." Refusing the blindfold, she blew a kiss to the firing squad, which thoroughly unnerved it, and fell gracefully dead and enduringly famous.

As final curtains go, this was a hard act to follow, but another grandstander outdid everyone.

Amelia Earhart was famous for flying planes. Plenty of other women were flying planes, but somehow Amelia got all the headlines. Endurance was her strong point; she was the first person to fly solo from Hawaii to California, the first to fly across the Atlantic twice, and the first woman to fly it solo, and to fly cross-country without stopping. (Other women tried to avoid the long flights because there were no airborne bathrooms and the "relief tubes" were designed for men. Presumably Amelia just let nature take its course.)

In the fame department she owed a lot to her husband. She'd always said she'd never marry, because wives were nothing but "domestic robots," and as far as we know she didn't care a snap about sex, but George Putnam insisted, and she could see he could do lot for a girl. He'd made a bundle of money promoting Charles Lindbergh, and he was struck by how much Amelia looked like Lucky Lindy, tall and leggy, with gray eyes and golden hair. He dubbed her "Lady Lindy" for the press and set out to make his fortune. Marriage would cement his share of the deal, and Amelia broke off a conversation she was having about autogiros, a kind of larval helicopter, spent exactly two minutes getting married, and went back to what she'd been saying.

She flew the planes and he worked out her book contracts, interviews, photo ops, lecture tours, newsreel footage, press releases, product endorsements, and corporate sponsors. He made her write magazine articles and books, though she hated writing. He made her write all but the last nine pages of a book called *The Fun of It,* about flying alone from Newfoundland to Paris; then he sent her off with a toothbrush and a thermos of soup to do it, so she could finish the missing pages. It was no fun at all. The plane staggered through the fog covered with ice; the gas gauge, the tachometer, and the altimeter all broke; gas dripped down her neck; the manifold cracked and shot out flames; and she wound up in the north of Ireland instead of Paris, but Putnam had her book in the stores a week after she got back.

The trouble with being famous for flying is that you have to push it a little farther each time or the public gets bored; if you've flown the Atlantic once, the next time you have to do it blindfolded, or upside down. And in certain circles, there were then, and still are, whispers about Amelia's skills. Certainly her style was a bit slapdash, or perhaps even sloppy. She was casual about navigation and often got lost—sometimes she'd had to land in cornfields to ask directions of the farmers—and she'd never bothered to learn radio telegraphy. She crashed, not once but again and again and again, on landings, on takeoffs, and for no special reason; in Abilene she crushed some parked cars by dropping her autogiro onto them.

Still, she had her public to think of. In 1937, Putnam decided she should go for broke and fly around the world. Wiley Post had done it already, but she would take a longer route, including four thousand miles of open water, and call it a new record. Her navigator, one Fred Noonan, was a serious drinker who, some said, should have been grounded long before, so Putnam got him cheap. Noonan didn't know Morse code either.

They took off from Miami, with Putnam in despair because Wallis Simpson's semiroyal marriage was hogging the front pages. Amelia got as far as New Guinea, where some say Noonan got so drunk he had to be dragged back on board. Then she made a hair-raising takeoff that cleared the bay at the end of the runway by a good five feet and disappeared forever.

She was expected on Howland Island, 2,556 miles out in the Pacific and roughly the size of the Cleveland airport. Several times they heard from her, asking them to take a bearing on her by radio, but she wouldn't stay on long enough to get located and she never mentioned where she was, or thought she was, and static was a problem since she couldn't do Morse. Last heard from, she'd been airborne for twenty-three hours with twenty-three hours' worth of fuel.

For over two weeks she was the most famous person in the world. It would be callous to suggest that Putnam was gratified, but certainly Wallis and the ex-king of England were blasted off the front pages while four thousand men in ten ships and sixty-five planes combed the Pacific for Amelia. Decades of rumors, speculation, movies, books, and theories followed: her old friend President Roosevelt had sent her as a spy; the Japanese had captured her; she was living in New Jersey under a new name; and her bones or her plane or her grandchildren, and recently a shoe, have been found on many an island.

She'd said she wanted to die in her plane, and some of her

previous mishaps would seem to bear her out. She'd said she was horrified at the thought of growing old, and she was already thirty-nine.

It cost the taxpayers a bundle, but it was one of history's most flamboyant exits. Even if she didn't plan it, she must have been pleased.

Seekers

Generations of otherwise docile Christian housewives have bristled inwardly at the tale of Mary and Martha. It seems that a certain woman named Martha received Jesus into her house, "And she had a sister called Mary, which also sat at Jesus's feet and heard his word. But Martha was cumbered about much serving, and came to him, and said, Lord, dost thou not care that my sister hath left me to serve alone? bid her therefore that she help me. And Jesus answered and said unto her, Martha, Martha, thou art careful and troubled about many things: But one thing is needful: and Mary hath chosen that good part, which shall not be taken from her." (Rudyard Kipling, some years later, observed that the division of labor continues and the Sons of Mary "sit at the Feet – they hear the Word – they see how truly the Promise runs. / They have cast their burden upon the Lord, and – the Lord He lays it on Martha's Sons.")

Luckily for the world and the children thereof, there have always been infinitely more Marthas than Marys, Marthas out bustling in the kitchen to make sure the guest gets his lunch while Mary cultivates her soul. Traditionally, the search for wisdom, enlightenment, the Holy Grail, and the true meaning of life has been an all-male occupation. The seeker's life is unsuitable for women as it tends to become obsessive and interfere with household duties. Many a wife has been quite proud to have her man spend all his time pondering the Torah or the Koran or arguing Original Sin or setting off on visionary pilgrimages, but few husbands would rather have their wives seek truth than cook dinner. Few children want to tell their friends that Mommy's in an ashram, or walking barefoot to Jerusalem, or even locked in her bedroom meditating; a peculiar father can be distinctive, but a mother must be, above all, *normal,* including clothes, hair, makeup, occupations, and concerns. It's also best for mothers to live in a world where all things are relative, since a passion for the diamond-pure absolute of goodness or truth is hard on the rest of the family.

Excessive religion or philosophy—or excessive anything, for that matter—is simply unbecoming in a woman. It is necessary for the future of humankind that women behave prosaically, deal with concrete facts, and keep their wits about them; *somebody* has to. Even among the saintly, men may live in a cave or wander the roads preaching; women should work in hospitals like Mother Teresa and maintain a proper mailing address.

Secular philosophers are male by definition, since they need females—mothers, wives, sisters, housekeepers—to feed and clothe them. Socrates may complain about the shrew Xanthippe, but who else would see that he got something to eat when he remembered to come home? Even the allegedly independent Thoreau, hermit of Walden, carried his laundry into town for a woman to wash and had most of his meals served to him at the Emersons' or his mother's. This philosophical gender imbalance is why so many established truths about human nature, widely held to be universal, actually apply to only half the population.

219

For practical matters, the religious fared better, sheltered in nurturing institutions where the cloistered life offered like-minded companionship and regular meals, even if the former was silent and the latter Spartan. Undomesticated women could get them to a nunnery, and did, whether because they'd dedicated their virginities to Christ or because they didn't like the man their father wanted them to marry or because their true love turned out a rotter. Here they could lead lives of prayer and introspection or be useful to the world by caring for the sick and orphaned. Except for Saint Joan and a few virgins who flung themselves from windows rather than marry a heathen, women saints, even the rebellious, distinguished themselves and worked their miracles under the protection of the Church hierarchy and accepted the rules. Their lives, however passionate, meshed with the political framework.

Then there was Saint Mary of Egypt, as wild and friendless as a hawk.

Many a male saint started out rollicking in wickedness before seeing the light; the women tended to be pious from childhood. Mary, however, was a slut, and loved it. She was only twelve, with two kind parents at home, when she ran away to the flesh-pots of fourth-century Alexandria and threw herself joyfully into them. She pursued fornication for the sheer fun of it, which was unusual at the time and still rare, women's sex lives being more often tied to either sentiment or finances, but we have Mary's own word on it.

The full account comes from the only person she seems to have met during her long later years, one Saint Zosimas, who swore to its truth.

Zosimas was staying at a desert monastery near the River Jordan, where part of the Lenten ritual involved all the brothers crossing the river and scattering separately alone into the desert to pray and fast until Palm Sunday. Zosimas went the farthest of any, walking for twenty days. Then, pausing for his regular prayers, he caught sight of a human form: "It was naked, the skin dark as if burned by the heat of the sun; the hair on its head was white as a fleece." He rushed to greet it, understandably glad to meet up with another human, but it ran away.

Convinced it must be someone saintly, he called after it, and it answered, "Forgive me for God's sake, but I cannot turn towards you and show you my face, Abba Zosimas. For I am a woman and naked as you see me with the uncovered shame of my body. But if you would like to fulfill one wish of a sinful woman, throw me your cloak so that I can cover my body and can turn to you and ask for your blessing."

She must have been more bone than flesh, after a diet of whatever desert plants she could pull up and gnaw on, and if the dates are roughly right she would have been in her mid-seventies, but she insisted on modesty. Zosimas threw her his shabby cloak to wrap up in and they conferred, each asking the other for a blessing. She said that only he was qualified to bless, being "dignified by the order of the priesthood."

Weeping with awe, he replied, "O mother, filled with the spirit, by your mode of life it is evident that you live with God and have died to the world. The Grace granted to you is apparent—for you have called me by name and recognized that I am a priest, though you have never seen me before."

She agreed to bless him and stretched out her hands and began to mumble. Zosimas lowered his head and waited, and waited, and finally, impatient, he looked up "and saw that she was raised about a forearm's distance from the ground and stood praying in the air." The harsh light of the desert can play tricks on the eyes, but he swears to God as witness that she was aloft. (Levitation was common, even usual, among saints, and a reliable distinguishing mark. A thousand years later, Saint Teresa of Avila rose up so frequently during communion that she had to hang on to the altar rail with both hands, and her fellow Carmelites had standing orders to keep an eye on her at all times and haul her back down when she started to float.)

Zosimas embraced Mary's feet and cried that obviously God had sent him there so he could report her story. She lifted him up and said that she was ashamed of her life, but since he had already seen her naked body, she might as well recount "with what shame and obscenity my soul is filled. But when I start my story you will run from me as from a snake, for your ears will not be able to bear the vileness of my actions."

She tells him of running off to Alexandria as a child, where she "unrestrainedly and insatiably gave myself up to sensuality. . . . I was like a fire of public debauch. And it was not for the sake of gain—here I speak the pure truth. Often when they wished to pay me, I refused the money. I acted in this way to make as many men as possible to try to obtain me, doing free of charge what gave me pleasure. Do not think that I was rich and that was the reason I did not take the money. I lived by begging, often spinning flax, but I had an insatiable desire and an irresistible passion for lying in filth. That was life to me. Every kind of abuse of nature I regarded as life. That is how I lived."

Then one fine summer day she noticed great crowds of people hurrying toward the port and asked where they were going. Hearing that they were off to Jerusalem for the Exaltation of the Precious and Lifegiving Cross, she decided the journey would be a fine chance for a few extra flings with the pilgrims—"to have more lovers who could satisfy my passion." Without money or food for the trip, she planned to pay her way as she went, and she did. "Whose tongue can tell, whose ears can take in all that took place on the boat during that voyage! And to all this I frequently forced those miserable youths even against their own will. There is no mentionable or unmentionable depravity of which I was not their teacher." Once in Jerusalem, she had a field day with the citizens and assorted foreigners in town for the Exaltation.

When the holy day arrived, she followed the crowds to the church where the Tree of the Cross was about to be shown, but when she tried to step over the threshold, the invisible air pushed her back. She tried again and again; the doorway refused her. Grieved at this rejection, she went and found an icon of the Virgin Mary out on the porch and prayed to it, vowing to reform and begging to be allowed in to see the Tree.

After that the doorway made space for her and she went in, and prayed, and then returned to the icon on the porch for advice. A voice told her, "If you cross the Jordan, you will find glorious rest." She'd always been game for adventure, and off she went.

At the Jordan she found a small boat, crossed the river, and went into the desert, where she stayed for forty-seven years, hiding from the rare voyager and seeing "not a beast nor a living being" before Zosimas came.

He was astonished, he said, that she'd managed to stay in health, eating and drinking next to nothing after the lush years in the metropolis, and she said it hadn't been easy. "Believe me, Abba, seventeen years I passed in this desert fighting wild beasts—mad desires and passions. When I was about to partake of food, I used to begin to regret the meat and fish of which I had so much in Egypt. I regretted also not having wine that I loved so much. For I drank a lot of wine when I lived in the world, while here I had not even water. . . . The mad desire for profligate songs also entered me and confused me greatly, urging me on to sing satanic songs that I had learned once."

Here is the most human of saints, alone in the desert, half starved, alternately scorched and frozen, wrestling for seventeen years with a wild urge to sing vulgar sailors' ditties. Sex was worse, of course. She was tormented with "thoughts that urged me on to fornication. . . . A fire was kindled in my miserable heart that seemed to burn me up completely and to awake in me a thirst for embraces." She would throw herself on the ground and lie there weeping, sometimes for a day and a night, until exhaustion drained her of lust.

Reading about the general run of saints, there's always the chilly feeling that they simply wouldn't like us much, not in our present condition; they'd pity our unworthiness, of course, but they wouldn't waste time chatting with the likes of us. Mary of Egypt, though, there's a lass who would have joined us in a flagon of wine and a naughty song or two, and matched us sin for sin. A fine saint for sinners.

Explaining herself to Zosimas, she quoted verbatim from Scripture, and he was surprised at her learning. Her former life was hardly conducive to Bible studies and it would be strange if she'd learned to read. It had just come to her, she said. So also had it come to her which monastery he was from, and its customs, and the name of his abbot.

She told him that the following year he wouldn't be able to cross into the desert with the other brothers, but please, would he bring down the wine and wafer of communion to his side of the river and wait for her there? And it so happened that the following year he was indeed ill with a fever during Lent and kept at the monastery, but when he was strong enough he remembered and set forth to meet her with the sacrament and some nourishing food.

He waited by the river, wondering how she was going to cross it. Then, on a moonlit night, she came, and of course easily walked across the water and asked for his blessing. He was impressed. She took the wine and wafer and received his blessing, but the food was less interesting; she selected three lentils and sent the rest back, making him promise to come find her the next year in the place where they'd first met. Then she walked back across the Jordan.

The next year he went back to her desert hideout, twenty days' walk from the river, and found her lying dead with her hands crossed, still wearing the tattered scraps of the cloak he'd given her. He kissed her feet, and prayed, and wondered whether or not he should bury her and why he had never asked her name. Then he saw, scratched in the dirt by her head: "Abba Zosimas, bury on this spot the body of humble Mary."

He found a piece of wood to scratch with and tried to dig a grave for her, but the ground was too hard and he couldn't make a dent in it. Exhausted, he sat back, looked up, and noticed a lion licking Mary's feet. It seemed friendly, so he addressed it politely, saying, "The Great One ordered that her body was to be buried. But I am old and have not the strength to dig the grave (for I have no spade and it would take too long to go and get one), so can you carry out the work with your claws?"

Even before he'd finished speaking the lion started digging industriously, flinging up piles of dirt. When the grave was deep enough, the big cat stood by respectfully while Zosimas laid Mary in it and covered her with earth. Then they went their ways, the lion into the desert and Zosimas back to the monastery to tell the tale. Some say he took the remains of the cloak and treasured it as a relic.

Officially, the modern church is a bit skeptical about the lion, and introduces it saying, "We are told . . ." I believe, though.

Who but a lion should dig a wilderness grave for such a wild saint? Tamer times were coming, and holy as they were, none of the convent saints in the following centuries ever made such a journey, with such a tale to tell.

Religious pilgrims of all denominations journeyed all over. They were overwhelmingly male, since the women, like Martha, had duties at home, but among the upper classes it was sometimes quite chic and social for a woman to ride forth with a retinue to some recognized shrine, grotto, spring, gravesite, or river for extra credit with the various gods. Not many invented their own journeys, though, or traveled unattended to visit the forbidden.

Alexandra David-Neel walked to Lhasa. In her frontispiece portrait she doesn't look like a religious scholar or a fearless traveler. She looks like my fourth-grade teacher, rounded and amiable but with formidable reserves of severity. She was the author of *Magic and Mystery in Tibet, Initiations and Initiates in Tibet, The Secret Oral Teachings in Tibetan Buddhist Sects, Immortality and Reincarnation, Buddhism—Its Doctrines and Methods,* and *The Power of Nothingness,* plus a translation of the ancient epic *The Superhuman Life of Gesar of Ling.* Works of serious Buddhist scholarship for the serious scholar, but she also wrote, for the frivolous, *My Journey to Lhasa,* an account of her four-month slog on foot, disguised as a begging pilgrim, across forbidden central Tibet to become, in 1924, the first Western woman to lay eyes on the capital of the Buddhist world, closed to foreigners.

To be honest—and she was honest—the Lhasa trip wasn't a necessary spiritual pilgrimage. She didn't need the capital city for her studies, being welcome in the ample libraries and lamaseries in the open, accessible parts of eastern Tibet. She'd been given access and privileges never before granted to any woman. She went to Lhasa because she was outraged at being told she couldn't.

Unlucky Tibet had recently shaken free of the Chinese and was now nominally ruled from Lhasa but much pushed around by the British, who saw the place as an essential buffer between their own India and a hostile East. She doesn't approve. Tibet, she says, was the loser in trading Chinese suzerainty for what she calls sham independence: "Most of those who rebelled against the far-off and relaxed Chinese rule regret it nowadays, when taxes, statute labor, and the arrogant plundering of the national soldiery greatly exceed the extortions of their former masters." (What goes around comes around, and by the century's end the British were long forgotten and the Chinese rule was back, this time neither far-off nor relaxed.)

David-Neel was born in Paris in 1868, child of a respectable bourgeois family. She was the sort of child who spent a lot of time staring at the railroad tracks, and imagining their destination in "wild hills, immense deserted steppes. . . ." From time to time she ran away from home. Her parents were unhappily married, which may have tilted her toward celibate solitude. She was raised by governesses and sent to a Calvinist boarding school and then a Catholic convent school, enough to rattle any child's religious identity; by thirteen she was immersed in Buddhism.

Her true calling took a while finding her. She went to India and Ceylon to do research, then found herself singing light opera on tour through North Africa and the East. In her middle thirties, in Tunis, she met and married Philippe François Neel, a perfectly ordinary civil engineer. Some say they separated within a week; others insist that she struggled with domesticity for seven years, making herself quite ill in the process, before giving up. In any case, she wrote to him almost daily for the rest of his life, addressing him as "bien cher Mouchy," and he subsidized her journeys and acted as her literary agent. She wrote, "I believe you are the only person in the world for whom I have a feeling of attachment, but I am not made for married life."

No doubt the psychologically minded would have a merry time plumbing the well-springs of her coolness; the very pages of her writing feel cool to the touch. She simply doesn't care for human companionship. In fact, she seems to loathe it, and takes great trouble to avoid people who might waste her time in conversation. Her only companion on her journeys, the young lama Aphur Yongden she'd adopted as a son, might have been a spare pair of socks for all the interest she takes in him. Though they travel together, she refers to the pair of them as "I." The landscapes that inspire her are uninhabited. As she wrote to Neel, "It is only in dreams that human beings are sweet and so good to have near us. . . . In reality they are the sharp stones in the corners that we hit against and are wounded by." The emotional detachment Buddhists strive for was her native soil.

She started for Lhasa in 1923, her fifth trip into Tibet. She'd loved the country since she first saw it, from beyond the closed border, and "the calm solitudes" over there told her she "had come home after a tiring, cheerless pilgrimage." Always, after that, she wrote, "the steppes, the solitudes, the eternal snows and the big skies up there have haunted me."

In 1911, she had gone to northern India to study. She spent a winter in a cave there with Yongden, wearing only a light cotton gown in the bitter weather. The thirteenth Dalai Lama was briefly in exile in Sikkim, hiding from a Chinese invasion, and somehow she got an audience with him, the first Western woman to be received by any Dalai Lama ever. He was impressed by her spirit and the knowledge she'd acquired without even a proper master, and decided she must be an emanation of Dorje Phagino, the thunderbolt woman. He told her to learn Tibetan. She did.

When the wartime regulations of 1914 wouldn't allow her into Tibet, she lived with the nuns in a primitive little monastery in the high Himalayas. The monks of Sikkim made her a "lamina," or ordained Buddhist clergywoman, and she built herself a tiny hermitage and studied with the Great Hermit of Lachen, one of those she admired for having "broken with all nursery games and who live alone with their audacious thoughts." In 1916 the Panchen Lama, second only to the Dalai, invited her to stay with him and study in his libraries in southeastern Tibet, where she won her honorary lama's robes and graduated as the Buddhist equivalent of a Doctor of Philosophy. Then the British, perhaps egged on by Christian missionaries, ordered her deported and knocked down her hermitage.

She went wandering. She and Yongden traveled from Calcutta through Burma, Japan, and Korea to Peking, then five thousand miles by mule, yak, and horse across China to northeastern Tibet, up into Mongolia and the Gobi to the Mekong River. The whole eight-thousand-mile trip to Lhasa took four years, a miracle of perseverance or, depending on your viewpoint, masochism.

The last, illegal leg of the journey, through largely unmapped country, was the tricky bit. If she was recognized as a Westerner, she would be deported and all the years be wasted. Yongden wore his robes as a lama of the Red Cap order and she went as his old mother (she was fifty-five), an *arjopa*, a simple pilgrim begging her way across the land, her feet bleeding from the Chinese rope sandals, her face and hands colored with soot from the bottom of their cooking-pot. She darkened her brown hair with Chinese ink and supplemented it with yak-hair braids.

"What had I dared to dream?" she mused. "Into what mad adventure was I about to throw myself? I remembered previous journeys in Tibet, hardships endured, dangers that I had confronted. . . . It was that again, or even worse, which lay before me. . . . And what would be the end? Would I triumph, reach Lhasa, laughing at those who close the roads of Tibet? Would I be stopped on my way, or would I fail, this time forever, meeting death at the bottom of a precipice, hit by the bullet of a robber, or dying miserably of fever beneath a tree, or in a cave, like some wild beast? Who knew?"

They threw away all their extra clothes and blankets and any Western conveniences, like spoons, that might give them away. Their shelter was a light cloth tent Yongden had made himself, but when setting it up might attract too much attention they simply lay down on the ground and used the tent as a blanket, covering it with leaves and snow for camouflage. "Small heads of rocks piercing through the earth made a really painful couch, even for me, who from youth upwards had been accustomed to the bare boards affected by the Greek stoics." (Why? And what had her husband, the respectable engineer, made of a wife who slept from choice on a board? Perhaps he was lucky it wasn't a bed of nails.)

Hidden in the folds of their robes they carried revolvers, writing paper, money, compass, watch, thermometer, the misleading and inadequate maps, and some handsome jewelry given by a Sikkimese prince. Traveling as an old beggar woman, she was obviously miffed that her adopted son, traveling as a lama, outranked her. She had always outranked him, she who had been allowed into the sacred libraries and spoken with the greatest of lamas; now, when they stayed with local families, it was Yongden who was asked to tell fortunes, make prophecies, bless the household, and cast spells to find a lost cow. "Years before, when we travelled in the northern country and I wore my beautiful lama robes, it was I who was requested to bless the people, blow on the sick to cure them, and prophecy about countless things. I performed a few miracles, chance, the faith and the robust constitution of those who were benefited making it diffi-cult to abstain from working wonders, and I had some gratifying success as an oracle. That glorious time was gone! Now I humbly washed our pot in the stream, while Yongden solemnly revealed to his attentive listeners the secrets of the future. . . ." (She had to be careful about washing that pot, too, as a careless splash of water washed the camouflaging soot off her hands.)

A family would bring out a bit of carpet, a cushion, or a goatskin for Yongden to sit or sleep on near the fire, while she was consigned to a corner on the bare ground with the other women. He was given the best food the family had to offer; she ate the scraps of leftovers.

His ministrations were useful as an exchange for gifts of bar-ley meal and protection from robbery, but she minded just the same. It's refreshing to find her so humanly jealous: Who was it taught him everything he knew about demons and spells, count-ing beads, tossing pebbles in the air to prophecy? Who is the more stoic traveler, never needing food, water, or sleep through the days of hard climbing, while he sometimes held up their progress to scramble down to a river for a drink?

When it was too cold to risk sleeping in the high mountains, they simply kept walking all night, picking their way by star-light, to stay warm. Things were thin at the best of times. Dinner was either tea made with river water, butter, and salt, or a soup made of boiled dried bacon, or, for a feast, both. The staple food of the area was tsampa, roasted barley flour eaten straight or mixed with butter, and when she had a chance she could put away quantities of it. She brags of her appetite and her good health, which she attributes to tea. (She was French, but her respect for the mystical, curative, and tonic properties of tea would do credit to the most dedicated British traveler.)

231

Having gone far out of their way to find a route never before taken by foreigners, they could relax a little; who would suspect them, here where no Westerner had ever been seen? They sleep with villagers instead of in caves, but the villagers are a bit of a disappointment. Setting out, she had looked forward to meeting the common people, having known only the elite of the Tibetan Buddhist hierarchy, but they're unwashed and unenlightened and their conversation, like most conversations, a waste of her time. Unlike other women travelers, she pays no attention to children and barely mentions them unless they're throwing stones at her.

She does notice animals. Of a pack goat, she writes, it was "bearing its queer head haughtily as if in utter disgust of the masters who had enslaved her frail body but had not tamed her wild little mind." (Shades of the child Alexandra in her Calvinist boarding school.) When Yongden is asleep on the ground beside her, a snow leopard comes to inspect them, and she whispers gently to it that it needn't think itself so special; she has seen a tiger just that close. A wolf trots by "with the busy yet calm gait of a serious gentleman going to attend to some affair of importance."

Buddhists, believing in the transmigration of souls, are allowed to take an interest in animals, who might, after all, have once been their grandparents. Besides, animals don't talk: "I like silence when traveling across the hills. So many voices may be heard there by trained ears and an attentive mind." Did Yongden sometimes long for a bit of casual chat to break the majestic silences? She doesn't ask him.

The going is rough. Passes 19,000 feet high are knee-deep in snow. The trails are unmapped and unmarked and easily lost. Bridges are rare, and the most luxurious method of crossing rivers involves being slung from a cable and hauled across to the opposite bank by a tow-rope. When the tow-rope breaks, David-Neel is left dangling high above the rushing torrent while an attendant makes his way out to her hand over hand, like a sloth, to mend it. Most rivers, however, involve breaking through the ice cover and wading, after which your wet clothes freeze solid.

To cross the Po Country into Lhasa, she had a choice of two routes, one following the valley and connecting villages, the other across the high passes, known only by local hearsay, with no food to be had on the way. Both were plagued by murderous traveling highwaymen and casual local robbers; in some parts, all the men were full-time robbers, leaving the farm work to the womenfolk. Although nobody knew much about the Po people, they were widely supposed to be cannibals, and everyone agreed that no stranger who made it into their country had ever been seen again.

Alexandra chose the wild trail; pilgrims and traders used the valley route and might be informers. They picked their way by guesswork in territory where a wrong guess could be fatal, high above the deserted summer cattle ranges, wading through snow in the thin cold air, staggering up what they thought would be the top of the pass, only to find more and steeper climbs ahead. This is the vertiginous scenery of *The Man Who Would Be King* and the flyover country of the renegade bomber in *Dr. Strangelove*. Crossing it on foot in midwinter is unthinkable. Crossing it illegally, disguised as a beggar, without supplies or equipment and in danger of being robbed, murdered, or arrested seems insane, but David-Neel reports it all with such calm that it takes the reader a while to realize what she's doing.

One night, finding no wood for a fire, they forged on until two in the morning, when some sticks and cow dung turned up. Alas, Yongden's flint and steel were wet from the deep snow and wouldn't strike. Alexandra had to remember what she'd learned of *thumo reskiang,* the Tibetan art of warming the body from within, so that naked hermits can sit meditating all night in the blizzards or thaw their frozen robes with the heat of their skin. She tucked the flint and steel and a piece of soggy moss inside her clothes and sat down to concentrate. She imagined flames leaping all around her; she felt warmer and warmer, and then quite uncomfortably hot; her face burned from imagined heat. The fire-makings dried and she struck sparks and built a fine fire.

She reports this as casually as if she'd been changing her shirt. The detachment of the Buddhist adept, regarding all worldly matters with a dispassionate eye, may be fine for freeing one's soul from the Wheel of Life but it works against an adventure tale. Her trip should be as gripping as Ernest Shackleton's story of the *Endurance,* but she slides through it as if buttered. Full moons come and go, snow falls, rivers run, vistas unfold, they walk and walk, climb and climb, but she seems, as befits a mystic philosopher, oddly out of touch with it all. The account lacks grit and texture; a fierce investment in the small irritations and satisfactions of the day brings the reader along with the traveler.

Not, of course, that she would have wanted the reader along. It was bad enough that she had to travel with Yongden, who now complicated things by falling and twisting his ankle and knee.

She tried to carry him but couldn't; he tried to hobble but couldn't. There was no fuel for a fire and nothing to eat but snow. The place was alive with wolves, bears, and snow leopards. "Yet, had it not been for my concern for my young companion, I should have found a peculiar charm in my situation. Indeed, that charm was so powerful that it triumphed over my preoccupations and my physical discomfort. Until late that night I remained seated, motionless, enjoying the delights of my solitude in the absolute stillness of that strange white land, sunk in rest, in utter peace."

Like Isabella Bird in the Rockies, she found nothing so soothing as huge vistas with no people in sight. It may be that thousands of years of narrow kitchen walls enclosing clamorous loved ones have etched themselves into women's brains and affected their eyes somehow; perhaps the female optic nerve carries an inherited passion for emptiness.

Her boots have fallen apart; she tries to patch them with scraps of hide. She and Yongden are both hobbling and limping and keep losing the track in the snow. Yongden begins to rave feverishly. For a change from plain snow, they make a soup from the bacon grease they'd been using to waterproof their boots and the leftover bits of hide from patching them; she muses a bit smugly on her fortitude and thinks of people she knows who would have fallen to pieces and wept and cursed.

After six days' struggle they reach the valley in the heart of Po Country, among the true Popas, who are just as disagreeable as described. Anyone coming from far away, which meant anyone they didn't already know personally, was assumed to be accompanied by demons, so hospitality was hard to come by. Villagers sicced the dogs on our half-starved wayfarers, who went back to sleeping in caves. Destitute as they looked, from time to time small bands of robbers with long swords stuck through their belts came to steal what they could; Alexandra had to fire her revolver to frighten them off. One murderous-looking bunch threw her into a rage and she cursed them, calling down their most fearsome deities: "There was Palden Dorjee Lhamo, who rides a wild horse on a saddle made of bloody human skin; there were the Angry Ones who devour the flesh of men and feast on the fresh brains served in their skulls; and the giant Frightful Ones, companions of the King of Death, crowned with bones and dancing on corpses." Not all Tibetan Buddhism involves peace and detachment. Horrified, the robbers gave back the two rupees they'd stolen and fled.

She wasn't above a show of witchcraft either, if the occasion warranted. Her years of study had been well spent.

Here where no other Westerner had ever been, she had reason to relax in her disguise, but then abruptly, as if fashioned from the air, a lone lama in hermits' robes appeared and called her by her Tibetan name, Jutsumna. He asked why she wasn't wearing her initiate's robes and trappings. Never mind trying to place him, he said; he had as many faces as he needed and she'd never seen this particular face before. They talked philosophy all night and then he vanished as inscrutably as he'd come.

And so they came to Lhasa. From far away they saw the huge and glorious Potala, the palace of the ruling lamas, and "the elegant outlines of its many golden roofs. They glittered in the blue sky, sparks seeming to spring from their sharp upturned corners, as if the whole castle, the glory of Tibet, had been crowned with flames." (It's still there, according to modern travelers, but now marooned in a dreary utilitarian Chinese metropolis.)

Half Tibet had trekked to Lhasa for the New Year's celebrations; Alexandra and Yongden joined the throng, and as they entered the city a blinding dust storm sprang up and hid them from all eyes, a sign, she believed, that she could wander all over unnoticed. The town was packed as tightly as New Orleans at Mardi Gras, not a room to be rented, but a woman stepped up and offered them a place in a cottage with a view of the Potala. She took them there, and then disappeared as abruptly as the anchorite lama. They never saw her again. (David-Neel explains that she doesn't believe in miracles or in magic, only in the supernatural, things with perfectly natural causes that just happen to lie beyond human understanding.)

The first foreign woman to see the city, she explored it for two months, undetected. She learned to haggle shrilly at market stalls like an upcountry cow-wife and to cringe when policemen pushed her around for being in the wrong places. When a lama child—"horrid little toad"—made her take off her hat in the Potala, her brown hair, the ink long since gone, drew a few stares, but Tibet is a big country that defies casual journeying and everyone supposed her to be from a tribe in some unvisited corner. (If she'd been born blue-eyed, of course, none of this could have happened.) She knew various dialects, and when questioned, she drew on her previous travels, filling in her imaginary history with details of her black tent in the Desert of Grass. Not lies, she insists, because "I am one of the Genghis Khan race who, by mistake and perhaps for her sins, was born in the Occident. So I was once told by a lama."

She roamed the temples and the treasure-houses, visited the images of deities draped with ornaments and jewels, some of which had been heard to speak on occasions, and ferreted out the aboriginal, magical, pre-Buddhist gods and demons that had been conscripted into the official religion, though the Malevolent and Invisible Ones were held in check only by a diligent repetition of magic charms. Pure scholarly Buddhism admits of no rites at all, but any religion is more popular embellished with dramatic flourishes for the unphilosophical; Jesus would still have been Jesus if he'd died in his bed of pneumonia, but that cross has done wonders as a rallying point.

The New Year's celebrations were splendid. Enormous towering bleachers were built to hold thousands of figures of gods, men, and animals, all molded out of butter and lighted by butter lamps. Alexandra was almost smothered in the crowd when the Dalai Lama was carried by to inspect them from his sedan chair, followed by streams of soldiers and bands playing old English

music-hall tunes, followed by a total eclipse of the moon that
excited the populace, many of them drunk, still further. Drums
were beaten to frighten the moon-eating dragon.

Later in the festivities the scapegoat was driven out of town,
into the Samye desert for a year. This ancient and widespread
custom carries away the sins and troubles of the country, and in
most times and countries it's an animal, usually a goat, but at
New Year's in Lhasa it was a human volunteer, called the King
of Impurity, carrying a black yak's tail. The event drew suffocat-
ing crowds, kept in check by policemen with whips. The Dalai
Lama attended in full regalia, mounted on a black mule. (Once
the only woman ever to have an audience with him, she was
now a beggar pushed and trampled by the crowds, and it ran-
kled.) Pursued by the mob, off ran the scapegoat, dressed in
goatskin, carrying away sickness and poverty. Cleansed, the
people celebrated.

The next day was the great "Serpang" pageant, a dazzling
production of drums, elephants, flags, paper dragons, fifteen-
foot trumpets, dancing, and reenactments of ancient battles.
"Under the blue luminous sky and the powerful sun of central
Asia the intensified colours of the red and yellow procession,
the variegated bright hues of the crowd's dresses, the distant
hills shining white, and Lhasa lying on the plain at the foot of
the huge Potala capped with glittering gold—all these seemed
filled with light and ready to burst into flames. Unforgettable
spectacle which alone repaid me for my every fatigue and the
myriad dangers that I had faced to behold it!" It was a far cry
from the years spent studying, translating, and meditating in a
freezing hut in the hills, and surely she'd earned a pageant if
anyone had.

The road home was long and cold, but she left in triumph:

she'd made it to Lhasa, and brought us back tales of a world now lost forever.

In France the following year, she was fêted and awarded the Gold Medal of La Société de Geographie, and after many more Asian travels she died, like Freya Stark, another valiant voyager, at the age of a hundred. Perhaps—who knows?—to be reborn as a higher form of life, an eagle, maybe, or a snow leopard, or Dorje Phagino the Thunderbolt Woman.

In olden times, the spiritual seekers were trying to burrow out through the self to something grander and wider, leaving the self behind like a sawdust doll; nowadays the self itself is the goal, and all are urged to track it down and cultivate and stroke and preen it. Courses, books, and sages everywhere are guiding our way to self-fulfillment, self-realization, personal growth, self-esteem, and self-actualization, and obviously once the self has been located and properly celebrated, no further journeying is necessary and nobody need bed down in the rocky desert or scramble over the Tibetan passes, or even join a convent. The self can be sought while the seeker loads the dishwasher or trades stocks on the Internet.

It may be that a certain grandeur of vision has been lost in the process, but it's certainly more convenient this way, and suitable for even the busiest of Marthas.

Radicals

For centuries, women with nerve enough to worry about matters beyond the home worried about personal threats like divorce and child-custody laws, and the right to their own money. Even crusader George Sand didn't take up politics until she had won or lost her own battles for her children and family property. Then, late in the nineteenth century, with a bit more domestic security in hand, women began to leave the house, with or without permission.

In the northern states of America, ironically, slavery seems to have been the door to freedom, inviting a long surge of women out into the streets and meeting halls. Influential ladies took up the cause of abolition and not even their husbands objected: abolition was a suitable cause for women, perhaps the first suitable cause since Lady Godiva's ride, essentially kindly, showing the gentle sympathies of a proper womanly heart. First they spoke in small private gatherings and then in public meetings. Many of them found they were good at speaking and organizing and petitioning, producing pamphlets and rounding up volunteers, and they enjoyed it.

After the Civil War, they were reluctant to sit back down and

240

be quiet. Other wrongs called out for righting. Some of them—temperance, votes, socialism, pacifism, labor unions—were much less suitable and simply none of their business, and the authorities were dismayed. Fierce Carry Nation, ex-wife of a drunk, went barging alone into saloons, singing hymns, praying, scolding the assembled rummies, and then smashing the bottles with a hatchet until Old Overholt laced with broken glass lapped at her shoes. Sometimes she stood up in unladylike places like carnivals and spoke loudly against alcohol, tobacco, and the eating of foreign foods. She was a joke. Everyone laughed at her but she didn't care, which was frightening. If women didn't care who laughed at them, how could they be controlled?

Southern women, lacking the initial baptism of abolition, continued working behind the scenes in the time-honored ways, coaxing and nagging their men to take action, until, as with Rosa Parks of Alabama refusing to give up her seat on the bus to a white man and Fannie Lou Hamer of Mississippi marching herself into the white man's restaurant, they gave up and did it themselves. In the North, though, a whole new breed of women started kicking up social sand. For the first time—and the last—women felt they could make a major difference in the ways of the world, and it went to their heads. For the most part they were wrong, as we can see now, and the world went on much as it always had, but they had a blazing fine time trying.

Susan B. Anthony and Elizabeth Cady Stanton met at an antislavery convention and struck up a lifelong partnership. Originally a temperance worker, Anthony had been to a temperance convention where she rose up to speak and was told to sit down: "The ladies have been invited here to listen and learn and not to speak." She went away and founded a separate women's temperance group but, since it was full of women, everyone ignored it and legislators laughed at its petitions, signed by the voteless. Stung, she took up the cause of women's rights and spent the rest of her long life in the struggle. She and Stanton started a newspaper, *The Revolution,* with the motto, "Men their rights and nothing more; women their rights and nothing less." Votes were the first step that would lead on to victories in divorce reform, child custody, property rights, education, careers, and a bit of respect from elected officials.

Anthony was, by all accounts, a wonderful speaker who "kept her audience laughing during an entire evening" and charming company in person. Gazing at her portraits, it's hard to imagine. The Susan B. Anthony dollar coin issued in the 1970s was rejected by the public, ostensibly because it was flimsy and easily spent as a quarter but perhaps really because Anthony looked so daunting nobody wanted her in their pockets. The problem haunts all the early radical women, with their cast-iron clothes and hairstyles, their stony visages in the gray forbidding portraits of the time, and, later, looking furious in blurry newspaper photographs of them speaking at meetings, mouths open, squinting into the sun. We know these women were brave and worthy, doing what they did not for themselves but for strangers, current and future; they were insulted and jeered at and ostracized and often jailed, but they soldiered on. Just the same, they look unlovable.

In 1896, when she was in her seventies, Anthony was interviewed by the pioneering reporter Nellie Bly, who called her "very lovable . . . always good-natured and sunny-tempered. Everybody loves her dearly and she never loses a friend." The camera often lies.

The memoirs don't make them any cozier. The radical women give us few personal details. They tend to lack the self-absorption that makes the writings of less public-minded women so richly endearing or enraging; the story of their days is the story of their cause. Impossible to imagine them eating or sleeping or laughing, picking out a pretty dress for the next rally. Were their childhoods unhappy, were they disappointed in love, is their hair turning gray, did their dog die? We'll never know. They may scarcely have noticed themselves. The crusade was all.

Anthony was called the Napoleon of the women's suffrage movement. She did the tactical leg work, traveling everywhere to speak and barging in to embarrass every Congress from 1869 to 1906, since she had no husband to complain. (She told an interviewer that she had "been in love a thousand times" but never quite enough to suppose it would last.) Stanton did marry and—this being decades before Margaret Sanger's even more indecent and impious crusade for birth control—produced seven children. She stayed home doing the writing and research, surrounded by a clamor of offspring. (Anthony said she was the greatest woman of the age, "a philosopher, a statesman and a prophet. She is wonderfully gifted—more gifted than any person I ever knew, man or woman—and had she possessed the privileges of a man her fame would have been world-wide." Possessing fewer children would have helped, too.)

After the Civil War, women's suffrage had stalled and its crusaders were told that suffrage for black men was their first duty; they should work and wait for that before muddling the issue with themselves. After Negro suffrage in 1870, the disapproval shifted to the general filthiness of politics and voting, no place for pure and innocent women.

The moral superiority of women was a Victorian given, but it needed careful tending, resting as it did on ignorance of the world and isolation from its wicked corruptions. If a woman were allowed into the smoke-filled rooms of politics, in no time her morals would crash and she'd be trading free beers for votes, telling improper jokes, and stuffing ballot boxes along with the scum of the precincts. Family life would collapse.

The women retorted that politics was foul simply because no women were allowed, and voting women would bring in a purer, loftier atmosphere, ennobling democracy from top to bottom. (As it turned out, the first president women helped elect was the handsome, square-jawed Warren G. Harding, who was probably too stupid to profit by it himself but presided over the sleaziest, most larcenous smoke-filled administration in American history.)

In 1872, Anthony and her sisters somehow convinced a dumbfounded Rochester registrar to let them register to vote, and they duly deposited their ballots. Two weeks later they were arrested. Anthony refused to post bail but her lawyer did it for her. Hoping to go to jail, she tried to have the bail canceled, but it was too late. The judge found her guilty and fined her a hundred dollars, which she refused to pay; prudently, he refrained from jailing her, perhaps to her disappointment.

It was a long road, and she never lived to see its end. She spoke, she collected signatures, she gave interviews, she badgered politicians, and she never gave up hope. She thought it would be the Sixteenth Amendment, "Citizens' right to vote shall not be denied on the basis of sex," and that it would surely happen by 1900. It was the Nineteenth Amendment, and didn't happen until 1920.

She said, "I don't want to die just as long as I can work. . . . I find the older I get the greater power I have to help the world. I am like a snowball—the further I am rolled the more I gain."

She died at eighty-six, still busy and still sure: "Failure is impossible," she insisted at the last.

It was 1906. The same year, in London, after the police broke up a demonstration of suffragettes, the lordly *Times* snorted editorially, "They all declined to find surety and went to prison. It is all excessively vulgar and silly. But it offers a very good object lesson upon the unfitness of women to enter public life."

Ten years later, in America, a total of 218 suffrage picketers were arrested for slowing down foot traffic on the sidewalk in front of the White House, and many served serious jail time for it. A long road indeed.

The plight of the poor had always been a proper concern for women, who were encouraged to carry soup and bandages to the grateful peasants in their hovels. This was charity, and charity was nice. Trying to better the lives of the poor through decent hours and wages, however, was invading the manly precincts of industry and threatening the profit margin. It was unladylike and extremely dangerous work.

Here in the postindustrial world the whole struggle seems faint and far away. The term "organized labor" is now dusted off only as a possible factor in elections, but once it divided the country. It meant Utopia to one side and the end of the world to the other, and everyone chose up sides; the aftermath roared through Senator Joseph McCarthy's Un-American Activities Committee and filled the file cabinets of J. Edgar Hoover.

Mary Harris Jones, known to history as Mother Jones and to her contemporaries as either the Miners' Angel or "the most dangerous woman in America," depending on your viewpoint, looked a lot like Whistler's mother. She was a tiny, frail, wisp of a woman with bright blue eyes and a low voice that carried easily for blocks and hypnotized crowds. Speaking was an art form in those days; people would travel for hours to hear a great speaker, regardless of subject matter, and Jones's impassioned prose could shift from wit to anecdote to tragedy to rage without breaking a sweat.

Her notion of philanthropy was far from womanly: "I'm not a humanitarian," she snapped, "I'm a hell-raiser." When the United States Senate denounced her as "the grandmother of all agitators," she said she planned to live to be the great-grandmother of all agitators, and she did.

She came by it honestly. As a child in County Cork, she'd watched English soldiers parading the heads of Irishmen on their bayonets; her grandfather was hanged during a rebellion and her father had to emigrate in haste when she was five. She grew up in Ontario and then moved around the United States, alternately teaching and sewing for a living, as women did in 1860. In 1861 she married George Jones, an iron-molder and loyal member of the iron-molders' union. They had four children in rapid succession, which might have kept her quiet, at least for a while, but in 1867 George and all four children died of yellow fever.

She dusted herself off and set up a dressmaking business in Chicago. Working long hours kept her out of trouble, and she might have made a life of it if Mrs. O'Leary's cow hadn't kicked over the lantern four years later and burned down the city, carrying off her home and business and everything she owned.

She rose like the phoenix from her second pile of ashes. A certain few resilient optimists seem to greet each devastating catastrophe as blasting open a new road to follow, and Mary Jones set off to work among the homeless and volunteer at the iron-molders' union office. (Her biographers tell us that she was "taught by her late husband to sympathize with labor," but it seems unlikely she'd needed much instruction.) She did the bookkeeping, kept the minutes, and got passed around among the union men for meals and a bed, as she would for the rest of her life. Later, when asked where she lived, she said, "Well, wherever there is a fight." Apparently her permanent home was a sturdy satchel repacked every morning with her night things, underwear, maybe an extra neat black dress, and fresh lace cuffs and collars. When you strip a woman down, peeling away first her husband and children and then her house and furniture and business, everything else fits into a satchel. It concentrates the mind wonderfully.

The iron-molders were part of the Knights of Labor, a recently organized federation of craft unions, and Jones signed on as a dressmaker. The unions operated underground, since anyone suspected of belonging would never find another job, and held secret night meetings in burned-out buildings in the slums. Times were hard. The depression of 1873 dragged on for seven years, millions were out of work, people starved in the streets. Protesters wanting jobs and bread got clubbed and hauled away. The industrial magnates of the day were kings, and not very nice kings at that: when the railroad tycoon Jay Gould was warned of a workers' uprising, he famously answered, "In that case, I can hire one half of the working class to kill the other half."

Jones hit the battlegrounds. The Knights of Labor sent her to the disastrous strike in the Pennsylvania coalfields, where she recruited and encouraged the miners, mostly Irish immigrants like herself, and bunked in their squalid quarters. The strike was doomed from the start. The mine owners hired goons to beat up the strikers. In a highly suspicious trial, the violent underground Molly Maguires drew ten death sentences for their activities and the hangings sent the miners running scared; the owners hired a private army, called "Cossacks," to keep the unions out. Jones was one of the last still daring to speak, but the union cause in the area lay dead for a long time.

In 1877 a handful of brakemen and firemen, bitter over yet another pay cut, impulsively walked out on the Baltimore and Ohio. The news spread through the B&O to the Pennsylvania, New York Central, and Erie lines and abruptly, with no planning or organizing, the nation's trains came to a stop. Jones was on the last one out of Chicago, on her way to Pittsburgh to represent the Knights of Labor.

It was fierce. The railroad moguls called for the National Guard. Shots were fired and strikers killed. Local citizens sided with the workers and ripped up the tracks; the troopers were told to shoot to kill. Freelance thugs, called "Specials," broke heads with clubs. A roundhouse was burned. The tycoons appealed to President Hayes, who sent federal troops to break the strike. Protesters gathered and were shot down. An army officer reported, "I told my men to shoot without compunction. I told them that the rabble in the streets was made up of foreign conspirators and that they should be treated as mad dogs." They were.

Jones was in the thick of it. A reporter compared her to Joan of Arc and wrote, "This wisp of a woman they call Mother Jones is a fiery speaker, with a surprisingly strong voice for one so frail-looking. Her words are full of fight and defiance. . . ." But she was no match for the United States Army.

The strike was broken but it left the country nervous. This is why today every established city still has an armory, not to defend the town but to stop any labor unrest in its tracks, though now they're useful mainly for flower shows and charity balls. Large factories had their own private armories, in case it was necessary to mow down the employees. Businesses sprang up and fattened by supplying strikebreakers and management spies; an employee spotted at a union meeting would be fired the next day.

Mother Jones fought on. Fresh waves of immigrants flowed into the slums, willing to work for even less, and those already here complained of the competition and wanted to shut them out. Jones was all for welcoming them, and especially the radical new idea they brought with them, the eight-hour day. She asked the unions for a birthday present, a general strike for the eight-hour day on her fifty-sixth birthday, May 1, 1886. "It's time," she said, "the American worker got a chance to sit in the sun or go fishing." The establishment considered this a full-strength Communist revolution and the *Chicago Tribune* declared, "Anyone favoring the eight-hour day is a scurrilous traitor who deserves a rope around his neck."

Her birthday present hit the whole country. In Chicago alone, sixty thousand workers struck and hundreds were bloodied and arrested. McCormick Harvester locked out a thousand union workers and replaced them with scabs. Jones was at every rally. "You are fighting for the entire working class!" she cried. "Don't yield! Hold fast! Your victory will be ours." Police fired on the strikers. At one meeting seven policemen and four demonstrators were killed and hundreds wounded; four anarchists drew the death penalty and a fifth died in his cell. The Haymarket Martyrs, they were called. "The dead were buried," said Jones, "but their cause was not buried with them."

Not buried, but severely ill: the unions had become a national enemy, with Jones as their evil angel, and breaking them was suddenly tops on the establishment agenda. The workers themselves gave up, and Jones yapped at their heels and tried to turn them like a sheepdog.

She was everywhere. She was in the front lines of the Carnegie steelworkers' strike in Homestead, Pennsylvania, where bullets flew; and she was rallying workers at the Pullman strike that the Army broke with guns and bayonets. "Labor's Joan of Arc," she was called, and "The Patron Saint of Picket Lines."

The United Mine Workers sent her back to the Pennsylvania coalfields, where life had grown steadily worse since the union's defeat in the 1870s. By the turn of the century the miners were working twelve or fourteen hours a day under hideous conditions and lived in moldering company shacks where their children, Jones reported, "die wholesale." Any miner who let her into his house would have been fired and evicted, so Jones, age seventy, slept in barns and sheds and abandoned mines, a different hideout each night to throw off the company police.

She tried to call out the men at the Drip Mouth mine, but the company brought in scabs and gunmen to guard them and the miners were discouraged. She glared through her little round spectacles and cried, "Quitters! A fine bunch you are! A disgrace to Ireland! If you can't win the strike, I'll get your wives, daughters, and sisters to fight your battles!" She told the men to stay home with the children the next day and all the women and girls to show up at the mine mouth with mops and brooms, pots and pans.

Brandishing a frying pan, she marched them up the hill to the line of company guards. One guard shouted, "You women go home before someone gets hurt!" A huge, ferocious-looking Irishwoman charged him, yelling, "Hurt, is it! Hurt! You slimy dog, I'll show you what hurt is!" and knocked him down with a mop. The women swarmed into the fray, cracking heads with rolling pins left and right, and fought their way to the mine entrance where scabs were leading the mules down into the pits. Shrieking and thrashing and banging pots and pans they swooped, and the mules stampeded in horror and the scabs scattered. The women set up a picket line.

250

Chagrined, the men joined them. It was a long strike and a hard winter; babies and old folks died; but if Jones could hold out, living on coffee and bread and scouring the countryside begging food from the farms for the strikers, so could the men. They did. At the end of February the mighty owners caved, done in by a tiny old lady and a mob of howling Irishwomen with brooms and mops.

John Mitchell was the boss of the United Mine Workers, and he and Jones had a basic disagreement: he favored outside arbitrators to settle matters between workers and owners; Jones, a hand-to-hand fighter at heart, wanted the unions to win on their own. In the anthracite coal region of Pennsylvania she led such a long strike that a national coal shortage loomed and President Teddy Roosevelt stepped in. He said the owners and miners had to submit to arbitration and settle the thing or he'd seize the mines and run them himself. The owners, of course, were outraged. One told a reporter, "I'll spend my whole fortune to hire gunmen to shoot the miners back to work before I'd have anything to do with the like of John Mitchell or that old harridan they call Mother Jones."

Nevertheless, with a shivering public behind him, Roosevelt forced them into arbitration. Some of the workers' demands were met, but they didn't get the credit, the unions had not been directly dealt with, and Jones was bitter. "It is Mr. Roosevelt," she said, "who won the strike, not the United Mine Workers' Union. Labor walked into the house of victory through the back door." Eventually she and Mitchell would part company over the issue.

The Pennsylvania victory made things even worse, if possible, in West Virginia as mine owners, lords of the state, cracked down. Conditions were appalling. One official company directive stated that a man who "even looked at a union agitator" would be fired, evicted, and "never again find work in the coal fields." It was considered certain death to talk union there, so naturally Jones went. All around her people were shot, beaten, or simply vanished. She was trying to get a strike together at Stanford Mountain when six union men were found murdered in their beds. It seems odd now, but at the time, killing union sympathizers wasn't considered murder at all, or even a misdemeanor, merely a sort of essential cleansing process, sometimes carried out by the state militia, or, from the corporate view, simple self-defense. It was effective, too. After the deaths, Jones's supporters melted away and she, grieving bitterly, left them to their misery.

Union folks called Lattimer, Pennsylvania, "Death Valley"; in just five years twenty-six union men and organizers had been murdered. The mine superintendent boasted to a reporter that any union organizer "stupid enough or foolhardy enough to come to Lattimer would leave as a corpse. And that includes Mother Jones." Off she went.

She swept through striking areas nearby and gathered up three thousand union miners and five hundred women and led them to Lattimer by night, along back roads. She hid the men down in the mines and guarded the entrance with the women. When the first shift showed up for work, leading the mules, she told them, "We've called a strike! Join the union!" but the men, long brow-beaten, went down into the mines. Presently the mules came thundering back up again, followed by the miners, pursued by the hidden union men. The company tried to hire scabs, but Jones and the women intimidated any who offered and the superintendent shut down the mine. The concession counted as a victory, and all over the Pennsylvania anthracite region mine owners gave in and offered to talk to the unions.

Jones turned her attention to child labor and organized the

Crusade of the Mill Children. This pitiful army, marching on Philadelphia, was made up of gray-faced, wizened children, mostly under twelve, who worked ten-hour days under dangerously unhealthy conditions, the boys earning thirty cents a day in the mines and the girls ten cents a day in the dust-choked textile mills, because their families needed the money. "I charge that Philadelphia's mansions are built on the broken bones, quivering hearts and drooping heads of these children," she told the crowd. Philadelphia's liberty bell was about to go on a tour to inspire the country with the joy of freedom, and she and her charges shadowed it, the mill children free to go because the mills were on strike. Jones followed the liberty bell, and spoke, and collected clothes and food for her band. In New York, on the Lower East Side, she spoke to thirty thousand assembled workers and curious citizens, crying out, "I say slavery was more decent than what's going on today! The black babies were sold for cash. Today the white child is being sold on the installment plan." They marched on Teddy Roosevelt's summer home, where he was relaxing with his own children, and asked to see him. The president refused, adding that Jones was "a dangerous demagogue and agitator."

The Philadelphia textile workers' strike failed, and the crusading children went back to work. The child-labor laws didn't get passed until the 1930s.

As a good Socialist, she spent a lot of time raising funds for the defense of Mexican revolutionaries being arrested or deported in the Southwest, but she always sprang forth to the bugle call of labor troubles. Colorado at the time was the personal property of John D. Rockefeller, Jr. and his Colorado Fuel and Iron Company; Rockefeller owned everything, including the schools and the graveyards. Mother Jones disguised herself as a peddler, in bonnet and old calico dress, with a wagon full of pots and pans and bolts of cloth, and moved around the coal-fields incognito, recruiting and agitating.

The miners struck. The governor struck back. Jones was arrested by the militia, put on a train, and told to get out of Colorado and stay out. She hopped off the train in Denver and sent a note to the governor saying she was right down the street from his office and "what in Hell are you going to do about it?" He couldn't think what to do, so she continued her travels to "wherever there is a fight." She was lecturing up and down California when she heard of the coal miners' strike in Paint Creek, West Virginia, and got on the next train east.

Conditions there and in neighboring Cabin Creek were desperate and dangerous; a trainman recognized Jones and told her, "The gunmen are the worst bums and criminals. Those rats would shoot you in a minute. Please don't go!" She thanked him for the advice but, she said, "they'll soon find out I'm rat poison." The thugs had machine guns, and quite a few miners had been killed. Jones gathered a thousand strikers and marched to the state capital and told the governor he'd have a civil war on his hands if he didn't replace the hired gunmen with a proper militia.

The governor agreed, but the militia wasn't much better than the thugs. In a night raid on a tent camp, machine-gun bullets killed and wounded a number of people, including a mine guard. Someone said it was Mother Jones's idea, and she was arrested and held in solitary confinement for weeks without being told why. Finally she was offered a lawyer and told she'd be tried by a court-martial board. She said she wasn't a soldier and refused to have anything to do with the proceedings. Along with five codefendants, she was convicted of conspiracy to commit murder and sentenced to twenty years; her only comment during the trial was that they must feel like idiots, considering she was already eighty.

She was held in solitary confinement in a military guardhouse for more than five weeks but didn't complain of anything but a lack of outside news. Then the popular *Collier's* magazine published a sensational exposé of the mine troubles, prompting a congressional investigation of the whole mess; she and the others were released, the mine owners recognized the union, and victory was sweet.

The Colorado miners were in trouble again. In Washington, Jones saw a statement from Colorado's governor that "outside agitators will not be permitted within fifty miles of the strike zone—especially that troublemaker, Mother Jones." She caught the next train west.

She smuggled herself by night into the strike zone and was talking with the strike leaders in a hotel room when the telegraph operator at the train station rushed in to warn her that orders had come from Denver for her arrest and the militia was on its way. She thanked him for the news and told the lads to put their revolvers away, reminding them that she'd been in jail before, and went on with the meeting. She must have seemed a supernaturally frightening figure by this time, because the militiamen burst into the room with fixed bayonets as if cornering a tiger and the lieutenant bellowed, "Mary Jones, I have a warrant for your arrest!" She said, "My goodness, sonny, no need to shout. I'm old, not deaf. Just give me time to gather my things."

They held her for nine weeks in a tiny room in the military prison, without mail or visitors, and then she was taken to see the governor. He said he simply wanted her promise not to go back to the strike zone. She said, as usual, that she went where she pleased. He shrugged, and she left and boarded a train to go back to the strikers. The train was stopped by a squad of soldiers. The engineer and the fireman protested, but Jones said, "Don't worry about me. I'll be all right," and they hauled her off.

Back to jail, this time an underground cell, "a cold, terrible place, without heat, damp and dark. I slept in my clothes by day, and at night, I fought huge sewer rats with an empty beer bottle. . . . I think the Governor and his bunch were hoping I'd catch pneumonia or the flu and they'd be rid of me that way. But I wasn't going to let them have that satisfaction." For entertainment, she speculated on the feet going past the little window up at sidewalk level.

She could have left at any time by promising to stay away from the strike, but of course she didn't. This was a woman who had watched her husband and four small children die within weeks of each other; anyone who hadn't been totally capsized by that would find the rest of life's troubles easy to sail through whistling. Perhaps she was even having fun, rats and all. Battle, as men have always known, is a stimulant.

After nearly a month, union lawyers got a writ of habeas corpus, she was free, and of course went back to the strike. It was January, 1914, and cold in Colorado where the miners and their families were camped out in tents. She wrote, "I sat through the long night with bereaved widows, I nursed men driven nearly mad with despair. I solicited clothes for children. . . . I helped bury the dead."

In the spring, the strikers refused to turn over a couple of men to the soldiers without a warrant, and the army sprayed the camp with machine-guns. Some of the miners had guns and fought back; the battle lasted all day. That night the soldiers got drunk and set fire to the tents. Everything was burned, including some people. Under the ashes of one tent they found the bodies of two women and eleven children, and this made the papers.

President Wilson himself was so shocked he sent the cavalry and asked the company to negotiate. It refused. More gunfire, more deaths. Finally, in January of 1915, the miners gave up and went back to work on the company's terms.

Jones traveled the country, speaking and raising funds. At Cooper Union in New York, after a ten-minute standing ovation, she scolded the cheerers that they'd better come up with something solider than cheers. "The Ludlow miners lost," she said, "because they had only justice and humanity on their side. The other side had bayonets. In the end, the bayonets always win."

Then she moved on, in 1915 and 1916, to the strikes of the garment and streetcar workers in New York, and in 1919 to the steel workers' strike in Pittsburgh (another loser). In 1923 she told a convention of the Farmer-Labor Party that "The militant, not the meek, shall inherit the earth." To Jones, fighting for a cause meant *fighting*, not talk. Her motto was "Pray for the dead, but fight like Hell for the living," and from the 1870s until 1924 she was on the front lines of every strike.

As previously noted, willful women make old bones; at ninety-three she was back in incorrigible West Virginia working another strike. At the reception for her hundredth birthday, in 1930, she made a speech for the newsreel cameras described by witnesses as "fiery."

They sprang up everywhere, the radical women. Their kind are gone now and what got into them we can only guess, but it seems related to the religious calling of bygone days that descended on a chosen few who were helpless to shake it off. New callings, unfriendly to religion, natural instinct, social imperatives, or personal gain, seized hold of these crusaders and pursued them like tireless dogs all their days.

The crusaders divided very loosely into Socialists, Communists, and anarchists, switching allegiances often and disagreeing on everything. Moderates favored reform; the more ardent felt reform was the enemy, a pacifier for the toiling masses, and the worse the conditions, the sooner the essential revolution.

Emma Goldman was an anarchist. Most of the old isms are still around in fragmented form, but anarchism seems to be dead, or surviving only in a few lone psychotics barricaded up in the hills, calling themselves libertarians and pouring their wrath onto the Internet. Once, though, anarchists were plentiful. It was said you could spot them by their beards and foreign accents and the bombs they carried around. Dedicated to stamping out tyranny, they stalked heads of state. After Leon Czolgosz shot and killed President McKinley—and many people believe Emma Goldman was the brains behind it—his dying words were, "I am an anarchist. I don't believe in marriage. I believe in free love."

Since anarchists also didn't believe in any sort of controlling institution or central authority, they were free to create their separate agendas. Goldman, a tireless writer and speaker, believed in free speech, labor unions, an eight-hour day, free love, and its corollary, birth control. She didn't believe in women's suffrage, which she thought was bourgeois, or in fighting World War I—a stand that earned her two years in jail for treason, but by then she was as much at home in jails as anywhere. Teddy Roosevelt said she was a madwoman and "a mental as well as a moral pervert." The *San Francisco Call* said she was a "despicable creature . . . a snake . . . unfit to live in a civilized country." Whether it was her ideology or her busy love life that upset them, we do not know. She wasn't attractive, being short and thick with distorted eyes behind sea-monster glasses, but she had plenty of lovers and advocated them as a lifestyle.

258

Goldman was born in Lithuania in 1869 and came to America in her teens. Her calling fell upon her after Mother Jones's May Day birthday riot and the jailing of the Haymarket Martyrs. When they were executed, she was so moved that she divorced her husband of less than a year and joined the Yiddish Anarchist movement in New York. A scholarly type, she studied all the literature, extracting what she wanted, and battled the world on intellectual rather than emotional grounds.

Jones believed unions were the whole answer; Goldman's larger vision called for bloodshed. She took up with fellow anarchist Alexander Berkman and the two of them worked up the assassination of the industrialist Henry Clay Frick, who had broken the Homestead strike. They had money for only one train ticket, so only Berkman went to do the job. He had a good try at it but Frick survived being stabbed and Berkman went to prison. Goldman did not.

She published the inflammatory *Mother Earth* until the government shut it down and in 1919, calling her the "ablest and most dangerous" anarchist in the country, deported her to Russia. She was disappointed in the tyrannical Bolshevik government there and wrote many articles and books about its shortcomings while traveling from country to country, not always exactly welcomed. She was exiled from the United States, Soviet Russia, Holland, and France, and many prudent countries saved themselves the trouble by not letting her in in the first place. She'd always been fiercely against patriotism, calling it a crippling trap to keep the world's downtrodden from making common cause, but perhaps never having a homeland, let alone a home, pushed her over the edge. Intellectual internationalism makes a chilly place to plant a garden.

For three years she threw herself into an exotic clash of creeds in Spain, supporting the anarcho-syndicalists in their battles against the Communists, Republicans, and Fascists. Then, in 1940, she was in Toronto trying to save an Italian anarchist from deportation when she died of a stroke. She was eighty-one. America finally let her back in, to be buried as she'd asked to be, near the Haymarket Martyrs who had saddled her with her destiny and started her off on the long wild ride.

As of this writing, Pope John Paul II is determined to make a saint out of Dorothy Day, another anarchist, and her loyal old-time followers are horrified. Her own granddaughter said the idea was "sick," and told the Catholic magazine that first suggested it, "You have completely missed her beliefs and what she lived for if you are trying to stick her on a pedestal."

When the saints go marching in, she'll make an unusual comrade in their ranks. Abbie Hoffman, fire-breathing sixties radical of the Chicago Seven, called her "the first hippie." And then there was that abortion, and all those lovers—the radical young of the late 1960s felt that they'd single-handedly discovered sex, but actually it had been around for a while. And surely she served more jail time than the average saint.

"Certainly the first time I went to jail—when I was eighteen—I felt a great sense of desolation," she wrote, "a great identification with all the hopeless people around me. I didn't have the faith. I spent a couple of days weeping and I just went into a state of melancholy. . . . I never feel unsure in prison any more. I feel it's a good place to be." She believed that whenever one person was jailed for speaking out, others outside would have to take over the work and new volunteers spring forward out of the downtrodden workers, and thus would the movement grow. What movement? Well, a kind of inspired spiritual anarchism, fiercely pacifist, committed to "an economy based on human needs, rather than on the profit motive," an effort to "build a new society within the shell of the old."

She was born in Brooklyn in 1897, grew up in Chicago, and came back with her family to New York, where she wrote for various Socialist and pacifist publications and mixed in the movements for women's rights, free love, and birth control; she was one of those White House picketers jailed in 1917. By night, she drank deeply of the merry bohemian life in Greenwich Village and hobnobbed with the famous literary lushes. Uncommonly beautiful, with wide-set eyes, a level jaw-line, and a generous, intelligent mouth, she had her pick of lovers in the free-wheeling twenties. She got pregnant by one and had an illegal abortion, then married on the rebound and stayed married for a whole year. After that broke up, she found herself pregnant again and this time had the child, Tamar Theresa Day. The father was a committed atheist, so when she decided to baptize the baby as a Catholic and join the Church herself, they parted sadly. (Little is heard of Tamar from then on; she may have served her purpose early in life.)

Day thought of the Church not as an ancient bureaucracy but as "the church of the immigrants, the church of the poor." Comfortably raised herself, she was inspired by poverty as an almost mystical condition and practiced it faithfully; recently a Cardinal called her a "romantic of poverty," but I suppose that could apply to a number of saints long before her time.

Catholicism gave her radical political views a piquant flavor, but the conflict never bothered her; she felt that communism and religion were no stranger a match than capitalism and religion. In 1933 she took up with a new man, Peter Maurin, a poet and speechifier, and together they started publishing the *Catholic*

Worker, a broadsheet still with us today, still a mix of labor, politics, religious faith, pacifism, and opinions ranging from the staunchly traditional to the lunatic left. Volunteers sold it on street corners for a penny apiece until they had enough to buy themselves a drink, then dumped the rest of them hither and yon. Oddly enough, its circulation soared.

At the same time Day opened the first of many "Houses of Hospitality" in New York's slums, a hands-on effort to help the helpless, deserving or otherwise, with food and shelter. She didn't expect to improve their lot or make them respectable and she didn't try to convert them. There was "nothing to do but love. What I mean is that there is no chance of rehabilitation, no chance, so far as we see, of changing them; certainly no chance of adjusting them to this abominable world about them—and who wants them adjusted, anyway? . . . What we would like to do is change the world—make it a little simpler for people to feed, clothe, and shelter themselves as God intended them to do." Until then, however, the Catholic Workers could at least "work for the oasis, the little cell of joy and peace in a harried world." Once derelicts had been taken in by the House, they became members of the family: "They live with us, they die with us, and we give them a Christian burial." Drunks and bums crowded in. More houses opened and rural farming communities were set up, with mixed success, and Day carried her own cot here and there among them.

Pacifism was her worst problem. She saw a lot of wars in her lifetime and she hated them all, including the Spanish Civil War, in which the Catholic Church massed solidly behind Franco and the *Catholic Worker* abstained, losing two-thirds of its readers. After Pearl Harbor, fifteen Houses of Hospitality closed and hordes of Day's young male followers went to jails or work camps for draft-dodging. During the Cold War, she and her people refused to take part in the dress rehearsals for nuclear bombs, drills that sent everyone else scurrying for shelters. They sat in front of City Hall and handed out leaflets instead. The first year they were only scolded, the second year, they went to jail for five days; the third year, thirty days. More and more peace protesters joined her, until in 1961 two thousand turned up and the police had to give up after forty arrests. Then there was Vietnam, with more uncooperative young Catholic Workers in jail than out. Day herself served her last jail time at seventy-five, in 1973, for picketing in a farm-workers protest; at the same time Notre Dame University gave her a medal for "comforting the afflicted and afflicting the comfortable."

Over time, her luminous early face aged into splendid, fearless crags and a look like eagles, if you can imagine an eagle with a sense of humor. As a good anarchist she laid down no rules or guidelines for the workers, and her followers opened up hospitality houses all over the country with wildly divergent themes and customs, but Day was one flag they all followed, often all the way to jail.

She died in 1980, eighty-three and still poor as a churchmouse, and now she's bound for glory, over, so to speak, her own dead body. "Don't call me a saint," she complained once. "I don't want to be dismissed that easily." Her comrade Daniel Berrigan, the radical renegade priest, wrote recently: "Her spirit haunts us in the violated faces of the homeless in New York. Can you imagine her portrait, all gussied up, unfurled from above the high altar of St. Peter's?" Of her hard-drinking early days, he says with a sort of reminiscent relish, she was "tumultuous, crazy in youth, sexually rampant. A spectacular sinner."

The Church, her old colleagues claim, will lobotomize her, take away the flophouses and tenements, the filthy streets of the despairing, the snores of the whiskey bums, the barricades and picket lines and all those jail cells, and replace them with a sweet smiling saint of the soup-kitchen. Thus some of the dangerous breakaway women can be defused and rendered harmless by wrapping them in gentler garments and leading them posthumously into politeness. Thus was the war hero Joan of Arc repackaged as an inspirational consultant. Niceness remains the essential female virtue.

Conclusion

In the 1960s, ardent young women joined ardent young men clamoring for civil rights reforms, peace, nuclear disarmament, sexual freedoms, equality, offbeat religions, and legalized pot. Then the silence fell.

Late in the twentieth century the restless, opinionated women found an outlet for their energies in jobs, the kind of jobs described as careers, and this made the world safer for the establishment. Who would stand and shout on a soapbox when a senior partner might be passing by? Who would get busted for picketing and spend Monday in jail instead of in the sales meeting? Who can get into any interesting trouble during a week's vacation? Careers, it turns out, keep women in line more effectively than policemen or repressive husbands. Freedom, according to the song, is just another word for nothing left to lose, and now the best and brightest of the women finally have something to lose.

Women obsessed by social questions can run for Congress now, and nothing is more effective than politics for neutralizing your opinions and toning down your wayward ways. America's first congresswoman, Jeannette Rankin, was a passionate pacifist who voted no to war in 1917 and lost her seat; she went back in 1941 and cast the only no on the next war, lost it again, and went back to Montana. Politics, like corporate and professional life, is no place for the passionate or the peculiar.

Opening *Who's Who in America—1998* to catch up on our progress, I choose the *L*'s at random and trudge through the first few pages and note, before I give up, eighteen hundred and fifty-five people, of whom fifteen hundred are men and three hundred and fifty-five are women. The ratio has improved since the nineteenth century but still leaves eleven hundred and forty-five missing women, women who aren't even famous for nursing or teaching.

Three of the included women are actually famous: Ann Landers the columnist, Angela Lansbury the actress, and Estee Lauder the cosmetologist. A third of the rest are schoolteachers, nurses, social workers, or librarians, and another forty-four engage in various arts. All still plowing the same gentle fields we plowed before the revolution of the 1970s. Of those in the manlier careers, we have twenty-nine lawyers, three judges, thirteen doctors and a dentist, seventeen "executives," two ministers, a bishop, a chaplain, two stockbrokers, and two chemists.

Apparently, as a group, some of us are making more money than we used to make. Some of us may be getting more respect from the neighbors. Few of us seem to be having independent adventures. Does the congresswoman really have more fun than the barmaid or more freedom than the housewife? Probably she spends her days in dull meetings, drops off the dry-cleaning, picks up some groceries, and spends her evenings with dull constituents.

Instead of casting off the shackles of yore, we may have buckled on a second set of them; instead of flinging ourselves out into endless possibility, we may have dug ourselves deeper into the cave. Those degrees and careers are time-eaters and demand ceaseless loyalty and attention. They're harder to leave than a husband, and unlike children, they never grow up and learn to take care of themselves. And their rules are stricter: a family may excuse eccentricities, but the CEO won't, not in a woman; an eccentric man at work might possibly be expressing genius, but an eccentric woman is terrifying.

The higher we rise professionally, the deeper the shackles bite. When we can manage a long weekend, we take the laptop along, and with the corner office finally in sight, who would buy a camel and vanish alone into the desert aboard it, or even lock herself in a bedroom for twenty years to write unpublished verse?

It may be that the taste for adventure is fading, at least in America, and the idea of risk now leads only to the stock market, with perhaps, at the farthest edge of daring, a hostile takeover; "frontier" now refers to computer technology. For the last mavericks, we offer freeze-dried or virtual adventure travel that simulates excitement by means of inconvenience, with tents and flashlights taking the place of cannibals, crocodiles, and the possibility of never being seen again. Experts have eliminated any possible risk, because of the insurance, and guarantee to get us back to the office by Monday morning.

There's space, of course, previously known as the sky, called the last adventure. In the new century, girls as well as boys can hope to grow up to be astronauts flashing through the galaxies, and from a distance space does have an old-fashioned, adventure-comics, science-fiction splash to it. Up close, though the media coverage and the scenery are both splendid, the actual astronaut functions within the most tightly controlled and organized sysem ever invented; strapped down and tube-fed and following orders, she has less autonomy than she would in Intensive Care, and at any minute may be replaced by a computer chip.

Dreaming about astronauts is better than being there. When Mattel designed Astronaut Barbie, its young customers rebelled vigorously against dressing her in a sexless NASA spacesuit. They wanted her to board that shuttle in knee-boots and silver mesh stockings and a miniskirt, not real life but a fantasy to set beside the fairy-tale princess dolls of yore.

Real life is a public accountant's certificate, piled on top of the dishes and driving and laundry. And always the children, or the prospect of children, to be tended and civilized. Buried under the weight of her own success, the roaring woman of the 1970s can barely mew. Chaucer's free-wheeling fourteenth-century Wife of Bath would laugh.

Perhaps freedom was never in the mainstream after all, but back there on the sidelines long ago.

Certainly women are better off now, at least in civilized countries, with all our fine new opportunities to behave ourselves and follow the rules. Still, it's nice to know there were Amazons out there, once upon a time.

Acknowledgments

The author is greatly indebted to all those genuine biographers whose patient work she has shamelessly plundered.

Index

271

About the Author

Barbara Holland was born in Washington, D.C., prod
three children, worked for many years in advertising,
now lives on a mountain in the Blue Ridge, where her cl
est neighbors are bears and there's nothing to do exce
write. She is the author of a dozen books and countles
magazine pieces. If she had it to do over, she'd be a pirate
instead.

About the Author

Barbara Holland was born in Washington, D.C., produced three children, worked for many years in advertising, and now lives on a mountain in the Blue Ridge, where her closest neighbors are bears and there's nothing to do except write. She is the author of a dozen books and countless magazine pieces. If she had it to do over, she'd be a pirate instead.